# FALL
## SCAPING

*Extending your garden season into autumn*

NANCY J. ONDRA *and* STEPHANIE COHEN
*photography by* ROB CARDILLO

# FALL
# SCAPING

Storey

*The mission of Storey Publishing is to serve our customers by*
*publishing practical information that encourages*
*personal independence in harmony with the environment.*

Edited by Gwen Steege
Art direction by Alethea Morrison
Cover design, text design, and text production by Ben Shaykin

Watercolor illustrations © Elayne Sears
Garden plans and plant identification diagrams by Alison Kolesar
Photographer's acknowledgments appear on page 240.

Indexed by Lina Burton

Printed in China by Dai Nippon
10 9 8 7 6 5 4 3 2 1

LIBRARY OF CONGRESS CATALOGING-IN-PUBLICATION DATA
Ondra, Nancy J.
    Fallscaping / by Nancy J. Ondra and Stephanie Cohen.
        p. cm.
    Includes index.
    ISBN-13: 978-1-58017-680-4 (pbk. with flaps : alk. paper)
    ISBN-13: 978-1-58017-681-1 (hardcover jacketed : alk. paper)
    1. Autumn gardening. I. Cohen, Stephanie, 1937-  . II. Title.
SB423.4O53 2007
635.9'53—dc22                    635.953
                                        2007017441

# CONTENTS

## 1 THE KEY PLAYERS 9

## 2 PERFECT PARTNERS FOR FALL 93

## 3 PUTTING IT ALL TOGETHER 147

## 4 FALL GARDEN CARE PRIMER 195

# THE KEY PLAYERS

WHY IS IT THAT SPRING AND SUMMER GARDENS GET SO MUCH attention, while autumn gardens often seem like nothing more than an afterthought? Fall has so much to offer: not just an abundance of beautiful blooms, but a rainbow of foliage colors, flashy fruits and berries, and showy seed heads, too — far more features than spring and summer gardens typically include. Fall temperatures tend to be comfortably mild, so it's a pleasant time to be outdoors, and rainfall is usually more dependable, which means that you can spend time enjoying your garden instead of worrying about watering. Admittedly, fall can be a bittersweet season, too, with the threat of frost creeping in just about any time and the prospect of a long, cold, dull winter looming ahead. But why let that stop you from enjoying the many benefits of this glorious gardening season? If you're not actively thinking about fall interest when you plan and plant, you're missing out on weeks or even months of beauty you could be enjoying — without any extra work on your part!

Most of you probably won't want to plan your garden specifically for autumn, although that's certainly an option if you want to pursue it. In fact, not so long ago, planting separate borders for each season was a standard bit of gardening advice. Trying to spread out the bloom times too much, the experts claimed, would dilute the effect of the entire border: Instead of looking absolutely glorious for the entire spring, or summer, or fall, it would look merely passable at any given point during the growing season. While there can be some truth to that, it's also true that few of us have the time or space to plant beds and borders to look at for just a few weeks and ignore for the rest of the year. The trick to creating rewarding multiseason borders is to base them on workhorse plants that offer a long summer-into-fall blooming period along with good form and foliage, so they look attractive even when they're not in flower. Adding in hardy bulbs or a few irresistible early perennials — or some of both — covers the spring season; then you're free to work in some fall-specific flowers and foliage to make the most of autumn as well. It's a simple recipe, but it really works!

**Simply stunning.** Fall color doesn't come from tree leaves alone! Closer to eye level, you can enjoy an abundance of beautiful blooms and bright berries, as shown in this perfect partnership of Tartarian aster (*Aster tataricus*) and tea viburnum (*Viburnum setigerum*).

# BEAUTIFUL BLOOMERS

When you think of flowers for fall, what comes to mind? Chrysanthemums, probably — maybe asters and goldenrods (*Solidago*) as well — and sure, these classic late-bloomers are key ingredients in many autumn borders. But they're only the tip of the iceberg when it comes to the dozens of fantastic flowering plants that can fill your beds and borders with color all through autumn: not just hardy perennials, but a wealth of annuals, tender perennials, bulbs, shrubs, trees, and vines as well. Some of them are exclusively fall-bloomers; others start earlier in the season and continue flowering straight through autumn, or else take a break during the hottest part of the summer and begin again when the more-moderate temperatures of fall return. Using a few time-tested gardening tricks, such as later-than-usual sowing, succession planting, and shearing, gives you even more ways to get flowers for autumn enjoyment. So, if you enjoy tucking mums into your gardens for fall color, go for it — but don't forget to make the most of your many other options, too!

**Look beyond the obvious.** Don't think you're limited to just asters and chrysanthemums for fall flowers! Cannas, for instance—such as the orange 'Pretoria' shown here—offer dramatic foliage all season, with a bonus of bold blooms through the autumn.

# Perennial Favorites for Fall

Have you ever heard someone say, "Well, perennials are nice, but if you want dependable color all season long, you really need to plant annuals"? Like the suggestion about creating separate spring, summer, and fall borders, that advice simply isn't all that relevant to today's gardens. Nowadays, we have access to many hardy perennials that bloom for just as long a period as many annuals — sometimes with a little help from us, and sometimes all on their own!

***Long-blooming perennials.*** Many of these amazing extended bloomers are perennials we commonly think of as summer flowers, but their long season carries them right into autumn as well. For instance, late-spring to early-summer classics such as Shasta daisy (*Leucanthemum*), catmints (*Nepeta*), coreopsis, golden marguerite (*Anthemis tinctoria*), lavenders (*Lavandula*), red valerian (*Centranthus ruber*), perennial sages (*Salvia*), yarrows (*Achillea*), some hardy geraniums (*Geranium*), and many pinks (*Dianthus*) can make a repeat appearance in late summer to early fall if you're meticulous about keeping the faded flowers picked off (a technique known

**Hardworking perennials earn their keep.** Despite their reputation for having short bloom seasons, a number of perennials — including golden marguerites (*Anthemis tinctoria* 'Kelways') [left] — flower for many weeks or even months each year. Mixing them with annuals and tender plants with showy flowers and foliage [right] ensures a spectacular autumn garden.

**The show goes on.** Removing the faded flowers of purple cone-flowers (*Echinacea purpurea* '*Kim's Knee High*') [left], anise hyssops (such as *Agastache* 'Black Adder') [right], and many other summer-bloomers can extend their show into early fall or even later.

as deadheading) or if you cut them back severely after their first flush of bloom. Regular deadheading also works wonders for extending the bloom season of perennials that tend to start a little more toward midsummer, such as anise hyssops (*Agastache*), border phlox (*Phlox paniculata* and hybrids), ornamental oreganos (*Origanum*), and purple coneflowers (*Echinacea*).

Although the need to deadhead your plants regularly can be a great excuse to spend time in your garden, sometimes you may not have the time or inclination to work outside during the summer. Perennials that can bloom over an exceptionally

long period even *without* deadheading are a big help for busy gardeners, supplying at least scattered rebloom into early fall and even later. (Many of these will flower even more abundantly if you do deadhead them at least once a week, or if you shear them back in midsummer, but it's not absolutely necessary.)

For long-blooming perennials at the front of the border, consider planting low-growers such as calamint (*Calamintha nepeta*), a compact clumper with small, aromatic leaves and tiny pink or white flowers; winecups (*Callirhoe*), with bright purplish pink blooms and bright green leaves on

# DEADHEADING: WHEN, WHERE, AND HOW

Besides the obvious benefits of preventing unwanted seedlings and possibly extending the bloom season into autumn, regularly removing faded flowers throughout the growing season makes your plants look nicer while they're blooming (and often afterward, too). Deadheading once a week is fine; spending a few minutes every day or two is even better. If you keep a bucket handy (tucked behind a border or near your back door), you can easily collect the spent flowers every time you take a quick stroll around your fall garden. That frees up your weekends for other garden projects!

**Pinching to a bud.** When you're deadheading most annuals and perennials, you'll pinch or cut off the spent blooms just above a leaf, above a side bud on that stem, or back to another bloom in the same cluster. That lets the plant produce a new shoot or a new bloom from the cut point without leaving an ugly stub on the stem. This technique is well suited for a wide variety of fall-bloomers, including asters, chrysanthemums, dahlias, goldenrods (*Solidago*), marigolds (*Tagetes*), yarrows (*Achillea*), and zinnias.

Removing a single bloom.

**Handling clusters and spikes.** Where flowers are borne close together on the same stem but bloom at slightly different times, you'll need a slightly different approach. On clustered medium to large flowers—daylilies (*Hemerocallis*) and rose mallows (*Hibiscus*), for example—carefully snip or break them off right at their base. Where many small blooms are grouped in a cluster or spike—as with veronicas and cardinal flower (*Lobelia cardinalis*)—wait until most of the spike is done blooming, then cut off the whole spike, either just above a leaf or leaf pair or (if the stem is leafless) down to the ground.

**Shearing entire clumps.** On plants that bear many small flowers, either singly or in clusters, deadheading individual blooms can be somewhat tedious or even downright impractical. Shearing off *all* the blooms at one time, by cutting just above the mass of foliage when most of the flowers are faded, is generally the most practical way to go. If you have only a few plants, regular handheld pruning shears can work fine. For larger plantings, use hedge shears or even a string trimmer to make the job go more quickly. Examples of plants that may respond well to this kind of deadheading are blanket flowers (*Gaillardia*), catmints (*Nepeta*), coreopsis, heucheras, and pincushion flowers (*Scabiosa*).

Snipping off a spike.

long, trailing stems that like to weave among other plants; 'Goodness Grows' speedwell (*Veronica*), with slender spikes of rich blue bloom over carpets of rich green foliage; and any of the many low-growing verbenas, which bloom tirelessly through most of the growing season in a range of bright and pastel shades. The red-and-yellow daisy-form blooms of blanket flower (*Gaillardia × grandiflora*) add zip to either the front or middle of the border, depending on the cultivar you choose. Pincushion flowers (*Scabiosa*) offer a somewhat similar flower form but in softer shades of blue, purple, pink, and yellow, as well as white. Other medium-height long-bloomers worth considering include gaura (*Gaura lindheimeri*), with airy wands of delicate pink or white blossoms; Mongolian aster (*Kalimeris pinnatifida* 'Hortensis'; also sold as *Asteromoea mongolica*), dotted with small but abundant white to pale pink daisies; mountain fleeceflower (*Persicaria amplexicaule*), with short, dense, reddish flower spikes; and any of the many reblooming daylily (*Hemerocallis*) hybrids, with trumpet-shaped flowers in many different colors and bicolor combinations.

**Late-summer bloomers.** Just as many summer-flowering perennials can also make an appearance in fall, quite a few perennials commonly associated with autumn actually begin blooming during the summer. Leadwort (*Ceratostigma*

*plumbaginoides*), for instance, can start flowering in midsummer or even earlier, but this ground cover is at its brilliant best when the rich blue flowers bloom against its bright red fall foliage. Toad lilies (*Tricyrtis*), too, are typically classified as fall perennials, even though some commonly available forms of these shade-lovers first open their intriguingly freckled flowers in late summer — especially those usually sold as selections of *T. formosana*, such as 'Amethystina' and 'Gilt Edge'. Glowing red cardinal flower (*Lobelia cardinalis*) and cooler-looking blue lobelia (*L. siphilitica*) are dependable for August color, but they'll often keep going well into fall. The same goes for the pink or white flowers of obedient plant (*Physostegia virginiana*) and turtleheads (*Chelone*); the tall white plumes of white mugwort (*Artemisia lactiflora*) and pampas grass (*Cortaderia selloana*); the white, pink, red, or purplish saucer-shaped blooms of rose mallows (*Hibiscus moscheutos* and hybrids); and the airy, purple-blue spires of Russian sages (*Perovskia*).

Though late-summer perennials are certainly welcome when they normally flower, the blooms they carry into fall often aren't as fresh-looking or abundant as they are in August. If your goal is to create a really fantastic fall display, cutting back the plants lightly just as the flower buds start to form can delay their first blooms until September or even later. Or,

**Delay the display** (facing page). In areas with long growing seasons, classic fall perennials may begin blooming in August or even earlier. That's not a problem on low-growing leadwort (*Ceratostigma plumbaginoides*) [above left], because it will keep flowering into autumn, but it can be a disappointment on purple ironweeds (*Vernonia*) [right], sunny yellow sunflowers (*Helianthus*) [bottom left], and others that may be done flowering by fall. Cutting these back in summer can postpone their show for the big finale.

you may choose to cut them back harder a few weeks earlier; that won't delay the bloom time as much, but it has the added benefit of helping to reduce the overall height of the plants at the same time — a real bonus for long-stemmed bloomers such as many asters, boltonias, chrysanthemums, ironweeds (*Vernonia*), Joe-Pye weeds (*Eupatorium*), perennial sunflowers (*Helianthus*), and sneezeweeds (*Helenium*).

# STAKING FOR SUPPORT

Fall-flowering plants tend to be on the large side, and little wonder: They've had the whole growing season to grow up, out, or up and out, and they make the most of it! This characteristic makes fall annuals and perennials challenging to use well in the garden. Because they take a while to get going early in the season, it's tempting to plant them close together or to give them bushy companions so there won't be large gaps in spring and summer. Once the late-bloomers hit their stride, though, they're competing for light and space, and this can lead to weak stems that sprawl onto paths or smother their companions. Fortunately, it's possible to arrange matters so fall-bloomers can hold their heads up without sacrificing the beauty of your borders earlier in the season.

The most common way of "stopping the flop" is to provide direct support for the plants in the form of stakes, hoops, or some other structure. It's possible to prop up plants *after* they've fallen, but it's far better to put in some kind of support system *before* they keel over. It's a real challenge to tie up or stake mature plants without ruining their loose, natural beauty—and without possibly damaging them or their companions in the process. A tight binding of stakes and string may do the job, but tightly corseted plants certainly don't add anything to the garden.

If your plants are leaning just a little, you may be able to help them straighten up a bit

Hoop-type stake.

by thinning out some of the blooms or by removing a few of the stems altogether. In other cases, you're better off admitting defeat and cutting the plants back to the ground, then resolving to place supports earlier in the season next year. (All is not lost in this case: Place the cut stems in an old watering can to decorate your front step, or bring them indoors to enjoy as beautiful fall bouquets.)

For a plant that you *know* will sprawl every year, advance planning is definitely in order. If it's been in the ground for several years and is overgrown, dividing it in spring or fall may be one solution. If crowding isn't the issue, you might dig up the clump and replant it in a drier or sunnier spot. Or leave the clump in place but cut around it with a spade, in a circle about 6 inches out from the crown. (That can sever enough roots to reduce the plant's vigor a bit, so it won't grow as tall as it did the previous year.) During the summer, holding off on water and fertilizer can encourage the stems to be shorter and sturdier, as can well-timed thinning and pinching. (For more information on using pruning techniques to affect plant heights and bloom times, turn to Staking, Pruning, and Grooming on page 211. If these tricks don't work, then spring staking is probably the best way to go. It's not the most fun gardening project, but it really doesn't take long, and you'll be glad you did it when your fall flowers are standing up straight and tall.

***True fall-bloomers.*** Then there are the perennials that are naturally at their full glory in fall, waiting until early or even mid-fall to open their blooms. Upright sedums — including *Sedum spectabile* and hybrids such as 'Autumn Joy' and 'Autumn Fire' — produce their flower-heads several weeks earlier and may start coloring up in late summer, but they usually don't come into full flower until September, gradually taking on darker shades of pink to red through the fall. 'Fireworks', a cultivar of *Solidago rugosa*, is by far the favorite goldenrod for fall color, but the much shorter 'Golden Fleece' (from *S. sphacelata*) and the medium-sized, shade-tolerant wreath goldenrod (*S. caesia*) are also great. Other goldenrod species are attractive, too, but they may come into bloom as early as midsummer and be finished by fall or may spread too aggressively to be good border plants.

Paying attention to the species you choose for fall bloom is important for other perennials, as well. You'll often see monkshoods (*Aconitum*) recommended for autumn borders, for instance, but that applies mostly to *A. carmichaelii*, not the more available summer-flowering species, such as common monkshood (*A. napellus*). The same goes for the shade-loving black snakeroots (*Actaea* or *Cimicifuga*): Most species typically start flowering in early fall, but the widely sold *A. racemosa* (*C. racemosa*) tends to bloom from mid- to late summer. And if you want to enjoy glorious anemones in your fall garden, be sure to buy those labeled as *Anemone* × *hybrida*, *A. hupehensis*, or *A. tomentosa* 'Robustissima' (*A. vitifolia*); there's an abundance of spring- and summer-flowering anemones as well. Even within one species, the bloom times of different cultivars can vary. Japanese silver grass (*Miscanthus sinensis*), for example, has many late-flowering selections that are ideal for an autumn display ('Morning Light' and 'Strictus' are just two), but some newer introductions come into flower weeks or even months earlier.

**Worth waiting for.** Perennials that wait until late to show their color add life and freshness to the fall flower garden. Among them are goldenrods (*Solidago*) [left] — shown here with 'Evan Saul' coneflower (*Echinacea*) — showy sedum (*Sedum* 'Karl') [middle], and the late monkshood *Aconitum carmichaelii* [right].

**Hunt for these treasures.** Looking for something different to grace your fall garden? Pink muhly grass (*Muhlenbergia capillaris*) [left] is a winner for late-season blooms in sun, while hardy begonia (*Begonia grandis*) [middle] is a star in shadier sites. For hues of blue, you simply can't beat gentians, such as closed gentian (*Gentiana andrewsii*) [right], with unique, bottle-shaped blooms.

***Some lesser-known stars.*** Seeking out some of the lesser-known late-bloomers is a symptom of the truly dedicated fall gardener. You're not likely to find these for sale at your local garden center — not because they're not garden-worthy, but mostly because they simply aren't all that exciting-looking in a nursery pot during the spring sales frenzy. It's worth tracking them down from mail-order nurseries, though! If you're usually not impressed with ornamental-grass flowers, you really need to seek out sun-loving pink muhly (*Muhlenbergia capillaris*): Its clouds of rich reddish pink autumn blooms are just as showy as many more-common perennials. Giant-sized *Persicaria* 'Crimson Beauty' is indeed a beauty for the back of the border, creating shrub-sized clumps of sturdy stems topped with creamy early-fall plumes that age to a rich reddish pink by mid-fall. For tall, lacy, lemon-yellow blooms, *Patrinia scabiosifolia* is a real beauty; *P. villosa* is about half its height, with white flowers. If crisp white daisies are to your taste, seek out Montauk daisy (*Chrysanthemum nipponicum*) or the taller *Leucanthemella serotina*. Medium-height gymnaster (*Gymnaster savatieri*) also has daisy-form blooms, but in a light shade of purple-blue instead of white. Similarly colored *Hosta tardiflora* is a treat for lightly shaded borders, producing its trumpet-shaped blossoms much later than other hostas do. Other shade-tolerant perennial gems for fall blooms are pink hardy begonia (*Begonia grandis*), yellow waxbells (*Kirengeshoma palmata*), and blue gentians (including *Gentiana asclepiadea, G. andrewsii, G. scabra*, and other species).

# SPOTLIGHT ON ASTERS

It's hard to imagine a fall garden without at least a few asters! To be fair, the plants themselves aren't especially exciting during most of the growing season, but once they burst into bloom, you'll know they were worth waiting for. Most asters need full sun, but you can find some for shade, too: Average soil usually suits them just fine.

*Aster laevis* 'Bluebird'

*Aster divaricatus*

*Aster lateriflorus* 'Lady in Black'

*Aster oblongifolius* 'Raydon's Favorite'

# Hardy Bulbs for Fall Borders

Sure, fall is a great time to add crocuses and other early-blooming bulbs to your yard, but bulbs aren't just for spring and summer interest; in fact, some of them don't put on their bloom show until the very end of the growing season. Like late-flowering herbaceous perennials, fall-blooming bulbs often get overlooked — in this case because of their out-of-the-ordinary life cycle. You see, most of these late-blooming bulbs send up their leaves in spring, then die back to the ground for their mid- to late-summer dormant period; their flowers come up by themselves in fall. Most of us aren't thinking about adding bulbs to our gardens during the height of summer, so it's easy to miss their ordering

and planting times. But for those of you who enjoy the unusual, these beauties are definitely worth a little extra effort!

***Fall crocuses.*** Two of the better-known options in this group are commonly called fall crocuses (*Crocus sativus, C. speciosus,* and other species) and autumn crocuses (*Colchicum*). Their goblet-shaped blooms can be anywhere from 4 to 10 inches tall, while their leaves are commonly in the 8- to 15-inch-tall range. It can be a little tricky to use these late-bloomers. They need a companion that will fill the empty space in summer but not cover up the flowers in fall — one with enough vigor to hold its own against the bulbs' spring foliage but not so much that it crowds out the bulbs altogether — a tall order! The ideal companion also helps support the delicate stems of the fall bulbs and keeps soil from splashing up onto the petals, so the bulbs' blooms stay in prime form for as long as possible. The true "fall crocuses" seem to work well with low-growers like ajuga and dwarf mondo grass (*Ophiopogon japonicus* 'Nanus'), while the larger "autumn crocuses" (colchicums) usually work well with somewhat taller ground covers, such as Alleghany pachysandra (*Pachysandra procumbens*).

***Other fall bulbs.*** If you're going to have crocuses in your fall garden, then why

**Spring into fall.** Late-flowering bulbs, such as *Colchicum byzantinum,* are guaranteed to stop garden visitors in their tracks. Who expects to see crocuses blooming in autumn?

not try some daffodils, too — specifically, autumn, or winter, daffodil (*Sternbergia lutea*)? While not a true daffodil (*Narcissus*), it does offer a cheery touch of bright yellow to the fall season. It shares the flower form of crocuses, as well as their liking for sunny, well-drained sites; unlike them, however, its foliage appears in fall and sticks around through the winter.

Hurricane lily (*Lycoris radiata*), also known as red spider lily, has a growth cycle similar to that of autumn daffodil: It produces its leaves in fall (in this case, usually a few weeks *after* the clustered red

flowers open in early autumn), then goes dormant in spring. Hurricane lily can be frustrating because its blooming habits tend to be unpredictable; newly planted bulbs, especially, may skip flowering for several years. They're worth the wait, though. The leafless, 12- to 18-inch-tall stems look best rising out of a low-growing companion, such as blue lilyturf (*Liriope muscari*) or another compact perennial. Slightly taller golden hurricane lily (*Lycoris aurea*) is a great companion for (or alternative to) the red species. When buying *Lycoris* bulbs, do keep in mind that some

**Brilliant resilience.** These dainty fall crocus (*Crocus speciosus*) flowers look delicate, but they're tough enough to tolerate a touch of frost and keep right on blooming.

# GROWING BULBS IN GRASS

Fall bulbs add unexpected beauty to beds and borders, but those aren't the only places to use them. Grassy areas can work well too, and they'll look all the better with a shot of seasonal color. "Naturalizing" bulbs in grassy areas takes a bit more effort than planting in already prepared soil, but the results can be delightful. The trick to success is choosing bulbs that are adapted to your site and climate, then giving them plenty of time to mature their spring foliage before you cut it off. That can mean delaying the first mowing until late spring or even early summer: a good reason to naturalize only in casual areas, such as a side yard—not in a high-visibility front lawn. You'll also need to stop mowing in late summer, so you don't damage the emerging autumn blossoms. Naturalizing is also a great way to work more spring bulbs into your yard, by the way, so you can use these same techniques when you plant early-flowering bulbs in autumn.

**Naturalizing small bulbs.** Tiny bulbs, such as fall crocuses and spring squills, make the best show when you plant them in large groups—at least a few dozen, and ideally many more. Fortunately, planting them is a snap! Get a narrow trowel and grab the handle in your fist with the blade pointing downward and the curve facing you. Stab the blade into the ground a few inches deep, rock it back toward you, then drop the bulb into the hole you've created. Pull the trowel blade out of the soil; the soil will fall back into place.

Naturalizing small bulbs.

Using an auger and drill.

That's it! (One other tip: If the ground is dry or very hard, water thoroughly the day before to soften the soil.)

**Naturalizing larger bulbs.** Autumn crocuses (*Colchicum*), daffodils, species tulips, and other larger bulbs also look best when naturalized in groups, so plan on planting a few dozen bulbs, at least. One option is to dig individual holes with a hand trowel: Cut out a plug of turf, dig the hole, set in a bulb, then replace the soil and the grass. If you are naturalizing many large bulbs, consider using a drill with an auger bit designed for bulb planting to create the holes. Sprinkle some grass seed over the whole area when you're done planting, if desired, or just let the existing turf fill in over the planting holes on its own.

**Planting bulbs in groups in grass.** Want another option for naturalizing all sizes of bulbs in grassy areas? Use a flat-bladed spade or lawn-edging tool to cut an "H" into the turf, with the sides 12 to 18 inches long and the center cut 6 to 12 inches wide. Slide the tool's blade under the grass to sever the roots ¼ to ½ inch below the surface, then carefully peel back the two "flaps" of turf. Loosen the exposed soil, plant your bulbs at the correct depth, then pull back the turf flaps to cover them. Use your feet to firmly settle the flaps back into the soil so the grass can grow new roots.

species (such as *L. squamigera*) flower mostly in late summer, rather than fall. Guernsey lily (*Nerine bowdenii*) produces a very similar effect to hurricane lilies in bloom, with slender-petaled flowers in various shades of pink.

Hardy cyclamen are a superb option for shadier borders, supplying dainty flowers and lovely silver-marked, deep green leaves to enjoy from fall through spring. As with *Lycoris*, not all cyclamen bloom in autumn, so if you want late-season flowers, seek out species such as *Cyclamen hederifolium* and *C. cilicium*. They bloom mostly in shades of

pink, but you can track down white forms as well. Hardy cyclamen are a great addition to the difficult, dry-shade sites under shallow-rooted trees. They don't offer any interest during their summer dormant period, unfortunately, but they're absolutely gorgeous during their fall-through-spring growth period!

**Lesser-known jewels.** Once you've experienced the thrill of late-blooming bulbs in your garden, you'll want to explore some even-more-unusual options, such as *Crocus medium* [left] and autumn daffodil (*Sternbergia lutea*) [right].

# Amazing Autumn Annuals and Tender Perennials

24

**Annual accents** (facing page). This early-fall combo features the moody maroon flowers and foliage of 'Hopi Red Dye' amaranth set against a sunny backdrop of 'Lemon Queen' perennial sunflower (*Helianthus*).

**Delay? That's okay** (below)! If you get a late start with spring planting, don't worry; that's just fine with many heat-tolerant annuals and tender perennials. Try the pale blooms of flowering tobacco (*Nicotiana alata*) [left] for a softening effect in fall borders, or add some intensity with an assortment of hybrid dahlias [right].

Late-flowering annuals and tender perennials offer a bounty of other options for brightening your late-season beds, borders, and container plantings. Sure, they last for only one growing season, but they're invaluable for adding colors, heights, and flower forms that you can't readily get from traditional hardy perennials.

*Tender perennials.* Many long-bloomers that we typically think of as annuals are actually tender perennials, but they grow quickly enough to go from seeds or cuttings to flowering in just a few weeks. That gives you several choices: You can start them yourself from seed each year; buy small transplants in spring; or dig up existing plants in fall, pot them up, and keep them indoors for the winter. (You'll find out just how to do that in Handling Cold-Tender Plants on page 102.) Whichever alternative you prefer, the extended flowering season makes these beauties worth the small investment of money or time. Among the classic "annuals" that keep the color coming from early summer to frost are begonias, cigar flowers (*Cuphea*), flowering maples (*Abutilon*), geraniums (*Pelargonium*), heliotrope (*Heliotropium arborescens*), impatiens, lantanas, salvias, verbenas, and rose periwinkle (*Catharanthus roseus*).

**Falling for tall annuals.** Later-flowering annuals can easily reach several feet in height by autumn, making them ideal for filling gaps in the middle to back of a border. Shown here are just two excellent options: spike celosia (*Celosia spicata*) [left] and common cosmos (*Cosmos bipinnatus*) [right].

***Late-season annuals.*** Then there are the plants — both true annuals as well as tender perennials — that take their time coming into bloom, often waiting until midsummer, late summer, or even fall to start flowering. Most of these tend to be on the tall side; some, such as spiky purplish pink *Plectranthus fruticosus*, get 3 to 4 feet tall, while others, such as red or green castor beans (*Ricinus communis*), can shoot up to 8 feet or more by autumn. Some other excellent options for late-season, back-of-the-border color include amaranths (*Amaranthus*), cosmos (*Cosmos bipinnatus*), kiss-me-over-the-garden-gate (*Polygonum*

*orientale*), and Mexican sunflower (*Tithonia rotundifolia*), as well as cannas and dahlias.

If you're always a little late getting your annuals going in spring, that's not necessarily a bad thing. Sometimes, when you try to get a jump on the growing season by starting seeds indoors and transplanting right after the last frost date, you end up with lots of color for the summer, but then the annuals fizzle out by fall. Sowing indoors a few weeks later than normally recommended, or even waiting until mid- or late June to sow the seed directly in the garden, means your annuals will come into their full glory some time in August, just in time for a terrific autumn display. Some annuals that are ideal for late planting include ageratum, California poppies (*Eschscholzia*), calliopsis (*Coreopsis tinctoria*), celosias, cosmos, flowering tobaccos (*Nicotiana*), four-o'clocks (*Mirabilis jalapa*), marigolds (*Tagetes*), nasturtium (*Tropaeolum majus*), shoo-fly plant (*Nicandra physalodes*), spider flowers (*Cleome*), sunflower (*Helianthus annuus*), and zinnias. This delayed-planting trick also works well for getting fantastic fall blooms from some tender bulbs, such as peacock orchid or Abyssinian gladiolus (*Gladiolus callianthus*) and the more common hybrid glads (*G.* × *hortulanus*). The latter take just about eight weeks from planting to flower, so you can wait until July to plant them for autumn color.

***Cool-season annuals.*** Fall really provides the best of both worlds when it comes to annual flowers: The weather is typically warm enough to keep the heat-loving types happy but cool enough to support those that simply don't thrive in very hot weather. If your summers normally aren't brutally hot, you may choose to plant these cool-season annuals for spring color, then expect them to take a break in the

summer and come back with blooms in the fall. Elsewhere, you can plant them in autumn for late-season color, and possibly enjoy them through most or all of the winter, too, where the weather is mild. (They're particularly handy as fall replacements for container plants that have bloomed themselves out by autumn.) Some good candidates to try are bachelor's button (*Centaurea cyanus*), diascia, edging lobelia (*Lobelia erinus*), nemesia, nierembergia, violas and pansies (*Viola*), petunias, pot marigold (*Calendula officinalis*), and sweet alyssum (*Lobularia maritima*).

**Late-season replacements.** Cool-season annuals are ideal for filling those spaces that inevitably appear as the growing season winds down. Pot marigolds (*Calendula officinalis*), for instance, grow quickly from seed sown indoors or directly in the garden, and their rich colors are a perfect addition to autumn gardens.

Part of the challenge (and thrill) of fall gardening is the uncertainty of when it's all going to end. While knowing the usual first-frost date for your area gives you some clue, that's just a rough guideline. Here in southeastern Pennsylvania, for example, our frost date is about October 10, but in any given year, our flower gardens may get zapped by a cold snap in mid-September or be blessed with an extended reprieve well into November, so it's tricky to predict just what flowers we'll get to enjoy, and for how long. Still, with a bit of planning—and a bit of luck, too—it's possible to enjoy bright new blooms in October or even November in much of the country. Here's a sampling of some true late-bloomers worth checking out:

*Actaea* (black snakeroot): *A. matsumurae* 'White Pearl' (also sold as *Cimicifuga simplex*), with brushy white flower spikes.

*Aster* (asters): Bushy, mound-forming, blue-to-purple fragrant aster (*A. oblongifolius*); tall, purple-flowered Tartarian aster (*A. tataricus*).

*Camellia* (camellias): Sasanqua camellia (*C. sasanqua*) selections and hybrids, such as pink 'Autumn Spirit' and 'Autumn Sunrise', and white 'Snow Flurry'.

*Chrysanthemum* (chrysanthemums): Gold-and-silver chrysanthemum (*C. pacificum*), with buttonlike yellow flowers over silver-edged foliage; double pink hybrid 'Mei-kyo'; single, apricot-pink hybrid 'Sheffield Pink'.

*Coreopsis* (coreopsis): *C. integrifolia*, with dark-centered, single yellow blooms on compact, bushy plants.

*Eupatorium* (hardy ageratum): *E. greggii*, with fuzzy-looking purple-blue flowers.

*Hamamelis* (witch hazel): Common witch hazel (*H. virginiana*), with fragrant yellow flowers.

*Helianthus* (perennial sunflower): Densely branched 'Low Down' (about 1 foot tall) and 'First Light' (about 4 feet), both with dark-centered, bright yellow daisies.

*Salvia* (sages): Brilliant red pineapple sage (*S. elegans*); deep purple-blue Mexican sage (*S. mexicana*); yellow forsythia sage (*S. madrensis*).

*Sedum* (sedum): Pink-flowered October daphne (*S. sieboldii*).

*Tricyrtis* (toad lilies): *T. hirta*, with purple-spotted white flowers; yellow-flowered hybrid 'Lemon Twist' and *T. macrantha*.

*Verbesina* (crownbeards): Extra-tall, yellow-flowered *V. microptera* and somewhat shorter *V. persicifolia* 'Autumn Sunburst'.

*Salvia elegans*

*Chrysanthemum* 'Sheffield Pink'

*Tricyrtis* 'Sinonome'

# Lovely Late-Flowering Trees and Shrubs

Shrubs and trees get attention mostly for colorful autumn foliage, but that's not all they have to offer: Some contribute beautiful fall blooms, too! Several common summer-flowering shrubs keep producing new blooms over an extended period, continuing into early autumn or even later. Glossy abelia (*Abelia* × *grandiflora*) is one of these, with small, fragrant, white to pale pink flowers that start in late spring and continue through early fall, at least. Butterfly bush (*Buddleia davidii* and hybrids) also has small, scented blooms, but they're grouped into much showier clusters that grace the garden in white or shades of purple to pink from early or midsummer well into fall (especially with regular deadheading). Rose-of-Sharon (*Hibiscus syriacus*) also flowers over the same period in a similar range of colors, with large single or double blooms. The flowers of blue mist shrub (*Caryopteris* × *clandonensis*) usually wait

**Not just for summer.** Roses aren't a flower you'd commonly think of for fall color—and that's a pity! Many hybrids, including Knock Out ('Radrazz'), produce some of their best blossoms in fall, when moisture is more abundant and temperatures are more moderate.

**The range of hydrangeas.** Why decide between fascinating fall flowers and colorful fall foliage when you can have both? The rich red blooms of 'Lady in Red' hydrangea (*Hydrangea macrophylla*) [left] linger over autumn-purpled leaves, while the rosy aged flowers of peegee hydrangea (*H. paniculata* 'Grandiflora') [middle] appear with usually yellow fall foliage. The white summer blooms of oakleaf hydrangea (*Hydrangea quercifolia*) [right] turn shades of green and rosy pink before turning to tan in fall, while its foliage ages from deep green to sumptuous shades of maroon.

until late summer to open but continue through early fall, supplying a rich blue color that's often fairly scarce in the late-season garden. And don't forget roses for beautiful fall flowers! After taking a break during the hottest part of the summer, the hybrids often respond to the cooler temperatures and more-dependable rainfall of autumn with another flush of high-quality blossoms.

**Hydrangeas**, too, are welcome in both summer and fall borders. The classic big-leaf hydrangea (*Hydrangea macrophylla*) usually opens its blooms in early to mid-summer on the previous year's growth, but its clustered blooms often stay attractive through the rest of the growing season. (Those in full sun typically age through lighter shades of pink before turning tan,

while those growing in some shade tend to turn deep pink or burgundy by autumn.) Several cultivars, however, produce new blooms in fall as well as summer, making for a very lush late-season show. Some of these generous rebloomers are 'Decatur Blue', Endless Summer ('Bailmer'), 'Lilacina', and 'Penny Mac', to name just a few. Two other popular hydrangeas with both summer and autumn flower interest are peegee hydrangea (*H. paniculata* 'Grandiflora') and oakleaf hydrangea (*H. quercifolia*). The tapered flower clusters of both go through a number of color changes as they age from mid- or late summer through fall, starting a green-tinged white, then turning pure white to cream before taking on various shades of pink and green in autumn. 'Amethyst' is a selection of oakleaf hydrangea that offers a particularly rich pink fall effect. If you'd prefer fresh white flowers for your autumn garden, try *H. paniculata* 'Tardiva' instead; it commonly waits until late August or September to open its buds.

**Lesser-known flowering shrubs.** To further expand your options for fall flowers, consider planting some lesser-known late-blooming shrubs in your borders as well. Bush clover (*Lespedeza thunbergii*), for example, deserves to be much more widely planted in Zones 5 to 8. It's adaptable and easy to grow, and it's absolutely glorious when its arching stems are covered with an abundance of purplish pink or white flowers in late summer and early fall. Mint shrub (*Elscholtzia stauntonii*) is equally easy to grow and may be slightly hardier (usually Zones 4 to 8), but it will probably take some effort to track down this out-of-the-ordinary beauty. It's worth the effort, however, with long, upright spikes of purple flowers in early and mid-fall and fragrant foliage on a compact, 3- to 5-foot-tall plant. Chaste tree (*Vitex agnus-castus*) also has spiky purple-blue flowers, usually starting in mid-summer and continuing into fall; it grows two to three times taller than mint shrub and tends to be a better choice for warmer areas (Zones 6 or 7 to 10).

**Warm-region woodies.** Gardeners in warmer areas have several more shrubby choices for fall flowers. Camellias, for instance, are a classic southern favorite for their showy flowers, which can grace the garden any time from early fall through spring, depending on the species or hybrid and cultivar you select. Sasanqua camellia (*Camellia sasanqua*) is a particularly popular choice for autumn because it can begin flowering as early as September, in white or many shades of pink. Tea-oil camellia (*C. oleifera*) and tea camellia (*C. sinensis*) bloom fairly early too, with white flowers. There are also a number of hybrids between *C. sasanqua* and *C. oleifera*, which offer the wider color range and more-substantial flowers of the former with the often-greater hardiness of the latter — a plus for Zone 6 gardeners who can't resist the lure of trying these elegant evergreens

**Out of the ordinary.** Deciduous bush clover (*Lespedeza thunbergii*) [left] is a stunner in its fall-flowering glory, covered with hundreds to thousands of small but bright blooms on arching stems that can cover an area up to 10 feet across. Tea-oil camellia (*Camellia oleifera*) [right] grows larger — to 20 feet tall and wide — but its flowers have a much more understated elegance, best appreciated at close range.

**Calling all connoisseurs.**
Franklinia (*Franklinia alatamaha*) isn't the easiest tree to grow successfully, possibly because of soilborne diseases. But with exquisite blooms like this as the reward, it's easy to see why gardeners want to try.

in their autumn plantings. Holly osmanthus (*Osmanthus heterophyllus*), another evergreen shrub, is better known for its handsome, glossy foliage than its blooms, because the small white flowers are mostly hidden among the leaves. However, you don't need to actually *see* the flowers to enjoy their delightful scent! It's a good alternative to thorny elaeagnus (*Elaeagnus pungens*), another evergreen shrub that has fantastic fall fragrance, but which is considered invasive in many areas.

**Late-flowering trees** provide yet another opportunity for celebrating fall in the landscape. Like camellias, crape myrtles

(*Lagerstroemia*) are usually best suited to Zones 7 and south, although some of them can survive the winter in Zone 6 as well. Their clustered blooms open in early to midsummer and often continue through early fall or even later, in white or shades of pink, red, or purple. Compact selections such as purple-flowered 'Centennial' (3 to 5 feet) and pink 'Hopi' (about 10 feet tall) are great in smaller yards; for larger landscapes, there are also species and hybrids that can easily reach 20 feet tall or more. Seven-sons flower (*Heptacodium miconoides*) isn't nearly as well known as crape myrtles, but it offers several of the same benefits — including showy autumn flowers and handsome peeling bark — on a much hardier, multistemmed small tree (Zones 4 to 8). Its clustered, creamy white, fragrant blooms open in late summer to early fall; after they drop, the remaining flowerlike calyces turn bright reddish pink, making it look like the tree is blooming for a second time through the fall months. Franklinia or Franklin tree (*Franklinia alatamaha*) is even harder to find than seven-sons flower and tends to be difficult to get established, but its cupped, single white flowers are so lovely in the late-summer-to-fall garden that it's definitely worth trying.

# Eye-catching Climbers for Autumn Bloom

If you're looking to deck your walls — and fences and arbors, too — with fall flowers, there are a number of colorful climbers to choose from. Classic morning glories (*Ipomoea*) and night-blooming moonflower (*I. alba*) commonly start blooming in mid- to late summer, then continue producing their large, showy flowers until frost. Dainty-looking canary climber (*Tropaeolum peregrinum*) is a more out-of-the-ordinary annual vine with small, bright yellow blooms over the same period. Two other equally delicate-looking, long-blooming vines are climbing gloxinias or chickabiddy (*Asarina*), with tubular white, pink, or purple blooms, and purple bell vine (*Rhodochiton atrosanguineum*), with pendant, moody purple flowers. Hyacinth bean (*Lablab purpureus* or *Dolichos lablab*) offers a much bolder effect, with twining stems that produce large clusters of purplish pink flowers from mid- to late summer until frost, along with amazing deep purple seedpods. Spanish flag (*Mina lobata*) can also fill quite a bit of space, with flashy, one-sided spikes of red buds that open to orange and age to yellow from midsummer to frost. But the biggest of the annual bunch has to be cup-and-saucer vine, or cathedral vine (*Cobaea scandens*): It can easily grow 20 to 30 feet tall in just one season! The cupped white to purple flowers often don't start until early autumn, but then they bloom with abandon until freezing weather.

***Tender perennial vines.*** Most of the flowering vines gardeners think of as annuals are actually tender perennials in very mild climates, but they bloom quickly enough that you can start them from seed

**Perfect partners.** Don't have room for trellises to support your fall-flowering vines? Large, sturdy, well-established shrubs can do the job too, as shown in this pairing of hyacinth bean (*Lablab purpureus*) mingling with Knock Out rose (*Rosa* 'Radrazz').

each spring and still enjoy their flowers in summer and fall of the same year. Then there are the tender vines that you need to buy as transplants every spring, or else bring indoors for the winter if you want to keep them from year to year. Passionflowers (*Passiflora*) are one good example of tender vines worth growing for fantastic flowers through much of the growing season. Mandevillas, too, can put on quite a show; one popular choice is 'Alice DuPont' (*Mandevilla × amoena*), with large, rich pink blooms that never fail to attract attention. Those of you who enjoy bright colors also need to try Mexican flame vine (*Senecio confusus*): Its glossy green leaves are handsome in their own right, but the clusters of fiery reddish orange daisies are what really catch the eye.

**Attention-getters.** Twining *Mandevilla* 'Alice DuPont', with *Verbena bonariensis* and petunias at its feet, makes an elegant display.

***Hardy climbers.*** Don't have the time or inclination to plant annual or tender vines

every year? There are several late-flowering hardy vines to choose from, too. Sweet autumn clematis (*Clematis terniflora*) is one that immediately comes to mind, with its dense blanket of fragrant white flowers in early to

mid-fall. It gets quite large, though (anywhere from 15 to 30 feet tall, depending on the size of its support), and its tendency to self-sow makes it qualify as invasive in many areas. Golden clematis (*C. tangutica*), with nodding, bright yellow blooms through much of the fall, tends to be a bit less vigorous and much less likely to produce unwanted seedlings. Quite a few summer-blooming clematis can also produce blooms into early fall, such as white 'Henryi', purple 'Jackmanii', blue 'Perle d'Azur', and cherry red 'Ville de Lyon', to name a few.

Honeysuckles (*Lonicera*) are another group of summer-bloomers that can keep going well into fall, even through light frosts. The tubular flowers of 'Dropmore Scarlet' (*L. × brownii*) are an intense orange, while 'Goldflame' (*L. × heckrottii*) bears fragrant pink-and-yellow blooms. Late Dutch honeysuckle (*L. periclymenoides* 'Serotina') is also very fragrant, with reddish pink-and-cream flowers. For something *really* out of the ordinary, consider climbing aster (*Aster carolinianus*). Best suited to Zones 6 or 7 to 9, it doesn't actively twine around a support; instead, its long, slender stems weave into or lean on a trellis, fence, or large shrub, then produce an abundance of small, purplish pink daisies from early to late fall.

*Vitis vinifera* 'Purpurea'

Options for fall foliage color among vines aren't especially abundant, but they make up for it by being absolutely spectacular!

Virginia creeper (*Parthenocissus quinquefolia*) and Boston ivy (*P. tricuspidata*), for example, typically turn clear red to burgundy in full sun but may also include bright orange, yellow, and purple; in shade, they can take on softer shades of the same colors.

Grapevines (*Vitis*), too, produce some exciting autumn foliage effects. Along with the regular edible types, ornamental species and selections such as crimson glory vine (*V. coignetiae*) and claret vine (*V. vinifera* 'Purpurea') commonly change to shades of red, orange, gold, and burgundy.

Best known for their clusters of white flowers in summer, climbing hydrangea (*Hydrangea anomala* subsp. *petiolaris*) and hydrangea vine (*Schizophragma hydrangeoides*) can also turn a lovely yellow in autumn.

*Parthenocissus quinquefolia*

# FABULOUS FOLIAGE FOR FALL

Colorful foliage is one of the hallmarks of fall gardens, although you don't necessarily have to wait until autumn to enjoy it. Thousands of annuals, perennials, bulbs, shrubs, trees, and vines have colorful leaves all through the growing season, providing a dependable source of red, orange, yellow, blue, pink, purple, silver, black, and variegated foliage for fall combinations. Cooler fall temperatures tend to enhance the hues of many colored-foliage plants, either intensifying the existing colors or encouraging the production of richly colored new leaves that rival their dramatic spring appearance. You can take advantage of the latter phenomenon by cutting many colored-foliage perennials to the ground if their leaves turn greenish in midsummer. This trick works especially well with variegated and chartreuse-leaved plants, such as gardener's garters (*Phalaris arundinacea* var. *picta*), golden meadowsweet (*Filipendula ulmaria* 'Aurea'), and 'Roman Bronze' columbine (*Aquilegia vulgaris*). Give them a thorough watering and a shovelful of compost mulch, and they'll send up a flush of fresh foliage that looks great well into autumn.

Planning for fall effects from plants that turn from green to other colors in autumn tends to be a much more challenging proposition. These color changes are due to varying amounts of pigments within the leaves, which in turn are dependent on environmental conditions such as sunlight, air temperature, and soil moisture. That's why the fall foliage show differs from climate to climate, and why it changes from year to year, too. A fall that is mild and cloudy or rainy is often rather dull, foliage-wise (at least if you like colors other than yellow), while cool-but-not-freezing temperatures and sunny, dry days usually produce brilliant reds, vibrant oranges, and rich purples. Early frosts and freezes damage the leaves before they have a chance to undergo their normal pigment changes, so even if weather conditions are perfect afterward, the result is drab greens and browns instead of a breath-stealing show of brightly colored foliage.

**Color to count on.** Predicting fall foliage colors may be tricky on some plants, but you can depend on most Japanese maples (*Acer palmatum*) to be absolutely spectacular. Some cultivars turn glowing tones of orange, as shown on facing page; below, rich red 'Crimson Queen' mingles with bright yellow Fiona Sunrise jasmine (*Jasminum officinale* 'Frojas').

While you're outdoors enjoying your colorful fall borders, take some time to really look at your perennials and see if any of them need to be divided. Fall can be a great time to divide those that flower in spring to midsummer, giving them plenty of time to settle back in before the next bloom season, and it's also

Separating loose clumps.

a fine time for many that you grow for foliage instead of flowers. (For more details on deciding exactly when and why to divide, check out Dividing Perennials on page 114.

Ready to try your hand at dividing a perennial? Most are so easy to separate, you won't even need tools to do it! You'll have to dig up the clump first, of course; to make that job easier, water thoroughly the day before if the ground is dry. And if the plant has lots of top growth, cut it down to 6 to 12 inches

above the ground either before or after you dig. Shake or brush off as much loose soil from the roots as you can, then you're ready to divide.

**Separating loose clumps.** On some perennials (including ajuga, asters, heucheras, geraniums, and phlox, to name a few), you can easily see that the clumps are made up of many smaller plantlets (crowns) grouped together. In this case, it's often possible to separate these plantlets simply by pulling them apart with your fingers. Remember, the more divisions you make from a clump, the more new plants you'll have, but the smaller they'll be and the more care they'll need to survive.

**Cutting apart spreaders.** Sometimes, perennial clumps appear more like a uniform carpet than a collection of individual plantlets. This is especially true with those that spread by runners, such as bee balms (*Monarda*) and obedient plant (*Physostegia*). Trying to pull these apart often leaves you with a stringy mess of roots and runners, so cut them apart instead, using an old pair of garden shears. The results will look much neater, and you'll do less damage to the roots this way, too. Make the new pieces about as big as the palm of your hand, and they'll re-establish quickly.

**Handling hard-to-divide clumps.** Some perennials, such as astilbes, peonies, and larger hostas, produce such tightly packed crowns that there's no way to pull them apart; you'll need to cut them apart instead. Just before or after digging, cut back the top growth to 6 to 12 inches. If a lot of soil is clinging to the clump when you dig it up, you might want to wash it off, either by rinsing the roots with a gently running hose or by swishing the clump around in a bucket of water. To make the cuts, you can use a knife made especially for garden use, although an old bread or steak knife with a sharp, serrated blade works just as well. If you can see where the crown separates naturally into sections, use those lines to guide your cuts; otherwise, just slice down through the center of the clump. Don't chop or saw too much; try to make a clean, straight cut. Keep dividing the sections until they are the size you want them. Remember, each new piece must have its own roots and *at least* one bud or shoot (ideally three or more).

**Dividing large crowns.** Perennials that form big clumps, such as hostas and many grasses, are easier to divide with a spade, ax, or mattock. Even with a sharp tool, dividing these monsters can really give you a workout. If possible, cut through the center of a clump to divide it in half, then keep dividing the halves until they are the size you want. If the center is too tough to cut, then work around the perimeter of the clump cutting off the outer parts in wedges. You can then divide those wedges into smaller sections, if needed.

**Discard the dead parts.** With tight-crowned perennials, new growth is formed around the edge of the clump and the center eventually weakens and dies out. So, when you divide them, keep the vigorous outer

pieces and toss the dense, dead-looking center into your compost or debris pile. (Even if it does have some live shoots, trying to make divisions from this weakened growth generally isn't worth the effort.) Before replanting any divisions, check them carefully for signs of weeds or other plants that may have mingled with the original clump and carefully remove the roots of the interlopers.

**Aftercare for divisions.** No matter how you divide, it's best to get the new pieces back in the ground quickly, so they don't have a chance to dry out. Replant good-sized pieces into compost-enriched soil at the same depth the original clump was growing, then water thoroughly. If you divided down to single crowns to get as many new plants as possible, it's best to give them some special care: Pot them up or plant them into a holding bed, and water carefully to make sure they don't wilt.

Dividing large crowns.

**Border workhorses.** Plants with great fall color *plus* other features are especially useful for small-space gardens, where each element has to add interest for as long as possible. Viburnums [left], for example, offer summer flowers and fall berries, too, while warm-season grasses, such as 'Shenandoah' switchgrass (*Panicum virgatum*) [right], can contribute pretty flower plumes as well.

Though you can't do anything about the weather, there are a few ways to improve the odds of enjoying beautiful fall foliage in your yard. First, start with plants that have a solid reputation for producing good autumn leaf colors, such as maples (*Acer*), sumacs (*Rhus*), switchgrasses (*Panicum*) and other warm-season ornamental grasses, and viburnums. Taking a drive around your community in fall, and visiting local arboreta, botanical gardens, and nursery display gardens, can also be enlightening; you can see for yourself which plants put on the best fall show in your particular area. Once you've selected your plants, give them a site with plenty of sun. (Even if they can grow just fine in some shade, their fall leaf colors will often be more on the pastel side there.) Then, cross your fingers and hope that the weather will cooperate with your wishes. If it does, so much the better; if not, you can always look forward to next year!

That brings up another point: Unless you have enough gardening space to plant *everything* you want to grow, make sure you choose plants that you'd find appealing even if they didn't have colorful fall foliage. Features such as showy blooms, great fragrance, and interesting leaf texture ensure that a plant earns its keep even in years when the fall color isn't at its best. The same advice applies when you're choosing partners for plants that can have showy fall foliage. If you include one or more companions with attractive autumn flowers, seed-heads, or fruits, and maybe one or more that have colorful or otherwise striking foliage throughout the growing season, then you'll have a combination that looks terrific in some years and absolutely fantastic in those when the weather cooperates to bring out the fall foliage color change.

# Perennials for Autumn Leaf Color

When it comes to fall foliage colors, perennials certainly don't get the same press that trees and shrubs do. Maybe that's why it's always a wonderful surprise to see how many perennials really *can* contribute extra autumn interest to our gardens this way.

*Yellow fall foliage.* Quite a few common perennials typically turn shades of yellow in autumn. Bluestars (*Amsonia*) are one of the best-known examples; balloon flower (*Platycodon grandiflorus*), burnets (*Sanguisorba*), daylilies (*Hemerocallis*), purple coneflowers (*Echinacea*), monkshoods (*Aconitum*), Siberian iris (*Iris sibirica*), and upright sedums (including *S. spectabile* and hybrids, such as 'Autumn Joy' and 'Autumn Fire') are other sun-lovers that can turn attractive shades of clear yellow to orange-yellow in fall. Although shady sites typically don't encourage brilliant fall colors, dwarf goat's beard (*Aruncus aethusifolius*), hostas, Solomon's plumes (*Smilacina*),

**Perennials with panache.**
The eye-catching fall color of Arkansas bluestar (*Amsonia hubrichtii*) would make it worth growing even if it didn't produce such beautiful early-summer blooms. Here, it's shown in its autumn glory against a mass of pink muhly grass (*Muhlenbergia capillaris*).

**Go for the gold.** Even if you're not a fan of yellow foliage in general, you have it admit that it's an integral part of the fall garden. Some perennials, such as 'All Gold' lemon balm (*Melissa officinalis*) [left], carry their leaf color all through the growing season; others, such as royal fern (*Osmunda regalis*) [right], wait until autumn to turn yellow.

and Solomon's seals (*Polygonatum*) are all fairly dependable for good-looking yellow fall color. Royal fern (*Osmunda regalis*) and cinnamon fern (*O. cinnamomea*), too, typically turn a handsome shade of yellow; so do hay-scented fern (*Dennstaedtia puncti-lobula*) and toothed wood fern (*Dryopteris carthusiana*).

*Gold-leaved perennials.* To further expand your options for yellow foliage in your fall combinations, check out some of the perennials that offer sunny-colored leaves through most or all of the growing season. 'Aztec Gold' veronica (*Veronica prostrata*) and 'Pee Dee Gold Ingot' blue lily-turf (*Liriope muscari*) are two low-growers that hold their foliage color well from spring through fall. 'All Gold' lemon balm (*Melissa officinalis*), golden meadowsweet (*Filipendula ulmaria* 'Aurea'), and 'Sweet Kate' spiderwort

(*Tradescantia*) can turn greenish yellow during hot weather, but if you shear the plants to the ground in midsummer, they'll sprout bright new leaves to grace your garden in autumn.

*Orange to red foliage.* Perennials with orange to reddish fall foliage offer even more dramatic color accents in late-season plantings. Those that produce distinctly orange foliage aren't all that abundant, but one option is 'Angelina' sedum (*Sedum rupestre*), with rich yellow, ever-present foliage that develops rich orange tips in fall and winter in sunny sites. Another is *Allium thunbergii* 'Ozawa', a hardy perennial bulb with slender green leaves that turn fiery orange in fall (along with its late-season reddish pink flowers). *Patrinia scabiosifolia* offers a mix of orange and reds in its deeply lobed leaves, while some hardy geraniums — including *Geranium sanguineum* and hybrids such as 'Brookside' and 'Rozanne' — can produce absolutely breathtaking shades of red. For other low-growing sun-lovers that turn reddish in fall, consider Chinese sedum (*S. tetractinum*), 'Dragon's Blood' sedum (*S. spurium*), bistort (*Persicaria bistorta*), and leadwort (*Ceratostigma plumbaginoides*). Taller options include some euphorbias (*E. polychroma* turns bright red, while *E. griffithii* can be deep red, orange, or yellow), Bowman's roots (*Gillenia*), and even some peonies. Yes, these flowering favorites can produce amazing autumn leaf colors as well. They'll vary from cultivar to cultivar and from year to year, but a few that tend to be dependable for great fall color are 'Buckeye Belle', 'Peter Brand', 'Sorbet', and 'White Wings'. For autumn reds in the shade garden, bergenias and 'Color Flash' astilbe are good bets. Foamflowers (*Tiarella*), foamy bells (× *Heucherella*), and *Mukdenia rossii* are great too: They often turn red to maroon but may also show some orange, gold, and pink in their fall foliage.

***Purple to maroon leaves.*** A striking addition to combinations all through the growing season, deep purple to maroon foliage can be especially handsome as a companion or underplanting for partners that turn red or yellow in autumn. Some favorites for good leaf color well into fall are black mondo grass (*Ophiopogon*

*planiscapus* 'Nigrescens'), 'Black Jack' and 'Purple Emperor' sedums, and 'Hillside Black Beauty' snakeroot (*Actaea* or *Cimicifuga*). And no list of dependable dark-leaved perennials would be complete without a mention of heucheras — there are dozens to choose from! Closely related foamy bells also offer some stunning colored-foliage selections, such as 'Burnished Bronze' and 'Chocolate Lace'.

**The king of crimson.** Rich reds aren't common among perennials where autumn leaf color is concerned, so leadwort (*Ceratostigma plumbaginoides*) is especially prized by fall foliage aficionados.

## THINK GREEN — AND SILVER, TOO

When you're working on filling your garden with fantastic fall foliage, don't overlook the value of companions that stay green for most or all of the autumn. Nothing sets off bright yellow, oranges, and reds as beautifully as a rich green background! A row or mass of broad- or needle-leaved evergreens makes a beautiful backdrop for deciduous trees and shrubs; hellebores (*Helleborus*), Japanese pachysandra (*Pachysandra terminalis*), wild gingers (*Asarum*), and similarly evergreen perennials and ground covers make great mates for other perennials, grasses, and small shrubs with showy fall color.

Silver foliage can be useful, too, providing a sparkling setting for jewel-like deep reds and purples. Options abound for stunning autumn silvers, including *Centaurea gymnocarpa* 'Colchester White', *Dichondra argentea* 'Silver Falls', 'Powis Castle' artemisia, *Senecio vira-vira*, and lamb's ears (*Stachys byzantina*).

Keep in mind that walls, fences, and other structures can serve a function similar to that of green or silver companion plants. A white picket fence or light-colored wall, for example, sets off red, purple, and rich orange tones perfectly, while a dark fence or outbuilding makes a striking contrast to bright and pastel yellows, as well as soft peach and pink foliage.

*Dichondra argentea* 'Silver Falls'

*Senecio vira-vira*

# Fall Foliage Color from Grasses

All too often, gardeners who are new to ornamental grasses bemoan the fact that these plants "aren't very colorful." Well, that couldn't be further from the truth — especially in fall. Warm-season grasses (those that do most of their growing in summer and flower in late summer to fall) can produce some amazing color changes in autumn, if not before.

***Reds and purples.*** Japanese blood grass (*Imperata cylindrica* var. *koenigii* 'Rubra'), for instance, emerges bright green with reddish tips in spring, gradually turning entirely red in time for a spectacular fall show. Quite a few switchgrass (*Panicum virgatum*) selections also go from green to reddish, including 'Rotstrahlbusch' (medium red) and 'Shenandoah' and 'Squaw' (purplish red). For even deeper purples in fall — and summer too, by the way — look to the annual purple millets (*Pennisetum glaucum* 'Jester', 'Purple Baron', and 'Purple Majesty'), tender perennial purple fountain grasses (such as *P. setaceum* 'Rubrum' and *P. macrostachyum* 'Burgundy Giant'), and 'Pele's Smoke' sugarcane (*Saccharum officinarum*).

***Gold grasses.*** There are many great grasses for yellow fall foliage as well. Selections of purple moor grass (*Molinia caerulea*) tend to be dependable for shades of yellow to gold; selections of Japanese silver grass (*Miscanthus sinensis*) are often in this color range, too, as is northern sea oats (*Chasmanthium latifolium*). And don't think switchgrasses and fountain grasses are good only for reds! Among the switchgrasses, look for 'Cloud Nine', 'Heavy Metal', and 'Northwind' for yellow fall foliage. Hardy fountain grasses (*Pennisetum alopecuroides*) that can be particularly pleasing for golden fall color

**Rose-colored grasses.** The striped leaves of golden Hakone grass (*Hakonechloa macra* 'Aureola') add a bright splash of yellow to shady gardens from spring through summer, then blush with shades of pink and red for the fall months.

**Grasses galore.** Tall or small, for flowers, seeds, or foliage, ornamental grasses are a must-have for glorious fall gardens. Yellow to orange is a common autumn foliage color for quite a few, including 'Cassian' fountain grass (*Pennisetum alopecuroides*) [top left], Japanese silver grass (*Miscanthus sinensis*) [bottom left], and many switchgrasses (*Panicum virgatum*) [right].

are 'Cassian' and 'Hameln'. Indian grass (*Sorghastrum nutans*) and prairie dropseed (*Sporobolus heterolepis*) are two more choices for shades of yellow, gold, and orange.

**Some surprises.** Many times, you can't easily predict what colors a particular grass will turn each year, but you can be well assured it will be beautiful. Frost grass (*Spodiopogon sibiricus*) typically turns shades of red and burgundy, but it may also take on some orangey tones. Flame grass (*Miscanthus* 'Purpurascens') shares

the same color range in full-sun sites, developing softer shades of pink and peach in shadier conditions. Little bluestem (*Schizachyrium scoparium*) can also vary quite a bit — often reddish orange, but sometimes with shadings of gold, pink, and/or purple as well. Golden Hakone grass (*Hakonechloa macra* 'Aureola') is bright yellow with thin green stripes in spring and summer; then in fall, it takes on reddish tones to appear in shades of maroon, rose, or orange.

# SPOTLIGHT ON GRASSES

Ornamental grasses are a great choice for fall borders, mass plantings, and even containers, contributing foliage and flower colors, showy seed heads, and terrific textures. Here's an overview of some glorious warm-season grasses that typically thrive in full sun and average, well-drained soil.

*Muhlenbergia capillaris*

*Pennisetum alopecuroides* 'Moudry'

*Miscanthus sinensis* 'Variegatus'

*Pennisetum setaceum* 'Rubrum'

*Chasmanthium latifolium*

*Imperata cylindrica* var. *koenigii* 'Rubra' with *Verbena bonariensis*

# Annuals and Tender Perennials for Autumn Foliage

Generally speaking, annuals and tender perennials don't offer much in the way of dramatic leaf color changes — but that doesn't mean they're not useful for fall foliage interest. As with hardy perennials, many annuals and tenders have colorful foliage from planting until frost, creating reliable color accents even if they never flower.

**Marvelous multicolors.** Coleus (*Solenostemon scutellarioides*), for instance, is a classic favorite for both sun and shade, and its leaves come in a wide range of bright and muted solid colors and patterns to complement just about any fall combination. Other marvelous multicolors that keep their great-looking leaves into autumn are fancy-leaved zonal geraniums (*Pelargonium × hortorum*) with shades of yellow and red in their foliage, such as

'Skies of Italy'; spiky-leaved phormiums, in many combinations of green, red, pink, orange, and yellow; showy sanchezia (*Sanchezia speciosa*), with deep green foliage heavily veined in yellow; and bold-leaved cannas, with green or purplish foliage striped with yellow or white, such as 'Minerva' and 'Pretoria'.

**Golden foliage.** If solid colors are more to your liking, there are plenty of options for you, too. Yellow foliage, for example, is a perfect complement to most other colors of fall flowers and leaves, and there are a number of excellent selections to select from. Some particularly good choices for clear, bright yellow foliage throughout the growing season are golden pigeonberry (*Duranta erecta* 'Aurea'), golden sweet potato vines (*Ipomoea batatas* 'Margarita' and 'Sweet Caroline Light Green'), Golden

**Love those leaves!** Annuals and tender perennials offer an abundance of fantastic foliage for fall gardens. Here, a mix of cannas and purple fountain grass (*Pennisetum setaceum* 'Rubrum') makes a striking backdrop for jagged silver cardoon (*Cynara cardunculus*) and rounded green nasturtiums (*Tropaeolum majus*) [*facing page*].

**Who needs blooms?** With all-season foliage this colorful, flowers are essentially incidental. Golden Lanterns Himalayan honeysuckle (*Leycesteria formosa* 'Notbruce') [below left] has vibrant yellow leaves that are flushed with red when new, while coleus (*Solenostemon scutellarioides*) [below right] comes in an array of colors and patterns to fit in anywhere.

**Rousing reds and pretty purples.** Bright fall blooms look all the better when paired with dark foliage, such as that of 'Carmencita' castor bean (*Ricinus communis*) [left], 'Redbor' kale [middle], and 'Maple Sugar' hibiscus (*Hibiscus acetosella*) [right].

Lanterns Himalayan honeysuckle (*Leycesteria formosa* 'Notbruce'), 'Kingwood Gold' jewels-of-Opar (*Talinum paniculatum*), and 'Sunshine' cape fuchsia (*Phygelius* × *rectus*).

***Deep red to purple foliage*** is invaluable for setting off both bright and pastel flowering and foliage companions from summer into fall, and options abound among both annuals and tender perennials. For low-growers well suited to growing in containers or near the front of a border, consider 'Black Pearl' pepper (*Capsicum annuum*), dark-leaved sweet potato vines (such as 'Ace of Spades' and 'Blackie'), 'Purple Knight' alternanthera (*Alternanthera dentata*), and 'Purple Lady' bloodleaf (*Iresine*). Dahlias, which are prized for their fall flowers, also come in a number of dark-leaved forms in a range of heights, from 12- to 18-inch-tall 'Chic' and 'Ellen

Huston' to 3-foot-tall 'Bishop of Llandaff' and 'Bishop of York', to name just a few. More mid- to back-of-the-border possibilities for moody maroon foliage are purple-leaved cannas, such as 'Australia', 'Black Knight', and 'Wyoming'; 'Carmencita' and other red-leaved castor beans (*Ricinus communis*); 'Red Shield', 'Maple Sugar' (also sold as 'Jungle Red') and other African rose mallows (*Hibiscus acetosella*); and *Euphorbia cotinifolia*. For something really unexpected, include some dark-leaved edibles in your autumn combinations. Cool-season crops like red lettuces ('Merlot' is one of the best), purple kale ('Redbor' is outstanding), and 'Bull's Blood' beet can make great fall replacements for border and container plants that look tattered by late summer.

# TAKING CUTTINGS OF TENDER TREASURES

If you have tender perennials that you'd like to keep for next year, taking cuttings in late summer or early fall is an ideal way to preserve them. The cuttings will take up much less space indoors than the original clumps, and you'll be able to enjoy their beauty all through the winter. Come spring, you can take cuttings from these pots to create even more new plants for your garden. Softwood cuttings provide quick results—you should have rooted cuttings in about a month. Fortunately, many of the most glorious frost-tender plants for showy foliage or flowers in autumn are also fairly easy to root from cuttings. Some good candidates to try are angelonias, begonias, cape fuchsias (*Phygelius*), coleus (*Solenostemon*), fuchsias, impatiens, plectranthus, salvias, and zonal and scented geraniums (*Pelargonium*).

**Choosing and preparing cuttings.** The day before you plan to take cuttings, water your plants thoroughly so they are not wilted or water-stressed. Then snip off healthy, 3- to 5-inch-long shoot tips, making the cut just below a node (the point where a leaf or leaves join the stem). Make sure each cutting has at least two nodes. Trim off the leaves from the bottom half of the cutting, and remove any flowers or flower buds.

**Planting softwood cuttings.** Fill 2- to 4-inch plastic pots with moistened potting mix. Use a dowel or pencil to make planting holes, then insert the cuttings to about half their depth, lightly firm the mix around them, and water well. A 2-inch pot holds one cutting; a 4-inch pot can usually hold three to five cuttings. (The leaves of the cuttings should not touch.) To keep humidity high around the leaves, set the pots in a clear plastic sweater box, or construct a light wooden or PVC frame, set the pots inside it, and drape it with a large sheet of clear plastic. If you wish, you can dip the cut ends of the stems in rooting hormone powder (available from garden centers), but softwood cuttings usually root rapidly even without this extra step.

**Aftercare for softwood cuttings.** Keep the cuttings in a bright spot but out of direct sunlight. The ideal air temperature is 65°F to 75°F, with the soil at 70°F to 75°F. (Setting the pots on a heated propagating mat can provide this steady warmth.) Most softwood cuttings start rooting within two to five weeks. Once you see new growth, gradually open the covering to reduce the humidity level and get the cuttings toughened up a bit. After a week or so, they should be well rooted and ready for transplanting into individual pots. Place the potted cuttings on a sunny windowsill, or set them under plant lights and treat them like houseplants for the winter; then set them outdoors after your last frost date next spring.

Preparing a softwood cutting.

# Fall Foliage from Shrubs and Trees

Now, we're at the traditional heart of the fall color phenomenon: the deciduous shrubs and trees that make a real spectacle of themselves at season's end. This feature isn't one that comes to mind during the frenzy of spring shopping; not surprisingly, flowers get most of the attention. Considering that few of us have unlimited space for these bigger, bulkier plants, though, it just makes sense to get as much interest as possible from the shrubs and trees that we *do* have room for.

***Colorful shrubs.*** Among shrubs, there are plenty of options that offer terrific fall color along with flowers, fruits, fragrance, and additional features to liven up other seasons as well. Deciduous viburnums are some of the hardest-working shrubs in the garden, producing clusters of cream to white, sometimes fragrant flowers in spring to early summer; showy fruits in a range of colors from late summer through most or all of the winter; and fall color mostly in shades of red and burgundy but sometimes with yellow and/or orange. Spireas (*Spiraea*) lack the long-lasting fruits, but their relatively compact size, handsome mounding to fountainlike form, and clustered pink or white spring and/or summer flowers make them a close runner-up in the most-valuable-shrub category. Their fall color a bonus: The green-leaved forms typically turn shades of yellow, orange-pink, and/or red, while those with yellow foliage throughout the growing season often take on bright orange to reddish hues in autumn.

Looking for more marvelous fall multicolors? Rugosa roses (*Rosa rugosa*) are best known for their fragrant flowers and showy scarlet "hips," but that's not all they have to offer. Depending on the cultivar and the weather conditions, their usual yellow autumn color can develop some dramatic shadings of orange, purple, and red as well. For a similar mix of leaf colors from a more shade-tolerant shrub, look to fothergillas (*Fothergilla gardenii* and *F. major*). Bush honeysuckles (*Diervilla*) are an out-of-the-ordinary choice for either sun or partial shade, with yellow flowers and

**Glamorous fall beauties.**
Whether you look to classics such as oaks (*Quercus*) [facing page] or something a little unusual, such as rugosa roses (*Rosa rugosa*) [below], colorful fall leaves are a must-have for the complete autumn experience.

**Expect the unexpected.** Shining sumac (*Rhus copallina*) [left] and sweetspire (*Itea virginica*) [right] are generally dependable for red hues, while dwarf fothergilla (*Fothergilla gardenii*) [middle] can take on a variety of autumn colors from year to year.

rich green foliage in summer and yellow, orange, and red autumn colors. Flowering currant (*Rubus odoratus*) offers a similar fall effect and also has yellow flowers, but its fragrant blooms appear in early spring; it produces edible summer fruits, too.

**Red-leaved shrubs.** If shrubs with reliably red fall leaves are more to your liking, sweetspire (*Itea virginica*) selections such as 'Henry's Garnet' and 'Merlot' are top-notch choices, with the added benefit of arching, fragrant white flower spikes in early summer. Chokeberries (*Aronia*) produce clustered white flowers in late spring that ripen into either black or red fruits by the time their deep green summer foliage turns striking shades of red in autumn. Those of you with acid soil are particularly lucky, because a number of distinctly acid-loving shrubs offer brilliant fall reds with

their other features; among them are dusty zenobia (*Zenobia pulverulenta*), enkianthus (*Enkianthus campanulatus* and *E. perulatus*), many deciduous azaleas (*Rhododendron*), and blueberries (*Vaccinium*).

A discussion of exceptional fall reds wouldn't be complete without mentioning burning bush (*Euonymus alatus*) and barberries (*Berberis*). These plants are considered seriously invasive in many areas, however, so other options are usually better for autumn interest. Cotoneasters, smokebush (*Cotinus*), and sumacs (*Rhus*), for example, can contribute some stunning scarlet leaf colors, while oakleaf hydrangea (*Hydrangea quercifolia*) and Diabolo ninebark (*Physocarpus opulifolius* 'Monlo') typically take on a mix of deeper red and burgundy shades. Yellowroot (*Xanthorhiza simplicissima*) is a sadly underused shrubby ground cover

# SPOTLIGHT ON DOGWOODS

Dogwoods (*Cornus*) come in a dizzying array of sizes, from good-sized trees to compact shrubs small enough to grow in a container, so there's no excuse for not tucking at least one or two into your yard. Most thrive in full sun to light shade with moist but well-drained soil.

Cornus florida

Cornus kousa

Cornus officinalis

# LET'S GET PLANTING!

Once you really start thinking about planning for fall color, you'll likely want to add lots more autumn-interest plants to your yard. Early fall is a great time to set out most container-grown plants, as well as to move existing clumps; in mild-winter areas (roughly Zone 7 and south), you can continue planting and transplanting potted plants into mid-fall. If you've mail-ordered bareroot plants, they probably won't arrive until mid- or late fall, but you don't have to wait until then to prepare their new homes. Get the holes ready earlier in the fall, while the weather is still pleasant, then you can quickly pop them into the ground when they finally do arrive.

**Go wide, not deep.** The trick to getting new plants well anchored before winter is encouraging their roots to spread, so don't skimp on digging the planting hole. Making it about as deep as the existing roots or rootball but at least twice as wide as its current spread provides a wide ring of loosened soil that new roots can easily creep through. (This advice isn't just for trees and shrubs, by the way—anything you plant in fall will appreciate the

Soaking bareroot plants.

Measuring crown depth.

extra attention.) Piling the soil you remove on a tarp makes for easy cleanup afterward.

**Handling a container-grown plant.** To make sure the rootball is thoroughly moist, sink the plant (pot and all) into a bucket of water and hold it down so the water covers the soil. Once no more bubbles are visible, lift out the plant, let it drain for a few minutes, then slide it out of the pot. Use your fingers to loosen any matted roots; if the roots are tightly wound together, use a sharp knife to cut shallow slashes every few inches around the rootball and on the bottom, too. Set the rootball in the planting hole, replace half of the removed soil around the roots, and water thoroughly. Replace the rest of the soil, then water again.

**Setting out bareroot plants.** Remove the packing material, then soak the roots in a bucket of warm water for an hour or two. Replace some soil in the planting hole to make a mound, then set the crown (center) of the plant on top and spread out the roots evenly over the sides of the mound. Lay a stake across the top of the hole to show the final soil level, then add or remove some soil from the mound if needed to ensure that the crown is even with the stake. (One exception: If you're planting bareroot peonies, set the buds about 2 inches below soil level.) Backfill with some soil, water thoroughly, replace the rest of the soil, and water again.

that can turn a wonderful reddish purple in fall, sometimes mixed with yellow. To bring some deeper purples into the mix, consider buttonbush (*Cephalanthus occidentalis*) or even ordinary forsythias.

**Gold-leaved shrubs.** Alone or combined with other bright fall colors, yellows are always welcome for brightening up autumn landscapes. Summersweet (*Clethra alnifolia*) is one superb multiseason shrub in this category, contributing an abundance of scented white flower spikes in midsummer and rich green foliage that commonly turns clear yellow in fall. Bottlebrush buckeye (*Aesculus parviflora*) produces a somewhat similar flowering and foliage effect in both summer and fall but on a much larger shrub. Japanese kerria (*Kerria japonica*) is best known for its golden spring flowers and bright green winter stems, but its soft

yellow autumn color can also be welcome. Though sweetshrub (*Calycanthus floridus*) isn't an especially showy shrub in bloom, the fruity fragrance of its maroon summer flowers, along with glossy green leaves that age to rich yellow in autumn, makes it a welcome addition to the multiseason garden. Beautyberries (*Callicarpa*) are, as you might guess, prized mostly for their attractive fruits, but their yellowish autumn leaf color also adds some interest — particularly on the purple-berried plants. The fall foliage color of winterberry (*Ilex verticillata*) tends to be more variable, but when it turns a good yellow, the contrast of the foliage with the bright red berries is also quite attractive. Spicebush (*Lindera benzoin*), too, combines yellow fall color and red berries. Shrubs that bear yellow foliage through the growing season usually hold their color into

**Mellow yellows.** If you love golden foliage, you're in luck — deciduous shrubs offer an abundance of options to choose from. Winterberry (*Ilex verticillata*) [left] typically takes on some shade of yellow in fall; bottlebrush buckeye (*Aesculus parviflora*) [right] gradually ages from green to gold as the season comes to an end.

**Showy combos.** It's not unusual to see colorful berries paired with fall foliage, as on this Korean mountain ash (*Sorbus alnifolia*) [left], but autumn-flowering Higan cherry (*Prunus subhirtella* 'Autumnalis') [right] is one of the few trees that produce scattered blooms among their showy fall leaves.

the fall as well; some, such as 'Dart's Gold' ninebark (*Physocarpus opulifolius*), appear an even richer gold as temperatures cool.

***Early-flowering trees.*** Where there's room for taller plants — at the back of a border, in small groupings, or as a single specimen — small to medium-sized trees that offer attractive flowers, fruits, *and* fall color are always welcome. Dogwoods (*Cornus florida*, *C. kousa*, and other tree-form species and hybrids) are among the most popular options here, and with good reason. Along with showy blooms in late spring or early summer, they offer an abundance of red fruits by late summer and autumn foliage color that's usually in shades of red, burgundy, and deep purple. Hawthorns (*Crataegus*) and mountain ashes (*Sorbus*) offer a similar progression — clustered white flowers in late spring or early summer, bright red fruits later on, and deep green leaves that typically turn deep red to bronze on hawthorns and yellow, orange, or red on mountain ashes. Also known as Juneberry or service-berry, shadbush (*Amelanchier*) too puts on a good show of white flowers, but its early-spring bloom develops into blue summer berries instead of red fall fruits. It's difficult to predict what its autumn color will be in any given year, but the brilliant shades of red, orange, yellow, and/or purple rarely fail to please. Both ornamental and fruiting cherries and plums (*Prunus*) can also have great fall color, usually in the orange-to-yellow range but sometimes with reds and purples as well.

If eye-catching or edible fruits aren't particularly important to you, there are many more small- to medium-sized flowering trees that are also outstanding for fall color, although not all are worthy of planting. The widely available Callery or Bradford pear (*Pyrus calleryana*), for example, is very pretty both in spring bloom and in its usual red, orange, and/or burgundy autumn color; however, its potential to become invasive (and its already established classification as invasive in some areas) makes it a poor choice when there are so many other beautiful multiseason trees to choose from.

Spring-blooming redbuds (*Cercis*) and fringetree (*Chionanthus virginicus*), for instance, often turn cheery yellow in autumn, at least in cooler climates. And witch hazels (*Hamamelis*) are practically a must-have for a dazzling autumn display: typically yellow for the fall-flowering *H. virginiana* and any number of glowing red, orange, and yellow shades for the late-winter-to-spring-blooming species and hybrids.

**Summer- and fall-flowering trees** that also offer good fall foliage color aren't nearly as common as early-blooming ones, but they're definitely worth seeking out. Sourwood (*Oxydendrum arboreum*), also known as lily-of-the-valley tree, flowers in early to midsummer, followed by yellow-green seedpods that show off nicely against the vibrant red to burgundy fall foliage. Stewartias are also welcome for their white, mid- to late-summer flowers as well as their red to golden orange autumn colors. Some other lovely late-blooming trees with excellent fall foliage are franklinia (*Franklinia alatamaha*) — it turns red, orange, and/or burgundy — and crape myrtles (*Lagerstroemia*) — typically with shadings of red and orange.

**Color standouts.** Some small- to medium-sized trees don't offer much in the way of flowers but they are so amazing in autumn that it's worth making a place for them if you can. Disanthus (*Disanthus cercidifolius*), for example, can produce such

an outstanding display of red to burgundy (and sometimes orange) autumn leaf colors that it's considered a must-try by many fall foliage aficionados. Japanese maples (*Acer palmatum*) and fullmoon maples (*A. japonicum*) are also justifiably popular, for their clear red and orange shades in particular. Paperbark maple (*A. griseum*) and three-flowered maple (*A. triflorum*) are two other

**A grand finale.** Franklinia (*Franklinia alatamaha*) puts on a spectacular show of fall foliage color while its camellia-like white flowers are still opening.

# SPOTLIGHT ON MAPLES

Maples (*Acer*) are practically a necessity for those of you who love fabulous fall foliage. Most of these small, medium, or large deciduous trees thrive in full sun to partial shade with average to moist but well-drained soil.

Acer trifolium

Acer palmatum

Acer pseudosieboldianum

Acer japonicum

exceptionally beautiful species worth considering for both their autumn colors and their beautiful peeling bark.

**Shade trees.** Finally, we come to the group of medium- to large-scale woody plants typically used as shade trees, which includes some of the most well-known trees for fall foliage color. The yellow autumn leaves of ginkgo (*Ginkgo biloba*) are a beautiful sight both on the tree and on the ground when they've dropped to form a pool of gold around the trunks. Katsura tree (*Cercidiphyllum japonicum*) is a treat to see in its orange-yellow fall color and even more of a pleasure to smell: Its

falling leaves have a strong, sweet scent that can carry through your whole yard! Other shade trees that typically turn yellow in fall are American yellowwood (*Cladrastis kentuckea*), birches (*Betula*), common hackberry (*Celtis occidentalis*), green ash (*Fraxinus pensylvanica*), hickories (*Carya*), honey locust (*Gleditsia triacanthos*), hop hornbeam (*Ostrya virginiana*), mulberries (*Morus*), pawpaw (*Asimina triloba*), poplars and aspens (*Populus*), striped maple (*Acer pensylvanicum*), and tulip poplar (*Liriodendron tulipifera*). Dawn redwood (*Metasequoia glyptostroboides*), larches (*Larix*), and swamp cypress (*Taxodium distichum*) are

**A feast for the senses.** Katsura tree (*Cercidiphyllum japonicum*) is a beauty for fall color, but that's not its only autumn attribute: Its aging foliage also has a distinct cotton-candy fragrance.

three oddities in the conifer world, because they are deciduous rather than evergreen. Dawn redwood's needles can turn coppery pink, golden orange, or rusty brown before dropping, while larch needles turn yellow to orange and swamp cypress is often a rich rust to reddish brown color.

Deciduous trees with brilliant red to orange fall foliage are some of the most exciting sights of the season. Some oaks (*Quercus*) can offer stunning scarlets in fall, among them northern red oak (*Q. rubra*), pin oak (*Q. palustris*), and scarlet oak (*Q. coccinea*). White oak (*Q. alba*) is typically a deeper red. Chinese pistache (*Pistacia chinensis*) is far lesser known, but it's considered one of the finest trees for bright red and orange shades in autumn. Sassafras (*Sassafras albidum*) also makes a spectacular show, although its tendency to spread by suckers makes it a less popular choice for most home landscapes. Black tupelo or sourgum (*Nyssa sylvatica*) is another good bet for knock-your-socks-off fall reds, either in solid shades or combined with orange, gold, and purple. Some other trees you can usually depend on for fantastic reds, oranges, and yellows in autumn are red maple (*Acer rubrum*), sugar maple (*A. saccharum*), sweetgum (*Liquidambar styraciflua*), and Persian parrotia (*Parrotia persica*). (If you choose to plant sweetgum, consider the cultivar 'Rotundiloba'; its fall color can vary, but it lacks the wickedly spiny seedpods of the species.) And then there's Japanese zelkova (*Zelkova serrata*), in shades of yellow, orange, and/or burgundy. With so many outstanding and colorful deciduous trees, why would you even consider planting one *without* autumn interest?

**Magical multicolors.** You never know exactly what colors they'll produce from year to year, but swamp cypress (*Taxodium distichum*) [left], sassafras (*Sassafras albidum*) [middle], and black tupelo (*Nyssa sylvatica*) [right] never fail to please where fall foliage is concerned.

Mahonia repens

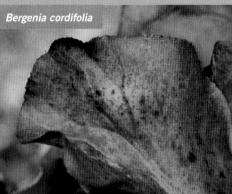
Bergenia cordifolia

Erica × darleyensis 'Mary Helen'

When you hear a plant described as being "evergreen," you naturally expect its foliage to be green all year 'round. Well, that's not always the case. Some "evergreens" are in fact green during most of the growing season, but then they take on shades of red to purple when cool temperatures return in fall and keep those colors until the weather warms up again in spring. Here's a brief rundown of some of these not-so-evergreens:

*Abelia* (abelias): Several species and selections take on reddish to bronzy colors in fall, then hold their leaves through part or all of winter.

*Arctostaphylos uva-ursi* (bearberry): Small, glossy leaves typically turn deep red to maroon for fall and winter.

*Armeria maritima* (sea thrift): 'Rubrifolia' turns deep purple for the colder months.

*Bergenia* (bergenias): Selections with exceptionally good burgundy color are 'Autumn Glow', 'Bressingham Ruby', and 'Winter Glow'.

*Calluna vulgaris* (heather): Many cultivars take on red, orange, or yellow foliage color for fall and winter.

*Erica* (heath): Several selections develop yellow, orange, bronzy, or purple tips in autumn and winter.

*Euonymus fortunei* (wintercreeper): Deep plum-purple for the colder months.

*Galax urceolata* (wandflower): Reddish fall and winter color.

*Gaultheria procumbens* (wintergreen): Glossy green foliage darkens to maroon or burgundy.

*Leucothoe* (leucothoes): Bronzy to deep purple fall-through-winter color in sun.

*Mahonia repens* (creeping grape holly): Many shades of plum-purple, bronze, and red, sometimes with yellow.

*Nandina* (heavenly bamboo): Bright red to reddish purple fall and winter color varies by cultivar; is considered invasive in some areas.

*Rhododendron* (evergreen azaleas and rhododendrons): A few that turn color in fall are 'Girard's Crimson' (reds and purples), 'PJM' (bright red, then deep purple), 'Silver Sword' (pinkish to red), and 'Stewartstonian' (red to burgundy).

# SHOWY SEED HEADS AND BOUNTIFUL BERRIES

**Take notice** [facing page]. Against the more common gold, red, and rust of the autumn garden, the violet-purple of Japanese beautyberry (*Callicarpa japonica*) is guaranteed to attract attention.

Fall gardens and landscapes offer yet another benefit you seldom find early in the growing season: a wealth of fascinating seed heads and fabulous fruits. Sometimes, these features carry over from late summer into fall; in other cases, they may appear in fall and last into or through winter. Either way, they give you even more ways to add excitement to autumn beds and borders.

## Seeds and Seed Heads

**A grain of salt** [below]. Airy sprays of sorghum (*Sorghum vulgare*) create a tall, dramatic accent.

If you're obsessive about picking off faded flowers and cleaning up your beds and borders as soon as frost hits, the idea of intentionally leaving "dead stuff" in your garden may sound like an oddball idea. Relaxing your standards a bit has several benefits, though. It gives you several more weeks or months of interest from your plantings, and it also provides a fall and winter feast for hungry songbirds. Admittedly, it can take a bit of effort to change your perception of seed heads from "unsightly" to "appealing." And even if you personally love the look of seeds and seedpods, you may choose to bow to conventional tidiness in high-visibility front- and side-yard areas. But in spaces where you feel free to enjoy every feature your plants can provide, good-looking seed heads make a perfect complement to the abundance of other autumn-flowering and fall foliage favorites.

*Annuals with stunning seed heads.* Once you've opened your mind to the possibility that plants can be attractive even when

**Delightful diversity.** Making seeds is what annual flowers are all about—and some do it in grand style! Some striking examples are [from left] the spiny green pods of swan plant (*Asclepias physocarpa*); the clustered seed heads of sunflowers (*Helianthus annuus*); and the hard, slender pods of 'Burgundy' okra (*Abelmoschus esculentus*).

they're not at their peak, you'll find ample opportunities for appreciating seeds and seed heads. Annual and tender perennial plants, for instance, aren't especially well known for looking good once their flowers fade, but if you're willing to broaden your planting palette beyond petunias and geraniums, you can find some truly interesting options. Love-in-a-mist (*Nigella damascena*) is one of the best, with puffy pods that are usually green aging to tan and striped with deep purple; 'Cramer's Plum', though, has totally purple pods. Spike celosia (*Celosia spicata*) offers a much different effect, with slender tan spikes of small, tightly packed seedpods. Cosmos (*Cosmos bipinnatus* and *C. sulphureus*) hold their dark brown seeds in tuftlike clusters at the shoot tips, creating a very airy effect. Castor beans, on the other hand, develop bold clusters of large,

spiny seedpods that are shades of deep maroon to bright red on red-leaved strains (such as 'Carmencita' and 'Impala').

Looking to some "heirloom" annuals can find you other superb seedpods to dress up your autumn borders. Shoo-fly plant (*Nicandra physalodes*), for example, is an old-fashioned favorite with pretty blue-and-white, bell-like blooms that mature into papery, brown, lanternlike husks around rounded seedpods. Another classic, money plant or honesty (*Lunaria annua*), is technically a biennial, but it's usually grouped with annuals in seed catalogs. The first year, it produces only foliage; in the second year, it sends up branching flowering stems that develop somewhat circular, flat, papery seedpods. If you carefully peel away the tan covering on each side of the seedpod, it reveals a fascinating silvery white membrane.

Specialty seed catalogs and seed exchanges are good places to hunt down some of the even-more-unusual annuals and tender perennials, such as jewels-of-Opar (*Talinum paniculatum*), with airy clouds of tiny pink flowers that develop into small, rounded, orange seedpods. Starflower or paper moon (*Scabiosa stellata*) is also fairly compact, but its pincushion-like pale blue or pink to creamy white blooms mature into rounded, papery, bronzy tan seed heads. Lacy-leaved cancer bush (*Sutherlandia frutescens*) is much showier in bloom, with bright red flowers that are followed by interesting inflated seedpods. The relatively ordinary-looking, pale pink flowers of devil's claw, or unicorn plant (*Proboscidea louisianica*), give no clue that they'll mature into large pods with long, curved, sharp-pointed spurs; nor do the hardly noticeable blooms of swan plant (*Asclepias physocarpa*), which turn into large, puffy green pods that are covered with small spines. They're guaranteed to attract attention!

***Grains and vegetables.*** Another group of annuals that you might not immediately think of for autumn interest is edibles, such as grains and vegetables. Wheat, barley, rye, and similar grains usually ripen in midsummer from fall or early-spring sowings, but if you plant them later in the spring, they'll mature later in the summer and can hold their beautiful seed heads into early fall. The plants of ornamental corn (*Zea mays*), also known as Indian corn, aren't all that attractive by this time of year, but you could peel back the husks while the colorful cobs are still on the plants for some garden interest, or else use them for fall decorations. Midsummer-sown sunflowers (*Helianthus annuus*) also mature in late summer to early fall. As with corn, the declining plants themselves aren't ornamental, but the seed heads are useful for fall decorating — not to mention for feeding hungry birds.

Broomcorn and grain sorghum (*Sorghum bicolor*) produce plumy seed heads in shades of cream, gold, rust, red, and brown. Amaranths (*Amaranthus*), too, have plumes, which can be greenish, rusty orange, or red. There are many single-color strains, among them 'Hopi Red Dye', which has deep red stems, leaves, and seed heads; and 'Orange Giant', with green leaves and orange plumes. If you'd prefer a mix of plume colors, look for seed blends such as 'Towers Mix' (green and red) and 'Magic Fountains Mix' (green, red, and orange). The distinctive ornamental love-lies-bleeding (*A. caudatus*), with long, trailing, reddish flower and seed heads, also falls in this group. And don't forget about the decorative value of okra (*Abelmoschus esculentus*): the green-stemmed types bear slender, pointed green pods; red-stemmed strains (such as 'Burgundy') produce deep red pods.

# AUTUMN COLOR FROM A CAN

**Make your own fall color.**
Purple coneflower (*Echinacea purpurea*) [left] takes on a distinctly different appearance with a glowing green coat, while a touch of pale pink perfectly complements the lacy seed heads of silverleaf hydrangea (*Hydrangea arborescens* subsp. *radiata*) [right].

If you like the look of autumn seed heads and stems but want a little more "zip" color-wise, simply give them a quick spritz with a can of spray paint! Choose a color that harmonizes with the other flowers, foliage, and fruits in your garden, or go for something really wild—like shocking pink, bright turquoise, or glittering gold—to add a real element of surprise. You don't need much to create quite an impact, so don't get carried away; light spritzes of paint, used on a few plants with particularly interesting seed heads, add just enough color to catch the eye without looking too intense or artificial. Spray the seed heads in place, using newspaper to mask the surrounding plants; or cut some of your favorites, spray them in a separate, well-ventilated area, then stick them back into your borders or into container plantings. If possible, wait until late fall to do this, so the birds have had a chance to eat the seeds first.

***Perennials for seeds and seed heads.***
Here's the key to the autumn seed head
show: the hardy perennials that hold their
good-looking post-bloom form well into
fall, if not through most or all of winter.
Some of the most dependable perennials
for handsome seed heads are those in the
daisy family; they lose their "petals" (technically known as ray florets) but usually
keep the densely packed center-disk florets. Several of the best-known perennials
for exceptional seed heads are called coneflowers: orange coneflowers (*Rudbeckia*),
purple coneflowers (*Echinacea*), and prairie
coneflowers (*Ratibida*). The seed-laden centers of all three are deep brown to black.
Orange coneflower seed heads typically
have a roughly rounded shape; those of
purple coneflowers are larger with pointed
centers and those of prairie coneflowers are
distinctly elongated. Golden marguerites
(*Anthemis*) and sneezeweeds (*Helenium*)
have much smaller, roundish seed heads,
whereas coreopsis and perennial sunflower
(*Helianthus*) seed heads are usually more
tuftlike but equally dark. And then there
are the asters, blanket flowers (*Gaillardia*),
and ironweeds (*Vernonia*), with fluffy, light-
colored seed tufts that are roughly rounded
to dome-shaped.

Of course, there are plenty of other
perennials with rounded seed heads that
*don't* belong to the daisy family. Giant sca-
bious (*Cephalaria gigantea* and *C. dipsacoides*),

for instance, are in the teasel family, but
their dark, dense, oval seed heads very
much resemble those of true daisies. Sea
hollies (*Eryngium*) are in the carrot family,
but they too have spherical to elongated
seed heads instead of the lacy heads that
are typical of many carrot-family members.
(The spiny bracts that form a ring or "ruff"
around the base of the seed heads also make
them look definitely different from daisy
seed heads.) Globe thistle (*Echinops ritro*),
as you may guess, is in the thistle family,
with perfectly rounded, steely gray heads
that never fail to attract attention long
after the tiny flowers have dropped off.
Verbena-family member Brazilian vervain
(*Verbena bonariensis*) holds its clustered
seed heads atop tall, slender stems. The
mint family also offers some splendid seed
heads, including the rounded heads of bee
balms (*Monarda*) and the small but sturdy
buttons of mountain mints (*Pycnanthemum*).

**An assortment of forms.** You
can depend on coneflower
(*Rudbeckia hirta* 'Gloriosa
Double Daisy') [left] to produce
dense, dark seed heads, while
ironweed (*Vernonia*) [right] blossoms end the season as much
smaller, silvery tufts.

Flowers that develop into plumelike or spiky seed heads provide a vertical effect that makes a welcome contrast to the many rounded forms. The best in the plume category include astilbes, goat's beards (*Aruncus*), many goldenrods (*Solidago*), and queen-of-the-prairie (*Filipendula rubra*); Russian sages (*Perovskia*), too, have a plumy effect in fall. And if you're searching for spiky seed heads, options are practically unlimited. On some, the actual seedpods are various shapes, but the strongly vertical stalk they're held on creates a distinctly spiky effect; examples here are sturdy-stemmed biennial mulleins (*Verbascum*), bear's breeches (*Acanthus*), gayfeathers (*Liatris*), monkshoods (*Aconitum*), and turtleheads (*Chelone*). False indigos (*Baptisia*) usually have an overall spiky effect, but their spikes are made up of individual, elongated black pods that are interesting in their own right. Jerusalem sages (*Phlomis*) also have strongly vertical stems, but their seed heads are held in ball-like whorls around the stems; *Salvia verticillata* creates a somewhat similar effect on a much smaller scale.

Other perennials produce much shorter, spiky seed heads at the tips of their stems. The taller anise hyssops (*Agastache*), such as *A. foeniculum* and *A. nepetoides*, are particularly striking for tan autumn seed heads, and they hold their form through the winter as well. Spike speedwell (*Veronica spicata*) and Culver's roots (*Veronicastrum*) also offer long-lasting, tapering spikes, while burnets (*Sanguisorba*) and black snakeroots (*Actaea* or *Cimicifuga*) have a more cylindrical shape to their seed heads. Siberian iris (*Iris sibirica*) seedpods are relatively large and very vertical, and their dark color really makes them noticeable. Lilies (*Lilium*), too, tend to have slender seedpods, but they're typically tan and held in clusters instead of singly; Formosan lily (*L. formosanum*) and martagon lily (*L. martagon*) are two species with particularly good-looking pods. Though ferns technically don't produce seeds, the spore cases of cinnamon fern (*Osmunda cinnamomea*) form on spiky-looking fertile fronds that age to a rich orangey brown color in autumn.

To complement the many spherical and spiky seed heads, consider some of the more unusual shapes. Yarrows (*Achillea*), for instance — particularly the sturdy-stemmed old favorite 'Coronation Gold' — produce interesting flat-topped clusters, as do many of the upright sedums, such as 'Autumn Joy', 'Autumn Fire', and showy stonecrop (*Sedum spectabile*). Joe-Pye weeds (*Eupatorium dubium, E. maculatum*, and *E. purpureum*) have larger, domed clusters; once their fluffy seeds blow away, the lacy "skeleton" remains for exceptional winter interest. Other perennials with lacy-looking fall seed heads are fennel (*Foeniculum vulgare*) and patrinia (*Patrinia scabiosifolia*). The small seedpods of Bowman's roots (*Gillenia*) and sea kale (*Crambe maritima*) also have a very dainty, delicate effect, and some of the ornamental onions (*Allium*) produce absolutely amazing, starburstlike summer seed heads that can last into fall if you're lucky. *A. christophii* and *A. schubertii* are two of the most striking seed head options; drumstick chives (*A. sphaerocephalon*) are much smaller but also appealing for autumn interest. Pineapple lilies (*Eucomis*) are another group of bulbs with exceptionally attractive fall seed heads: essentially large, cylindrical clusters of individual seedpods topped with a tuft of foliage, creating a remarkable likeness to real pineapples.

A few other perennials produce relatively undistinguished pods, but once they split open, they're quite showy in the autumn garden. Blackberry lily (*Belamcanda chinensis*), for example, reveals round black seeds in clusters that are about the size and shape of real blackberries, while crocosmias offer one-sided sprays of small pods that split to reveal red seeds. Despite its awful common name, stinking iris (*Iris foetidissima*) is a stunning multiseason perennial, with swordlike evergreen foliage, interesting (though not tremendously showy) light purple-and-yellow flowers in early summer, and large pods that burst to display bright orange-red, rounded seeds that

usually stick around into winter. There is also a selection with bright white seeds sold under the name 'Fructo Albo', 'Fructo Alba', or 'Albo Fructa'. Even peonies (*Paeonia*) may get into the act in autumn, with large, multipart pods that enclose rounded, glossy blue to black seeds sometimes mingled with smaller orange, pink, or red sterile seeds or set into a red to pink lining. Some that can produce a particularly eye-catching autumn show are *P. cambessedesii*, *P. japonica*, *P. mlokosewitschii*, *P. mollis*, and *P. obovata*.

One more perennial often praised for its showy fall seedpods is Chinese lantern (*Physalis alkekengi*). Its puffy orange pods are beautiful, but I definitely don't recommend letting this aggressive spreader loose in your garden unless that's all you want to grow. If you must have it, keep it in a large pot set on a paved area so the roots can't creep out of the bottom.

**Seed heads for show.** If you're not too quick to cut them down, perennials can provide an exciting array of seed heads for fall and winter. Facing page, from the top: Miss Willmott's ghost (*Eryngium giganteum*), spike gayfeather (*Liatris spicata*), and Culver's root (*Veronicastrum*). This page: blackberry lily (*Belamcanda chinensis*) [top], *Paeonia obovata* [bottom left], and Persian onion (*Allium aflatunense*) [bottom right]

# SAVING AND SOWING SEEDS

Seed-savvy gardeners get double pleasure from their fall plantings. They enjoy seeing the array of beautiful seed heads on their plants, and they revel in the wealth of free seeds just waiting to be collected and sown to create new plants.

If you're used to buying your seeds every year in tidy, colorful packages, you may wonder why anyone would bother collecting his or her own. Well, for one, it can save you a bundle of money! No more having to buy a whole packet when you need only a half-dozen plants, or multiple packets when you need lots of new plants. Collecting seed from your favorite annuals also ensures that you'll have them to enjoy year after year, even if seed catalogs stop selling them. It's a terrific way to preserve special heirloom varieties or unique colors of annual flowers that appear in your garden.

You do need to keep in mind that in some cases, the seedlings you get from saved seeds will not exactly resemble the plants you gathered them from. They may differ only slightly, or they may be very different in height, vigor, bloom color, or other traits. This is especially true if you are dealing with hybrids—carefully controlled crosses between specially selected parent plants. To get identical-looking plants of annual hybrids every year, you'll need to buy the seeds instead. The same is true of many named cultivars of perennials and shrubs; to get exact copies, you'll need to use a technique such as division or cuttings rather than seed. If you enjoy experimenting, though, the unpredictable results you often get from home-collected seed can be quite exciting!

For specific details on when and how to collect seeds, check out Gathering Seeds on page 124. Keep in mind that when you gather seeds from your garden, you're not just getting the seeds—you're also likely to collect pieces of seedpods, leaves, insects, and other bits of debris. Getting rid of this chaff makes

*Nigella damascena*

the seeds less bulky to store, and they'll be much easier to deal with at sowing time, too. As soon as possible after you collect them, spread out each kind of seed on a plate or shallow tin in a warm, airy place to dry for a week or so. After cleaning, place the seeds in labeled paper envelopes and store them in a cool, dry dark place.

**Picking out the big bits.** First, rub the seed-chaff mixture with your fingers to break up any large clumps and to help release the seeds from any covering they might have. If the seeds are in pods that are too hard to break with your fingers, tap the pods with a hammer or run a rolling pin over them to help release the seeds. Then pick out the largest debris with a pair of tweezers. Or, tilt the plate or tin slightly and tap it gently to encourage the heavier seeds to roll to one side, then use a small paintbrush to remove the remaining chaff.

**Cleaning with screening.** For even quicker results, use wire mesh to separate the seeds and chaff. Larger mesh lets the seed fall through and retains the larger debris; finer mesh catches the seed but lets the very fine chaff fall. You can buy sets of commercially made sieves designed specifically for cleaning seeds, and they're invaluable if you save lots of seed

each year. But if you have only small amounts to clean, it's possible to get great results with several small handheld tea strainers in various mesh sizes. With just two or three siftings, you can remove most or all of the debris in just a few minutes.

**Breezing along.** Once you've removed most of the debris, your seeds are probably plenty clean enough to store. But if you want to clean them further, try a technique called winnowing. This involves pouring the seeds from one container to another in front of a fan. Experiment with winnowing at different distances from a fan set on its lowest speed, starting at roughly 18 inches away for fine seeds and 1 foot for larger seeds; then move nearer or turn up the fan, if needed. You want the air movement strong enough to blow the chaff but light enough that it doesn't blow the seeds too. Don't have a fan handy? You could also try this outdoors on a day with a light

Using a brush to remove chaff.

Winnowing with a fan.

breeze or simply puff gently over the seeds to blow away the chaff.

**Smart storage.** Most of the seeds you can collect in fall are dry when they're ready to harvest, and they like to be stored dry in paper envelopes in a cool place, such as a refrigerator. (It's a good idea to place the seed envelopes in an airtight container before storage, to protect them from humidity.) Some, though—such as roses and hollies (*Ilex*)—are formed within berries or fleshy fruits, and if you try to store these as they are, they're likely to rot. One option is to rub them against a screen to crush the fruits; another is to rub them with your fingers or run a rolling pin over them. Place the crushed fruits in a bowl of water and skim the debris and pulp off the top. Drain off the water, spread the seeds on a fine screen or a piece of paper to dry, then store them in a cool spot or, better yet, plant them right away.

**Sowing for winter chilling.** While spring is still the ideal sowing time for most annuals, the seeds of some perennials, shrubs, vines, and trees sprout best when you sow them outdoors in autumn, either in pots or in holding beds. Some need a certain period of cool temperatures to germinate, while others benefit from the alternating cool and warm temperatures of fall and spring. With purchased seeds, the sowing directions on the packages will usually tell you if autumn sowing is appropriate. If you've saved seeds from your own plants, it's smart to check a reference book,

such as *The Gardener's A–Z Guide to Growing Flowers from Seed to Bloom* by Eileen Powell (Storey Publishing), for the ideal sowing time. Or, you could experiment by dividing the seeds into two batches, then sowing one outdoors in fall and another indoors in early spring, to see whether those seeds sprout better in warm or cool conditions. For more details on sowing seeds outdoors, turn to Making More Plants on page 204.

Unlike indoor sowing, which often produces results in just a few days, outdoor sowing requires some patience on your part. You'll usually see the seedlings come up the following spring after sowing, although some seeds take two or even three years to appear. If you plan on doing a lot of fall sowing, it's smart to set aside a special nursery bed or a cold frame to hold your sown seed pots, so they can sit for a few years without being in the way. Also, remember to mark the sowing year on a pot or row's name label. Then, if you don't see any action by the fall of the third year, you'll know it's safe to dump that pot in your compost pile or to sow other seeds in that part of the nursery bed.

***Gorgeous grasses for fall seed heads.***
Even gardeners who are immune to the charm of other seed heads have to admit that ornamental grasses have a lot to offer autumn beds and borders. The species and selections that are in seed at the end of the season are typically "warm-season" grasses: the ones that do their growing during summer's heat, then flower and set seed as the growing season winds down. The actual blooms on grasses are so small that it's often hard to tell exactly when the flower heads turn into seed heads, but that's really not as important as how they look in the garden. Some, such as the tall, dense, creamy white to pink plumes of pampas grass (*Cortaderia selloana*), are showy enough to be visible from several hundred feet away. Ravenna grass (*Saccharum ravennae*), sometimes called hardy pampas grass, is also quite dramatic, with relatively open, silvery pink to bronzy plumes. Both of these can easily reach 8 to 12 feet tall, so you need a lot of space to show them off to their best advantage.

Would you prefer grasses that show their seed heads closer to eye level? You might consider selections of Japanese silver grass (*Miscanthus sinensis*), with whisklike heads of reddish to silvery flower clusters that mature into fluffy seeds in fall. Even after the seeds blow away, the seed heads hold their form well through the winter. Or, if you're among the gardeners who are

concerned about the tendency of these and other exotic grasses to seed into natural areas, look toward U.S. natives such as switchgrass (*Panicum virgatum*) and Indian grass (*Sorghastrum nutans*). Switchgrasses have airy, many-branched plumes that last from late summer to early spring, long after their tiny seeds are gone. Their plumes are typically red-tinged green — or

**Heads above the rest.** Shown here with orange coneflowers (*Rudbeckia*) and Russian sage, the plumy seed heads of dwarf pampas grass (*Cortaderia selloana* 'Pumila') add a distinctive touch to fall gardens in warmer parts of the country.

sometimes distinctly pink, as on 'Dallas Blues' — during the growing season, turning tan after frost. Through the larger, reddish brown seeds of Indian grass are usually devoured by birds as soon as the seed heads are ripe in mid- to late fall, the plant's tan, vertical stalks stick around for winter interest.

For somewhat shorter warm-season grasses that fit well into smaller-scale borders and foundation plantings, fountain grasses (*Pennisetum*) are a popular option. Their long, cylindrical, brushy-looking spikes remain attractive in the garden into early winter, at least, and they're packed with seeds that many birds find appealing. Northern sea oats (*Chasmanthium latifolium*) is more upright in overall form, with dangling, flattened seed clusters that turn coppery to brown in autumn; unlike many other grasses, it can perform well in partly shaded areas as well as full sun. Pink muhly grass (*Muhlenbergia capillaris*) creates an effect distinctly different from that of both of these, due to its dense clouds of reddish pink fall flower- and seed heads.

Fall isn't exclusively for warm-season grasses, of course; some cool-season or intermediate grasses bloom in early to midsummer, then hang on to their showy seed heads for fall. Feather reed grass (*Calamagrostis* × *acutiflora*), for example, blooms with airy, pinkish plumes in summer, turning tan and lasting into winter.

It holds its stems and plumes very vertically — as does frost grass (*Spodiopogon sibiricus*) — whereas those of Korean feather reed grass (*C. brachytricha*) tend to radiate out in all directions, creating a very different and exciting effect. Silver spear grass (*Achnatherum calamagrostis*) is another summer-bloomer, somewhat similar to Korean feather reed grass, but its bronzy seed plumes are much more arching and relaxed-looking. Purple moor grass (*Molinia caerulea*) and giant needle grass (*Stipa gigantea*) are taller, but their summer-into-fall seed heads are airy enough to let you see through them, so they don't appear as massive as many equally tall grasses do. Hair grass (*Deschampsia cespitosa*) also produces very delicate, cloud-like seed heads, and its compact clumps fit nicely even at the front of the border.

**Shrubs and trees with showy seed heads.** For post-bloom beauty among woody-stemmed garden residents, hydrangeas generally take the prize. For most, their claim to fame is not so much their seed heads as the large clusters of sterile florets that remain once the fertile ones wither away. On some species, such as oakleaf hydrangea (*Hydrangea quercifolia*) and peegee hydrangea (*H. paniculata* 'Grandiflora'), the clusters are long and tapering; on others, such as bigleaf hydrangea (*H. macrophylla*) and smooth hydrangea (*H. arborescens*), the clusters are distinctly domed to nearly rounded. Most age through shades of pink to red before turning tan for the winter, so they're showy enough to be considered fall flowers as well as fall seed heads. In either category, they're practically a must-have for autumn gardens.

The attraction isn't quite as obvious on most other shrubs, but once you've developed an eye for interesting seed heads, there are several others worth considering, such as the spiky, light brown seed clusters of summersweets (*Clethra*) and the dark, spherical seed heads of buttonbush (*Cephalanthus occidentalis*). Bladdernuts (*Staphylea*) and golden rain trees (*Koelreuteria*) both have puffy brown pods, while hop hornbeam (*Ostrya virginiana*) produces pale green to brown, conelike clusters that dangle below the branches. The small, rounded, yellow-green seedpods of sourwood (*Oxydendrum arboreum*) aren't especially attractive on their own, but they certainly catch the eye when set against the bright red of this tree's fall foliage. While magnolias are justifiably famous for their beautiful flowers earlier in the growing season, they can contribute to the autumn landscape too, with conelike brown fruits that split open to show their good-sized red seeds.

***Vines for seeds and seed heads.*** A couple of climbers can also supply some autumn interest in the "seeds and seed heads" category — most notably, summer- and fall-flowering clematis. Their clustered seeds have long, curved tails covered with pale, silky hairs, decorating the vines with fluffy-looking, cream-colored to silvery tufts. Love-in-a-puff (*Cardiospermum halicacabum*) isn't nearly as showy as clematis in bloom — in fact, you'll barely notice this annual vine's tiny white flowers — but its balloonlike green to brown seedpods are intriguing to look at and fun to pop with your fingers. And let's not forget hyacinth bean (*Lablab purpureus* or *Dolichos lablab*), which continues to produce its clusters of purple-pink flowers and magenta-purple pods into fall. Combine it with midsummer-sown pole beans, such as yellow-podded 'Marvel of Venice', deep purple 'Trionfo Violetto', and slender, green-podded 'Yardlong', for a fun mix of colors and shapes that lasts until frost. The vigorously twining, woody-stemmed American bittersweet (*Celastrus scandens*) is well known for its bright orange autumn seed capsules and showy red seeds, but it's often confused with the very invasive Oriental bittersweet (*C. orbiculatus*) in the nursery trade, due to their similar appearance and ability to hybridize with one another.

**Many shapes and sizes** [facing page]. Grasses are winners for fall seed heads. From the top: purple fountain grass (*Pennisetum setaceum* 'Rubrum'), northern sea oats (*Chasmanthium latifolium*), and 'Karl Foerster' feather reed grass (*Calamagrostis* × *acutiflora*). **Pretty pods** [above]. Shown here are the inflated brown seedpods of golden rain tree (*Koelreuteria paniculata*) [top] and the flat magenta-purple pods of hyacinth bean (*Lablab purpureus*).

While showy seed heads and colorful fruits are invaluable for brightening up autumn gardens, they can have a dark side, too. The plants don't produce them just for us to admire, after all; they're a means of reproduction, and sometimes an alarmingly efficient one at that!

Every time you allow seeds to form and mature on your plants, you're taking a chance that those seeds will fall, blow, or be dropped by birds some distance away to sprout and produce new plants. In your garden, self-sown seedlings can be useful for filling new areas or to serve as replacements for parent plants that have died out over the winter. If you don't want them, you can easily pull or dig them out while they're small or else top off your garden with a fresh layer of mulch each spring to stop many of them from sprouting.

A more serious issue is the seeds that end up sprouting in nearby natural areas and crowding out the native vegetation. The potential for a particular plant to become invasive varies widely, depending on the climate and growing conditions. It may be a serious problem in one region—or state or even county—and perfectly well behaved in another. Even within a relatively small area, it may be fine in dry soils and a menace in wet areas, or vice versa. The list at right contains some plants that you might be tempted to include in your garden for autumn flowers, foliage, or fruits but are considered invasive in some areas.

*Verbena bonariensis* with *Miscanthus* 'Morning Light'

*Koelreuteria paniculata*

*Euonymus alata*

Remember, these are just a few of the most common problem plants; some of them might be fine in your area and others not mentioned might be more seriously invasive in your region. Don't assume that a plant is safe to grow just because your local garden center is selling it; it's up to you as a responsible gardener to do your homework before you buy.

Local nature preserves and conservation organizations can be a good source of information, or do a Web search for lists of problem plants in your area. The "Alien Plant Invaders of Natural Areas" list compiled by The Plant Conservation Alliance's Alien Plant Working Group is one handy reference (www.nps.gov/plants/alien/).

## POTENTIAL INVASIVES

*Acer campestre* (hedge maple)

*A. ginnala* (Amur maple)

*A. palmatum* (Japanese maple)

*A. platanoides* (Norway maple)

*Ampelopsis brevipedunculata* (porcelainberry)

*Arum italicum* (Italian arum)

*Berberis thunbergii* (Japanese barberry)

*B. vulgaris* (common barberry)

*Buddleia davidii* (butterfly bush)

*Celastrus orbiculatus* (Oriental bittersweet)

*Clematis orientalis* (Oriental clematis)

*C. terniflora* (sweet autumn clematis)

*Cortaderia jubata* (purple pampas grass)

*C. selloana* (pampas grass)

*Elaeagnus angustifolia* (Russian olive)

*E. multiflora* (cherry elaeagnus)

*E. pungens* (thorny elaeagnus)

*E. umbellata* (autumn olive)

*Euonymus alatus* (burning bush)

*E. fortunei* (climbing euonymus)

*Hibiscus syriacus* (rose-of-Sharon)

*Ilex aquifolium* (English holly)

*Kerria japonica* (Japanese kerria)

*Koelreuteria paniculata* (golden rain tree)

*Lagerstroemia indica* (crape myrtle)

*Lantana camara* (lantana)

*L. montevidensis* (creeping lantana)

*Lonicera japonica* (Japanese honeysuckle)

*L. maackii* (Amur honeysuckle)

*L. morrowii* (Morrow's honeysuckle)

*L. periclymenum* (European honeysuckle)

*L. tatarica* (Tartarian honeysuckle)

*Miscanthus sinensis* (Japanese silver grass)

*Morus alba* (white mulberry)

*Nandina domestica* (heavenly bamboo)

*Poncirus trifoliata* (hardy orange)

*Populus alba* (white poplar)

*Pyracantha coccinea* (scarlet firethorn)

*Pyrus calleryana* (Callery pear)

*Rosa rugosa* (rugosa rose)

*Saccharum ravennae* (Ravenna grass)

*Verbena bonariensis* (Brazilian vervain)

*Viburnum dilatatum* (linden viburnum)

*V. lantana* (wayfaring tree)

*V. opulus* (cranberrybush viburnum)

# Beautiful Fruits and Berries

An abundance of brightly colored fruits and berries has to be one of the greatest joys of the fall garden — and it's also one we gardeners most overlook when planning for fall interest. Admittedly, creating a great fruit display isn't nearly as easy as filling your garden with fall flowers and colorful foliage. You need to put extra care into selecting the plants, keeping in mind that some will produce berries by themselves, while others will need one or more compatible companions to set fruit (more about this in Grab Your Partners on page 90). Patience is a big part of the equation as well; shrubs and trees, especially, can take several years to mature enough to set a good batch of berries. You also need to keep your pruners in your pocket during the growing season! If you snip off the spent flowers on fruiting plants as you do on your others, you're also removing any possibilities of getting berries that year. Still, when everything comes together and your plants are filled with bright berries and colorful fruits, you'll know it was worth the effort. Besides brightening your garden, fruit-filled plants will lure a number of beautiful birds to your yard for fall and winter — and some fruits are great for people to eat, too!

***Border beauties for fruits and berries.*** Annuals and perennials are hardly the first plants that come to mind when you think of fall fruits, but they do offer a few interesting options. Some that we normally think of as vegetable-garden crops, for instance, can also be fun additions to autumn borders and container gardens. Peppers come in an amazing array of sizes, shapes, and colors, from the tiny purple-to-red fruits of black-leaved 'Explosive Embers' to the elongated, bright orange fruits of 'Bulgarian Carrot' and the multicolored, berrylike spheres of 'Marbles' — to name just a few. Watermelons rarely make the grade as ornamental plants, but 'Moon and Stars' has intriguing yellow-speckled foliage as well as deep green, yellow-splashed fruits that keep forming and ripening well into fall. Its spreading vines can easily travel 6 feet or more in all directions, so

**Fruits for flower gardens.** From the fiery red to sultry purple hues of 'Black Pearl' peppers (*Capsicum annuum*) [below] to the plump scarlet hips of rugosa roses (*Rosa rugosa*) [facing page], showy fruits add that feeling of abundance we all associate with the harvest season.

**A bounty of berries.** Some autumn berries can become a little *too* prolific in certain regions. If you start finding too many seedlings of Italian arum (*Arum italicum* var. *pictum*) [left] or pokeweed (*Phytolacca americana*) [right], for instance, you might want to clip off their berries for a few years.

it's not something you'd include in a border, but it can make an intriguing (and tasty) temporary ground cover in sunny, open areas. The same goes for large-fruited gourds and pumpkins, while smaller varieties (such as orange 'Jack Be Little' and white 'Baby Boo' pumpkins) look great growing on fences and arbors. Or maybe you'd like to try Queen Anne's pocket melon (also known as plum granny), with small, rounded, orange to yellow fruits that are nice to look at and sweetly fragrant.

More traditional ornamental perennials typically have much smaller fruits than annuals, but they can still make a significant contribution to the fall garden. In the evergreen ground cover category, consider bearberry (*Arctostaphylos uva-ursi*), partridgeberry (*Mitchella repens*), or wintergreen

(*Gaultheria procumbens*) — all with small, bright red berries. Lilyturfs (*Liriope*) and mondo grasses (*Ophiopogon*) can also produce berries, although their blue-black to deep purple fruits are usually hidden among the leaves and not especially eye-catching unless you can see them up close. Somewhat larger options (typically in the range of 8 to 12 inches tall) for showy, spiky clusters of rich red berries are Italian arum (*Arum italicum*), Jack-in-the-pulpits (*Arisaema*), and Japanese sacred lily (*Rohdea japonica*).

Tender flax lily (*Dianella tasmanica*) is definitely something different for borders and planters, with 2- to 3-foot-tall, arching spikes of blue spring-to-summer flowers that ripen into brilliant blue berries later in the season. Hardier spikenard (*Aralia racemosa*) is another out-of-the-ordinary fruiting perennial, producing large clusters of small purple berries in autumn on 3- to 5-foot-tall plants. And for something *really* unusual in the border, you might consider pokeweed (*Phytolacca americana*), with clusters of deep purple berries that dangle from the 6- to 10-foot-tall, branching stems in fall. Just be aware that it can self-sow enthusiastically, and it has huge taproots that make removing it a challenge once the plant settles in.

# SPOTLIGHT ON HOLLIES

Evergreen hollies (*Ilex*) have long been one of those good-news/bad-news plants. Their foliage provides year-round interest, and the berries on the female plants are beautiful in fall and winter, but many of them also have sharp spines on the leaf edges. That's not so much a problem on the plants themselves, but when the older leaves drop into nearby plantings, they can be a menace to gardeners who don't wear gloves. Still, you don't have to give them up altogether; you could site them where the dropped leaves won't be a problem, or choose spineless species or cultivars. Or consider some of the many delightful deciduous hollies—they offer pretty yellow fall foliage and a bounty of berries. Generally speaking, hollies can grow in full sun to light shade with average to moist but well-drained, acidic soil.

*Ilex* × *meserveae* 'Blue Angel' and *Amsonia hubrichtii*

*Ilex verticillata* 'Winter Gold'

*Ilex verticillata* 'Winter Red'

*Ilex opaca*

***Edible-fruiting shrubs and trees.*** When you're considering fruit-bearing shrubs and trees for your fall gardens, the traditional edible fruits of the season can be a great place to start. You can appreciate their good looks and then harvest the ripe fruits for eating, or leave them on the plants and let birds and other critters feast on them in fall and winter. Apples and pears are two obvious choices, and they come in several fruit colors. If you don't have room for full-sized trees (they can reach 30 feet tall or more), you can sometimes buy them grafted onto semidwarf, dwarfing, or sometimes even minidwarf rootstocks; the latter usually stay 4 to 6 feet tall, so you can even grow them in containers. Persimmons (*Diospyros*), with showy orange fruits and red fall foliage color, and pawpaws (*Asimina triloba*), with yellow fruits and leaves in autumn, are two more options in the 15- to 30-foot-tall range. Chinese dates or jujubes (*Ziziphus jujuba*) fall into this size range too, with small, sweet fruits

**Looking good.** American persimmons (*Diospyros virginiana*) are a treat to eat when they're fully ripe, but they're so striking on the tree that you may wish they'd stay up there all winter.

that ripen to bright red in fall; the yellow autumn foliage is another plus.

Grown in a pot, trained against a wall, or pruned into a tree form, figs (*Ficus carica*) bear plump fruits with yellow-green, purple, or rich brown skins, in both summer and fall on some varieties and mostly in fall on others. Fruiting quince (*Cydonia oblonga*) is yet another handsome small- to medium-sized tree, with large, fragrant, bright yellow fall fruits used mostly for making jelly; 'Aromatnaya' is one variety sweet enough for fresh eating. Where a tree wouldn't suit your purposes but you'd still like useful fruits, you might instead choose flowering quince (*Chaenomeles speciosa*); it's best known for its early-spring flowers, but it also produces a few good-sized yellow fruits in autumn. It takes a brave soul to taste the sour fruits of hardy orange (*Poncirus trifoliata*), but the round, bright yellow fruits look great clinging to the wickedly thorny, leafless green stems from fall into winter.

Elderberries (*Sambucus*) will get rather large if left undisturbed — usually in the range of 10 to 15 feet tall and wide — but it's not difficult to keep them smaller with pruning. European and American elders (*S. nigra* and *S. nigra* var. *canadensis*) bear large clusters of small fruits that typically ripen to deep purple in late summer to early fall, although there are some yellow-fruited varieties, such as 'Goldbeere'. Blue elder

(*S. caerulea*) has light blue berries that, like those of European and American elder, can be useful for preserving or wine-making. Red or scarlet elder (*S. racemosa*) has red berries that normally aren't harvested for human consumption, but they're popular with birds and other wildlife (as are those of the other species of elderberry).

***Ornamental fruits.*** Among the more traditional shrubs grown as ornamentals, you can find other fruits and berries in a range of shapes and sizes and a veritable rainbow of colors. Viburnums and hollies (*Ilex*) are two particularly useful groups with both deciduous and evergreen species: you can find out more about them in Spotlight on Hollies on page 83 and Spotlight on Viburnums on page 87.

If you're interested primarily in red berries for your fall garden, some decidu-

ous shrubs to consider are cotoneasters, hearts-a-burstin' (*Euonymus americana*), red chokeberry (*Aronia arbutifolia*), silver buffaloberry (*Shepherdia argentea*), and spicebush (*Lindera benzoin*). Many roses (*Rosa*) also produce showy red to orange-red fruits, usually referred to as hips. Blueleaf rose (*R. glauca*), eglantine (*R. eglanteria*), Moyes rose (*R. moyesii*), and rugosa rose (*R. rugosa*) are a few of the showiest, but you may also get a good fruit display from the more common hybrids if you stop deadheading them in mid- to late summer. Sumacs (*Rhus*) produce their fuzzy red fruits in dense, elongated clusters that look great in fall and winter, too.

Though hollies are often the first evergreens to come to mind for red fruits, there are many other options as well. Yews

**Share the wealth.** Keep in mind that many birds find bright fruits and berries as attractive as we do. They're particularly attracted to small berries, such as those of 'Brilliant' red chokeberry (*Aronia arbutifolia*) [left] and 'Kiftsgate' rose (*Rosa filipes*) [middle], but they'll feast on the bigger "hips" of rugosa roses (*R. rugosa*) [right], too.

**High impact for fall borders.** Berries are especially striking when they form in dense clusters, as shown here with heavenly bamboo (*Nandina domestica*) [left] and American beautyberry (*Callicarpa americana*) [right].

(*Taxus*), for example, have small, bright "fruits" (actually, they're seeds with a fleshy covering) set among their foliage, while aucubas, heavenly bamboo (*Nandina*), and skimmias hold their clustered berries at the shoot tips. Strawberry tree (*Arbutus unedo*) offers a double feature in fall of white flowers and clustered fruits that ripen from cream through peach to red. Many red-berried plants get picked clean by hungry birds soon after their fruits ripen; however, you can usually depend on firethorns (*Pyracantha*) to hold their bright red (or orange, or even yellow) fruits through the winter months.

Deciduous shrubs with blue to purple berries aren't as dramatic as their red-fruited counterparts, but they can still add to the feeling of autumn abundance and make a pleasing complement to bright flowering and foliage companions. As you might guess from the common names, sapphire-berry (*Symplocos paniculata*) is known for its bright blue berries in late summer to early fall, and blue bean shrub (*Decaisnea fargesii*) produces denim blue to gray-blue fruits that look like bean pods. Harlequin glorybower (*Clerodendrum trichotomum*) actually offers two colors: bright blue, rounded berries that are each set into a star-shaped red base for an amazing autumn fruit display. And Himalayan honeysuckle (*Leycesteria formosa*) is practically in a class by itself, with long, dangling clusters of reddish purple bracts and red berries that mature to deep purple in late summer and fall.

Early-summer blooms, beautiful berries, and fabulous fall color: Viburnums have it all! These medium-sized to large shrubs generally grow well in average garden soil and can adapt to either full sun or partial shade, although their fall colors are brightest in sunny sites. To get a good fruit display, make sure you grow at least two seedlings or two different cultivars of the same species.

*Viburnum opulus* var. *americanum* 'Bailey's Compact'

*Viburnum* 'Chippewa'

*Viburnum carlesii*

*Viburnum opulus* var. *americanum* 'Wentworth'

*Viburnum nudum*

**Think twice.** Tea crab apple (*Malus hupehensis*) is a beauty both in bloom and in fruit, but it's also very prone to a bacterial disease known as fireblight. Where this disease is a common problem, look for resistant crab apple cultivars instead.

Coralberry (*Symphoricarpos orbiculatus*) isn't an especially eye-catching shrub in itself, but its long-lasting fruits are a unique coral-pink to pinkish purple color. The hybrid Amethyst (*S.* × *doorenbosii* 'Kordes') has distinctly pink berries, while those of the closely related snowberry (*S. albus*) are bright white. Beautyberries (*Callicarpa*) are usually an almost unreal shade of bright purple, although they can have white fruits (as on *C. japonica* 'Leucocarpa' and *C. americana* var. *lactea*).

Looking for more shrubby possibilities for white and other light-colored berries? Gray dogwood (*Cornus racemosa*) and red-osier dogwood (*C. sericea*) both produce attractive white to pale blue berries that ripen in late summer to early fall, with the added benefit of red stems for winter. (Red-twig dogwood — *C. alba*, also known as *C. stolonifera* — also produces white berries, but they ripen earlier in the season and are usually eaten by birds before autumn arrives.) Northern bayberry (*Myrica pensylvanica*) holds its small but abundant waxy, gray-white berries along its stems, where they become increasingly more visible as the leaves drop in fall and winter. And for yellow berries, don't forget the many selections of deciduous and evergreen hollies and viburnums. Besides bringing an unexpected splash of color, these paler fruits seem to be less appealing to birds, so they're likely to be around longer than their red counterparts.

Where space allows, berry-bearing trees can provide the perfect finishing touch to the fall fruit display. In the small- to medium-sized tree category, it's tough to beat dogwoods, whether you're looking at the clusters of red-stalked, deep blue berries on pagoda dogwood (*C. alternifolia*); the brilliant red, oval fruits on Eastern flowering dogwood (*C. florida*) or corneliancherry (*C. mas*); or the larger, pinkish red globes that dangle from the branches of kousa dogwood (*C. kousa*). Crab apples (*Malus*) are another classic for showy summer-into-winter fruits in all shades of red to yellow. Those with larger fruits — in the 1- to 1½-inch-diameter range — make quite an impact in the landscape and can be useful if you'd like a harvest for jelly-making, while those with small to tiny fruits seem to be more of a hit with birds. Hawthorns (*Crataegus*), mountain ashes (*Sorbus*), and hybrids between the two genera are also outstanding choices for late-summer and autumn (and sometimes even winter) berries in many shades of red, orange, and yellow, as well as white.

Adventurous autumn gardeners with plenty of space might look in to some of the more offbeat trees for fall fruits. Ginkgo (*Ginkgo biloba*), for instance, can produce a generous display of seeds, each of which is encased in a fleshy yellow covering. They're not something you'd want to plant close to a residential area, however, because the "fruits" are positively foul-smelling when they drop and start to decompose. For a less odiferous option, consider Chinese pistache (*Pistacia chinensis*), which can produce clusters of small, rounded, red-to-blue fruits, or the showier iigiri tree (*Idesia polycarpa*), with long chains of orange-red berries.

***Fruiting vines.*** Whether you harvest them or leave them on the vines for hungry wildlife to feast on, grapes (*Vitis*) are a traditional symbol of the harvest season. Passion-flowers (*Passiflora*) are a much less obvious fruiting option for fall, but they too can be quite attractive, with good-sized, oblong to egg-shaped fruits that will be that yellow, orange, or purple, depending on the species. And don't forget kiwi vines (*Actinidia*); the oval to oblong, smooth green or fuzzy brown autumn fruits aren't especially eye-catching, but they're a treat to eat. The rather obscure magnolia vine (*Schisandra chinensis*) is also edible, but the clustered red berries are so beautiful in the garden that you won't want to spoil the show.

**Do your homework.** White flowers followed by bright berries and showy fall color make both flowering dogwood (*Cornus florida*) [left] and Korean mountain ash (*Sorbus alnifolia*) [right] possible selections for multiseason interest. Unfortunately, they're both susceptible to several pests and diseases, so if you have a small yard, you may want to consider a more trouble-free tree.

You may have heard the design "rule" that you shouldn't plant just one of anything—and if you're like most gardeners, you've probably ignored that advice many times. But when it comes to seeds, fruits, and berries, growing more than one of a particular plant is important for more than just good looks; it can make the difference between a great display and no display at all!

You see, some plants are "dioecious," which means they have female flowers and male flowers on separate plants. The female plants are the ones that bear fruit, but they need a compatible male plant nearby. One male can usually provide enough pollen for several females. It doesn't have to be planted immediately next to the females, but it does need to be nearby, so unless you can convince a neighbor to include a non-fruiting male in his or her landscape, you'll need to make room for it in your own yard. In other cases, plants have the usual arrangement of both male and female parts in the same flowers, but they need pollen from another seedling or cultivar of the same species that blooms at the same time to set any fruit (or to set *more* fruit). Cross-pollination is an issue mostly with edible fruits, but it can come up with ornamentals, too. Below is a list of fall-fruiting plants that typically require partners to produce fruit.

*Malus hupehensis*

*Ginkgo biloba*

Ilex verticillata 'Winter Red' [left]; Viburnum nudum [right]

Malus toringoides

*Actinidia* (kiwis):
Need both male and female plants.

*Asimina triloba* (pawpaw):
Most need cross-pollination.

*Celastrus scandens* (American bittersweet):
Needs both male and female plants.

*Cornus mas* (corneliancherry):
Most need or benefit from cross-pollination.

*Diospyros virginiana* (American persimmon):
Most need cross-pollination.

*Ginkgo biloba* (ginkgo):
Needs both male and female plants.

*Humulus lupulus* (hops):
Needs both male and female plants.

*Idesia polycarpa* (iigiri tree):
Needs both male and female plants.

*Ilex* (hollies):
Need both male and female plants.

*Malus* (apples and crab apples):
Need cross-pollination.

*Passiflora* (passionflowers):
Most need cross-pollination.

*Pistacia chinensis* (Chinese pistache):
Needs both male and female plants.

*Pyrus* (pears):
Need cross-pollination.

*Rhus* (sumacs):
Need both male and female plants.

*Sambucus* (elderberries):
Most need cross-pollination.

*Schisandra chinensis* (magnolia vine):
Needs both male and female plants.

*Shepherdia* (buffaloberries):
Need both male and female plants.

*Skimmia* (skimmias):
Need both male and female plants.

*Taxus* (yews):
Usually need both male and female plants.

*Vaccinium* (blueberries):
Benefit from cross-pollination.

*Viburnum* (viburnums):
Need or benefit from cross-pollination.

*Ziziphus jujuba* (Chinese date or jujube):
Most need or benefit from cross-pollination.

# PERFECT PARTNERS FOR FALL

**P**ART OF THE CHARM OF FALL GARDENS IS THEIR UNPREDICTABILITY. Frost may come unexpectedly early, cutting the display short, or unusually late, extending the flowering season for weeks longer than you anticipated. Leaves may turn amazingly bright colors or muted shades; fruits may appear in abundance or barely at all. Still, you can have a glorious autumn garden every year, if you plan your combinations carefully.

First, be sure to include lots of different plants with fall interest — not just the usual perennials and shrubs, but annuals, bulbs, grasses, and vines as well — to increase the odds that *something* will look great, no matter what the weather. Try for a mix of flowers, berries, seed heads, and fall-colored foliage too. That way, even if the weather doesn't cooperate for good autumn leaf color, or if hungry birds devour your berries in one swoop, you'll still have something to enjoy.

If you're fanatical about particular colors, you can certainly use your favorites in fall combinations just as you would for those in spring and summer. It's funny, though — there's something about fall that makes almost any color combination look great. Purple asters with red holly berries, orange dahlias against bright pink roses: During the bright light of summer, they might make you cringe, but in fall, they just *work*.

To get you thinking, I've put together a gallery of some outstanding plant partnerships for a variety of sites and purposes. You might choose to reproduce them exactly, or else use the basic ideas to create combinations custom-tailored for your particular taste. Either way, they're guaranteed to get your creative juices flowing!

**Worth the wait.** Part of the fun of fall gardening is the surprising combinations that appear as late flowers bloom and leaves change color. This partnership of Arkansas bluestar (*Amsonia hubrichtii*) and a late-blooming chrysanthemum is a quiet interplay of greens for most of the growing season, but come autumn, it's absolutely eye-catching!

# A FALL FLORAL EXTRAVAGANZA

Sun-drenched gardens are a perfect canvas for generous drifts of flower-filled perennials, providing an explosion of color to celebrate the arrival of autumn. Where you have plenty of space, you can create a seasonal spectacle such as this one with masses of purple and pink New England asters (*Aster novae-angliae*), spiky blue Russian sage (*Perovskia*), and bright yellow 'Fireworks' goldenrod (*Solidago rugosa*). Interplantings of long-flowering perennials and shrubs, such as catmints (*Nepeta*), salvias, coreopsis, and butterfly bush (*Buddleia*), add some color to the space earlier in the growing season as well. To extend the impact even further, tuck in an abundance of spring bulbs and early-flowering perennials that will go dormant by midsummer, giving the late-bloomers plenty of space to fill in and grow freely. In any season, repeating colors and flower shapes — such as the yellow goldenrod and coreopsis, and the spiky catmint, salvia, and Russian sage, in this giant-sized border — is a great trick for tying everything together.

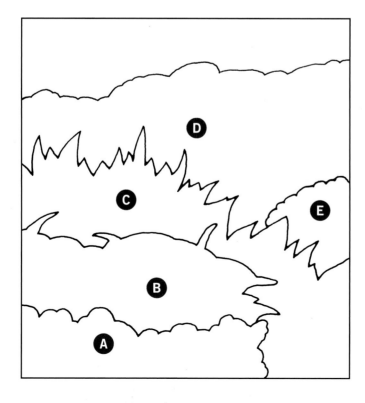

A  *Nepeta* (catmint)
B  *Solidago rugosa* 'Fireworks' (goldenrod)
C  *Perovskia* (Russian sage)
D  *Aster novae-angliae* (New England aster)
E  *Coreopsis grandiflora* (coreopsis)

Borders filled with late-season flowers are worth waiting for—but with a little planning, they can contribute color earlier in the year, too. Spring-flowering bulbs are ideal bedmates for late-bloomers, because the bulbs put on their show while their partners are dormant, then die back to the ground just as the late-risers start filling in.

Admittedly, planting hardy bulbs in fall may not be the most exciting task you'll tackle. But it's a lot more fun if you think of it as an investment that'll pay off big-time in just a few months. Come spring, no one ever regrets planting too many bulbs—instead, people wish they had planted *more*. Bulb companies know this, and many start sending out their catalogs for next year's bulbs while this year's are still in their glory. In a way, that's a good thing; it's easy to see the kinds and colors of bulbs you'd like to add to your yard and to figure out where you could plant them. Plus, the earlier you place your order, the lower the price you'll pay. The combination of beautiful photographs and great bargains is enough to send just about any gardener into a frenzy of preordering, envisioning carpets of crocuses and huge drifts of daffodils.

Just remember that when your order finally arrives in fall, you'll need to have the time to get all those bulbs in the ground. The great discount you got on an early order of 250 crocuses or 100 daffodils may not seem like such a good deal when they arrive on your doorstep come autumn, needing to be planted as soon as possible! If you know you tend to overestimate your available gardening space and energy level, you might want to put off your bulb orders until later in the summer (once the memory of the spring bulb show has faded a bit) or even limit yourself to buying locally. You'll pay a bit more, and you'll probably have a smaller selection to choose from, but planting a few dozen bulbs isn't nearly as daunting as facing several hundred—and it's better than wasting money on bulbs you simply don't have the time or space to get in the ground.

No matter how many bulbs you plant, the task will go far more quickly if you've done some advance planning. In spring, decide how you'll mark the location of your existing bulb plantings: by drawing their exact location on a garden map, by using a ring of pebbles or golf tees to circle each clump, or by taking lots of photographs for later reference. That way, you can plant your new bulbs in autumn without worrying about digging into those already in the ground. Another approach is to plant just one particular bed or part of your yard each year, then move on to filling another area the next fall. Be sure to keep a record of which areas you've already planted, and what you put in them.

Marking planted bulbs.

# THE SHOW GOES ON

Where space is limited, you don't have to give up valuable border room to plants that wait until autumn to do their thing. Concentrate on those that earn their keep all through the growing season, with features such as an extended bloom season and foliage that looks great from spring to frost (or even longer). This simple but effective combination provides a surprisingly long show while still changing through the seasons, so it never gets boring. The perennial 'Blue Fortune' anise hyssop (*Agastache*) blooms from early or midsummer well into fall even without deadheading, and its attractive seed heads look great in winter. The 'Shenandoah' switchgrass (*Panicum virgatum*) is green when it emerges in spring, gradually taking on red tinges through the summer and fall before turning tan and lasting all through the winter. The third member of the trio, the conifer 'Blue Point' juniper (*Juniperus chinensis*), provides a year-round counterpoint to both of its companions, echoing the distinctly upright form of the grass and the soft color of the anise hyssop's blooms. Best of all, this combination needs practically no maintenance: Simply cut the perennial and grass to the ground in spring, then stand back and enjoy the show!

A *Juniperus chinensis* 'Blue Point' (juniper)

B *Panicum virgatum* 'Shenandoah' (switchgrass)

C *Agastache* 'Blue Fortune' (anise hyssop)

# PLANNING AHEAD

When it comes to creating a fantastic fall garden, investing a few minutes during the summer can pay off big-time later. You see, depending on your climate, and on the particular weather conditions during any given summer, some classic fall plants can begin blooming much earlier in the season. By the time autumn actually arrives, they may be well past their peak or even finished flowering altogether! In this combination, for example, a light trim in mid-July delayed bud formation on the 'Lemon Queen' perennial sunflower (*Helianthus*) by several weeks. Having blooms just starting to open in early fall adds a welcome touch of "freshness" to companions that have already been flowering for weeks or even months, such as the *Salvia coccinea* and 'Karl Foerster' feather reed grass (*Calamagrostis × acutiflora*) shown here. Looking for other ways to perk up your fall flower borders? Sow a few pots of cosmos, flowering tobaccos (*Nicotiana*), or other annuals in midsummer, then tuck them into the bare spots that inevitably appear as autumn approaches. They'll be in bloom by early fall and add a burst of bright blossoms and lush foliage until nipped by frost.

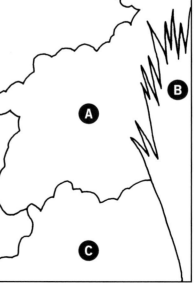

A *Helianthus* 'Lemon Queen'
(perennial sunflower)
B *Calamagrostis* x *acutiflora*
'Karl Foerster'
(feather reed grass)
C *Salvia coccinea*
(scarlet sage)

Delaying bloom a few weeks is a great reason to give some perennials a summer trim, but it's not the only reason to prune your perennials. A simple snip here and there can work wonders for improving the shape of your plants, increasing the number of blooms, and preserving their overall health and vigor.

Proper pinching is one of the easiest—as well as one of the most complex—techniques for gardeners of all levels to use. The actual act of pinching is simple: You literally pinch off shoot tips with your fingers, or else cut them off with pruning shears or some other tool. The art comes in the timing you use, the number of times you use it, and how much you remove. For instance, a single cut in late spring or early summer, removing the top half of each stem, will produce distinctly shorter but bushier plants that will likely bloom at their normal time. If you wait until midsummer to take off the same amount, the plant will be somewhat shorter than usual, and probably also bloom a week or so later. And if you wait until the flower buds just begin to form, then take off the very tops of the stems, the height will basically stay the same, but the bloom will be delayed by several weeks.

Different perennials react differently to pinching, so the challenge comes in deciding what effect you want, then experimenting with removing varying amounts at different points during the growing season. It's critical to keep good notes of what, when, and how much you cut and what the results were, so you'll know what to try again once you get the effect you are going for.

Keep in mind that when you remove the tip of a shoot, side buds along the shoot will sprout. Each of these side shoots will eventually flower, but the individual blooms are typically smaller than those on an unpinched shoot; the result, then, is more but *smaller* flowers. If you'd rather have *bigger* blooms and don't mind having fewer ones overall, there's a technique for you too: It's called *disbudding*. Technically, this refers to removing any flower buds, but in this case, you leave the center bud or stalk on each main stem and remove any side buds or stalks around it. (You can even extend this to removing all the side shoots from each main stem.) All the energy in each stem then goes into producing one showstopping bloom. This trick doesn't work with every plant, but dahlias, mums, bee balms (*Monarda*), and monkshoods (*Aconitum*) are a few worth experimenting on, if you're so inclined.

Pruning perennials.

# TROPICAL ABUNDANCE

If you're fond of the lush look that tropicals and tender perennials can bring to borders anywhere, then fall must be one of your favorite seasons. These heat-lovers tend to be slow to get started after planting, waiting until warm summer weather to put on luxurious growth. Some don't start flowering until mid- or late summer; for others, it's early autumn or even later by the time they even start setting buds. Late-bloomers, such as the spiky purple Mexican bush sage (*Salvia leucantha*) in this combination, are certainly worth waiting for, but you don't have to do without color in the meantime if you pair them with partners that produce striking foliage all through the growing season. The showily striped leaves of the 'Pretoria' canna shown here are one spectacular option; caladiums, dahlias, elephant's ears (*Alocasia* and *Colocasia*), and coleus (*Solenostemon scutellarioides*) are just a few of the many excellent alternatives for fancy foliage. And don't overlook walls, fences, and other landscape features as year-round color accents. A little paint can work wonders in any area, and you can easily change the color any time you wish!

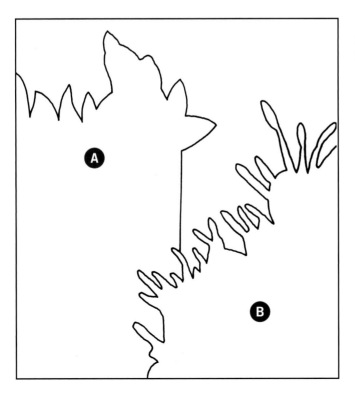

A  *Canna* 'Pretoria' (canna)
B  *Salvia leucantha* (Mexican bush sage)

Pots ready to bring indoors.

As the return of cooler temperatures signals the approach of winter, it's time to start thinking about what you're going to do with your cold-tender garden plants. The choices about which ones to bring indoors in fall and which to leave outside for the winter are some of the toughest gardening decisions you'll make. It's tempting to just leave everything outdoors, then buy whatever replacements you need next year, but that's a tough resolve to keep; most of us end up bringing at least a few special favorites inside at the last minute, if not before. It's equally tempting to try to bring in *everything* that might not survive outdoors—at least until you try to find space in the house!

To make a realistic assessment of what you're going protect and what you'll leave outdoors, you need to consider several factors. The most important criterion is whether or not you can easily replace a particular plant if you lose it. If it's simply a pretty red-flowered geranium (*Pelargonium*) you bought at the local garden center back in the spring, it probably doesn't belong at the top of your must-save list. But if it's a rare variegated cultivar that you had to get by mail order years ago and haven't seen for sale since, it definitely deserves a place indoors for the winter. When space is limited, saving only plants that are difficult to find, expensive to buy, or impossible to replace due to sentiment can take some of the guesswork out of the decision-making process.

If you have some space left over, think about which plants you'd really *enjoy* having inside with you for the winter. For example, it's easy to buy a new rosemary plant each spring, but its flavorful foliage, warm fragrance, and pretty flowers make it a delight indoors. Coleus, impatiens, and begonias are three other common but beautiful plants that are worth potting up for welcome winter color.

A couple of practical considerations can also influence your decision of what to save and what to sacrifice. Obviously, if the plants are small, you can fit more of them indoors. But a particularly large specimen that's taken years to mature clearly deserves special consideration—at least if it hasn't grown too large to move. In that case, leaving it outdoors and seeking a replacement in spring might be a wiser option. (Taking a few cuttings at the end of the season is another way to preserve a large plant, as these will take up much less space indoors.) Remember, too, that not all of the plants you might want to save will compete for the available windowsill space. Yes, some need a warm, sunny space to thrive, but others—including begonias and geraniums—can get by just fine in a bright but cool spot, such as an enclosed but unheated porch. And some tenders, such as cannas, go totally dormant, so they can survive in no light at all, at least until they start growing in spring. (Keep them in a cool but frost-free place; water sparingly—just enough so they don't dry out.) Considering the many overwintering options, you may find that you can bring in a lot more plants than you ever imagined!

Searching for more options to provide a long season of flowers and foliage to your garden? Fall is a great time to visit your local garden center and see what still looks good—and to shop the end-of-the-season sales.

**Look for late-bloomers.** If you shop only in spring, there's a good chance that your garden has mostly early-flowering perennials and shrubs, as they are the stars in sales displays at that time of year. It also means that your garden probably looks pretty boring by mid-summer! Fall-flowering plants tend to emerge late in pots in spring, so it's easy to overlook them during early-season shopping sprees; for that reason, some outlets don't even start stocking them until mid- or late summer. This makes late-summer and fall shopping a must if you're trying to track down many autumn-flowering plants.

**See beyond the obvious.** Don't expect container-grown plants to look as lush and full in fall as they do in spring. You want to avoid those with noticeable pest or disease problems, of course. But a couple of dropped leaves or broken stems generally don't matter much, because the plants will be going dormant soon anyway and they'll send up perfect new growth next spring. The important thing is that your potential purchases have a strong, healthy root system. It's common to see roots peeking out of a pot's drainage holes at this time of year; if they're not visible, carefully slide the plant out of the pot. If you don't see many (or any) roots on the outside of the rootball, or if the roots look discolored, mushy, or dried out, it's probably best to pass over that plant.

**A plant divided saves you dough.** As you shop in fall, keep an eye out for full pots of easy-to-divide perennials and ground covers, such as hostas and sedums. Often, you can separate these overgrown clumps into several pieces, giving you two or more plants for the price of one! That means significant savings, especially if you're installing a new garden or establishing a patch of ground covers. For best results, don't divide the clumps into many tiny pieces; two to four divisions per pot will produce good-sized sections that are much more likely to survive the winter.

Checking for healthy roots.

# COOLING THINGS DOWN

Whether you grow them yourself from early-summer-sown seeds or buy already-started transplants in late summer to early fall, cool-season annuals are invaluable for bringing fresh foliage and flowers to autumn gardens. Here, frilly-leaved ornamental kales (*Brassica oleracea*) show their true colors long after their companions were zapped by frost, pepping up a scene that has plenty of textural interest but not much color otherwise. Diascias, pansies and violas, and pot marigolds (*Calendula officinalis*) are just a few of the many easy-to-grow cool-season annuals that look just as good in late-season plantings as they do in spring. Work them into your borders as soon as gaps appear in late summer so they'll be ready to burst into bloom as soon as the temperatures cool off a bit. Or, keep them in pots for spots of mobile color, then pop them into your garden to perk things up as the perennials and shrubs start to go dormant.

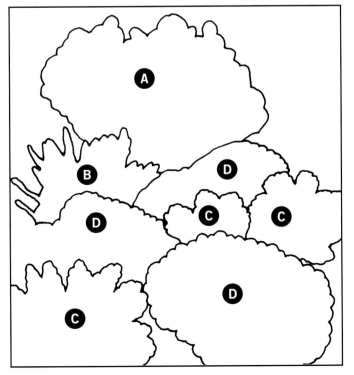

A *Hydrangea* (hydrangea)
B *Pennisetum alopecuroides* (fountain grass)
C *Brassica oleracea* (flowering kale)
D *Chrysanthemum* x *morifolium* (mums)

If your borders have a few bare spots that detract from the autumn display, don't despair—they are easy to fix. When the empty space is due to an earlier-bloomer that's gone dormant or been cut back, a temporary filler may be all you need to fill in that void—at least for this year. Then you can think about permanently replacing it with a late-bloomer to ensure a fuss-free fall show, or perhaps pair it with bushy partners that will naturally fill the space left when the early-riser dies back. Or, simply plan on using your creativity to find fun ways to fill that space each year!

**Exterior decorating.** Having on hand a stash of garden ornaments in various sizes is a perfect solution to empty spaces during any season. Try to match the colors and style of your garden with the ornament that you choose. A crockery jug or quirky sign can add a perfect touch of whimsy to a casual, country-style garden, for example, whereas a small metal sculpture or elegant urn might better suit a more formal setting. Don't forget to remove the accent piece by late winter (if not sooner), so the plant it's filling in for can emerge again in spring. Or, if you really like the ornament there, move the plant and make the ornament a permanent part of the design.

**Containers on the move.** Autumn is really a time for container plantings to shine—and not just on your deck or doorstep! It's a snap to pop potted plants, containers and all, right into bed and border gaps, where they'll instantly add height as well as flowers and foliage. As with ornaments, try to choose container plantings with colors and textures that complement the plants they'll be paired with. Don't limit yourself to using only perennials with perennials, or annuals with annuals; mixing up annuals, perennials, tropicals, and grasses can add extra excitement to your fall display. The only drawback to using potted plants as garden fillers? Sometimes they blend in so well that it's easy to forget to water them!

**Perfect partners.** Sometimes, the best fillers for dormant plants are other plants. Bushy late-bloomers like compact asters are a little slow to start in spring, but they begin to bulk up by midsummer—just in time to fill the space formerly occupied by earlier-flowering bulbs or perennials. Pinching off the shoot tips of taller fall flowers can produce a similar bushing-out effect (see Shape 'Em Up on page 99 for details). Annuals are another excellent option for seasonal fillers. Set out transplants or sow seeds right around the declining foliage of the early-bloomers. Annual vines, in particular, can work great for gaps near the front of a border because they grow quickly and look great weaving among their companions, filling in any empty space as they sprawl instead of climb.

Transplanting annuals as fillers.

# PRIMARY COLORS FOR FALL

You probably wouldn't ever think to plan a border around bright red, blue, and yellow together, but in the autumn garden, anything goes! Shrubs and trees with richly colored fall leaves are always a welcome sight during this season, and flowering companions, such as the deep blue monkshoods (*Aconitum*) shown here, are ideal for supplying colors you simply can't get from foliage. Looking for more ideas for great fall combinations? Walk around your yard in autumn and snip pieces of anything that looks good: flowers, leaves, seed heads, berries, and so on. Then sit down with them and try out different groupings to see what you can come up with. If you find an appealing color combination, you're in luck. You already have the plants on hand and know they'll grow for you; all you have to do is move them around to re-create the winning combo in your autumn garden. Who knows — you might decide you like these colors so much that you'll figure out a way to use them in other seasons, too!

A  *Acer palmatum* (Japanese maple)
B  *Aconitum carmichaelii* 'Arendsii' (monkshood)
C  *Cornus alba* 'Bloodgood' (red-twig dogwood)

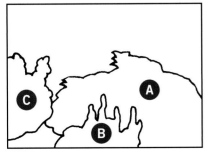

# SHOCKING CONTRASTS

Even if you don't normally consider yourself adventurous when it comes to color, you might decide to change your mind as the growing season winds down — or your plants might do it for you! Fall gardens often showcase combinations that are as stunning as they are surprising, such as this striking contrast of tiny, bright purple beautyberries (*Callicarpa*) against the feathery, golden fall foliage of Arkansas bluestar (*Amsonia hubrichtii*). This pairing provides interest earlier in the season too, with the bluestar's domed clusters of pale blue blooms in late spring or early summer and the beautyberry's flattened clusters of pink flowers a bit later in the summer, but neither plant even hints at its electrifying color potential until fall arrives. It's easy to create ample opportunities for other amazing autumn effects; simply select ground covers, perennials, vines, shrubs, and trees that typically produce dramatic fall foliage along with their other seasonal features. The specific colors and shades they turn can vary from year to year, so you'll never know exactly what to expect from them — but you can be pretty sure it'll be beautiful, no matter what.

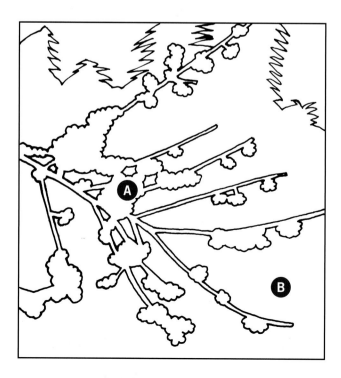

A  *Callicarpa japonica* (Japanese beautyberry)
B  *Amsonia hubrichtii* (Arkansas bluestar)

# CREATING A NEW GARDEN SITE

If you'd like to try a color scheme that simply doesn't fit with an existing border, then why not create an entirely new planting area? Fall is a fantastic time to get a new garden started: the weather is perfect for working outdoors, and there aren't so many other critical chores to do as there are in spring.

Digging isn't a leisurely way to get a new garden started in any season, but it does have several points in its favor. (If you're interested in learning about creating a new garden using the layering technique—which has benefits of its own—check out Starting New Gardens on page 200.) First, by removing the existing sod and weeds, you're greatly reducing the chances of those unwanted plants popping up in your new planting. In seriously compacted sites, digging or tilling helps to break up the soil again, improving drainage and giving soil organisms a generous supply of much-needed air. These techniques also give you an opportunity to work organic matter and lime (if needed) into your soil. In addition, cultivation brings soil-dwelling pests up to the surface, where birds can feast on them.

**Getting rid of the grass.** It may seem like an extra step, but removing existing grass and weeds before you start digging is a critical part of this process. Otherwise, you'll simply chop them into small bits and spread them all through your new garden. Using a flat-bladed tool (such as a spade or a half-moon lawn edger), cut all along the outer edge of the bed. Then, starting at one point along the

Removing sod.

edge, slip the blade horizontally into the soil about ½ inch below ground level. The point is to remove the growing points and runners of the grass while taking as little soil away as possible. Use the sod pieces you remove to fix bare spots in other parts of your yard, or pile the pieces upside down in an out-of-the-way place, where they can decompose.

**Checking the soil.** Next, make sure that the soil moisture level is right by troweling up a handful of earth and squeezing it. If the soil crumbles as soon as you open your hand, it's too dry; water thoroughly and test again the next day. If the soil clumps together but crumbles when you tap it, it's just right; if it doesn't crumble, give it a day or two to dry out. When it's ready, spread a 1- to 3-inch layer of chunky compost, livestock manure, roughly chopped leaves, or other organic matter over the site, along with any lime, sulfur, or other amendments indicated by soil-test results.

**Digging in.** Finally, you're ready to use a shovel, spading fork, or rotary tiller to loosen the top 8 to 12 inches of soil. Start at one edge of the bed and work backward toward the other side, so you're not stepping on the loosened soil. As you dig or till, remove any rocks, large roots, or other debris you find, and break up large clods as best you can. When you're finished, use a rake or hoe to level and smooth the surface. Finish with a light layer of organic matter (about an inch or two deep) as a mulch to protect the soil from pounding rains, which can cause crusting.

While your garden is in its fall glory and summer is still fresh in your mind, autumn is a super time to take a close look at your landscape. Grab a notebook and pencil, then take a leisurely stroll through your yard. In one section, make notes of what worked great during this growing season: plants that performed well, new techniques that you tried, and exceptional flower and foliage combinations that you noticed in your beds and borders.

Next, evaluate your property as impartially as possible to see what could be improved. Look first from your normal vantage points—your front door, your existing paths, and so on. Check for areas where weeds have gotten a roothold among your flowers, or where lawn grass has crept into planting areas. Note which perennials would benefit from being divided, or where your plants simply aren't growing as well as you'd expect. Also note where established trees and shrubs have filled in over time, casting shade on garden areas that were once sunny. If you've been gardening for more than a few years, the first few gardens you created may now look a little boring; your notes might include a list of new plants you want to try or changes you'd like to make to those gardens to better suit your current needs.

Consider your yard from other perspectives, too. From indoors, look out of the window of your kitchen, family room, home office, or other room where you spend a lot of time. Are overgrown shrubs blocking your view or are your neighbor's trash cans making your view less than appealing? Your notes might include a plan to do some pruning or to add some shrubs and tall perennials to provide some screening. Walk away from your house, then turn around to check the view from the street or from your driveway. Does a boring foundation planting detract from the beauty of your home? Does a sparse, weedy lawn make your flowers look bad? Would a new flower bed make the entrance more welcoming? Jot down your ideas of what could be fixed and how you might approach the task.

While you're at it, think about some ways to make your yard work harder for you. If you usually get to enjoy it only in the evening, installing a lighting system could be a perfect project. Want a quiet seat where you can relax with a book or do some bird-watching? A combination of shrubs, grasses, and perennials can create the ideal sheltered spot. And adding a well-planned path is a project from which any garden could benefit.

Once you're done taking notes, choose a few projects to complete this fall, then put aside your notebook for perusing over the winter. Now, make the most of the beautiful autumn weather and get busy!

Evaluate plantings in fall.

# PASTEL PERFECTION

Bright reds and yellows are often among the first colors that come to mind when we think of fall, but they're not the only palette we can "paint" our gardens with. Plenty of flowering and foliage plants show off their softer sides during this season too. In the sunny-site combination shown here, fluffy, blue hardy ageratum (*Eupatorium coelestinum*) forms a delicate background for the rosy to coppery pink fall foliage of 'The Blues' little bluestem (*Schizachyrium scoparium*) and the moody purple flowerheads of 'Moudry' fountain grass (*Pennisetum alopecuroides*). Keep in mind that this grouping isn't well suited to a small garden — the hardy ageratum is a vigorous creeper, and 'Moudry' (and the similar-looking selection called 'National Arboretum') may self-sow prolifically, especially in warm climates. But there are plenty of other plants you could use instead, such as light blue 'Bluebird' smooth aster (*Aster laevis*) in place of the hardy ageratum, and perhaps the pinkish tan–flowered 'Karley Rose' oriental fountain grass (*P. orientale*) instead of 'Moudry'. Besides asters and grasses, there are loads of cool-colored perennials to consider, including anemones, Joe-Pye weeds (*Eupatorium*), and turtleheads (*Chelone*), to name just a few.

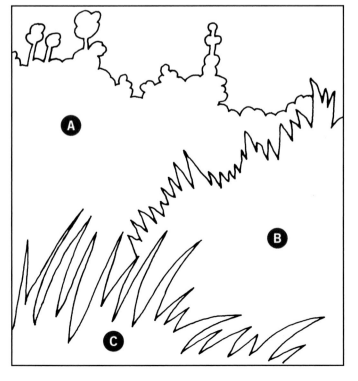

A  *Eupatorium coelestinum* (hardy ageratum)
B  *Schizachyrium scoparium* 'The Blues'
    (little bluestem)
C  *Pennisetum alopecuroides* 'Moudry'
    (fountain grass)

# DIVIDING PERENNIALS

Fall-blooming perennials aren't the only ones to possibly be a little overenthusiastic when it comes to filling space in beds and borders. Some spring- and summer-bloomers, too, can fill out quite quickly, and autumn is an ideal time to get those earlier-flowering perennials into good shape for the next growing season. (One exception is early-spring-bloomers, such as pulmonarias and primroses; these generally do best if you divide them as soon as they're done blooming in mid- to late spring.)

If you're new to the process of dividing your plants, don't be nervous! Learning how to divide perennials is one of the most practical gardening skills you'll ever pick up. With this one simple technique, you can give new life to old plants, reduce the size of overlarge clumps, and make lots of new plants from the ones you already own.

You'll know that old plants need division when they start looking crowded and blooming less; you may also notice a dead spot in the center of the clump. Some perennials can get to this stage in just a few years; others can go five years, ten years, or even longer before needing rejuvenation. The more vigorous the plants are and the more fertile your soil is, the more frequently they're likely to need this kind of attention.

For propagation, you can divide as soon as the plants are large enough to separate into at least two parts. Generally, it's best to give new perennials at least a full year (ideally two or three) to "bulk up" before dividing them; otherwise, the new pieces may be too small and weak to recover. After you replant the pieces, give them the same amount of time to recover before dividing them again. Remember, it usually takes a plant at least three years to really settle in and look its best, so if you divide it too often, you'll never get a chance to appreciate its full beauty.

Whenever you divide, it's a great opportunity to enrich the soil in the site where the original plant was growing. Toss a shovelful or two of compost into the hole and work it into the soil before you set out a new plant there, or before you replant the divisions in that spot. That'll really help the new roots get off to a great start.

Overgrown perennial bed.

# PLANNING A PATH

Sometimes, gardens are designed to be seen only from a distance, and that's fine. But if you like to get up close and personal with your plants, a well-planned path will make your gardening time much more of a pleasure. Besides giving you a way to get from one place to another, paths and walkways can complement the style of your home, make visitors feel more welcome, and make garden maintenance easier. The size of the paths you make and the materials you make them out of have a great influence on how well they'll serve their purpose in the long run.

**The path to success.** Doing some careful planning *before* you install a new path will save you a lot of regrets later on. It sounds obvious, but first you need to decide where the path will start and where it will end: at a door, perhaps, or a bench, or maybe another path. Next, think about the route you want to take. A straight path will get you from point to point quickly, but it's not very interesting. Curves can add mystery if the point they lead to is at least partially hidden; a path that twists and turns for no reason is often more annoying than charming. Make your path wider than you think is needed: 4 to 5 feet for main paths and at least 30 inches for side paths.

**On a firm footing.** For heavily used paths, a hard surface—such as pavers, brick, or flagstone—is a must for safe footing. These kinds of paths are also the most expensive and time-consuming to build, partly because they need careful site preparation (usually several inches of crushed stone topped with a layer of sand). But the investment of time and money is definitely worthwhile, because they'll give you many years of pleasant strolling in every season and they'll need only minimal maintenance. Hard-surface paths also make it easy to reach your garden with a wheelbarrow or garden cart. Installing pavers or bricks set in sand is something most gardeners can do on their own; it's usually worth hiring a professional to design and install brick or flagstone with mortared joints.

An inviting path.

**Hit the nature trail.** For lesser-used paths, loose materials such as gravel, bark chips, and pine needles are a perfectly practical option. It's ideal to prepare a gravel base for them just as you would for hard-surface paths, because they'll drain much more quickly that way. But if you're in a hurry, you can get away with simply covering the area with landscape fabric to smother weeds while still letting water drain through, then covering it with several inches of your chosen path material. Installing edging strips on both sides of the path will help keep the material in place. Loose-surface paths are easy to install and don't cost much, but if you use an organic material such as bark, you'll have to add more once or twice a year as it breaks down.

# MADE FOR THE SHADE

Shady autumn gardens tend to lack the brilliant flower and foliage colors of sunnier sites, but they have an undeniable charm all their own, thanks to shade-loving late-bloomers such as toad lilies (*Tricyrtis*). These curiously shaped and spotted blooms show off best where you can admire their intricate beauty up close — next to a bench, for instance, or right next to a path. They're lovely on their own; pairing them with a fantastic foliage companion, however, provides interest earlier in the growing season as well. This combination showcases the perfect partnership of a toad lily with Japanese painted fern (*Athyrium goeringianum* var. *pictum*), a deciduous species with ghostly gray-green fronds that are typically tinged with some purple, especially along the stems. Though the purple is most noticeable earlier in the growing season, enough remains to provide the perfect echo to the purple spots on the toad lily blooms. This fern would also look lovely with another late-blooming shade-lover: hardy cyclamen (*Cyclamen hederifolium*). While the cyclamen is summer-dormant, the fern is still there to add interest; in winter, the cyclamen fills in for the now dormant fern. In spring, you can enjoy the interplay of both plants' foliage, and in autumn, the cyclamen's delicate pink flowers look great against the lacy fern fronds.

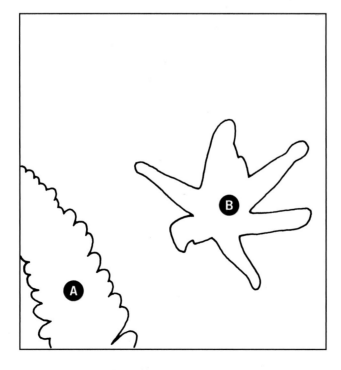

A *Athyrium niponicum* var. *pictum* (Japanese painted fern)
B *Tricyrtis* 'Sinonome' (toad lily)

# BOUNTIFUL BULBS

Most of us think of fall as a time to put bulbs down into the ground — not as a time for them to be coming *up!* So if you're a little tired of the usual fall flowers and foliage, late-blooming bulbs may be just what you need to bring a touch of the unexpected to your autumn beds and borders. This combination shows three fantastic fall plants: Arkansas bluestar (*Amsonia hubrichtii*), with yellow to gold fall foliage; bushy, purple-blue 'October Skies' aster (*Aster oblongifolius*); and the rosy pink blooms of 'Ozawa' ornamental onion (*Allium thunbergii*). As if its late-season flowers weren't enough, 'Ozawa' offers another outstanding ornamental feature: Its slender, rich green leaves also turn an amazing orange color in mid- to late autumn. Most other fall-flowering bulbs send up their foliage in spring, retreat underground for the summer, and then send up leafless blooms in fall. The trick of planting them around the edge of a bushy perennial works as well with them as it does with 'Ozawa'. The bulb foliage can easily come up and ripen in spring, the perennial fills the space in summer, and then the bulb flowers can poke up through the tips of the perennial in autumn.

A  *Amsonia hubrichtii* (Arkansas bluestar)
B  *Allium thunbergii* 'Ozawa'
   (ornamental onion)
C  *Aster oblongifolius* 'October Skies'
   (fragrant aster)

# PLANTING BULBS IN BEDS AND BORDERS

Warm-season grasses aren't the only plants that make perfect bedmates for spring-flowering bulbs. The early-risers pair perfectly with all kinds of autumn favorites, adding a whole different look to the garden in their season. The same goes for autumn-flowering bulbs, which can do wonders perking up areas where spring-flowering companions have long since lost their luster. Either way, adding bulbs to existing garden areas is a terrific way to get more blooms from the same amount of space. Most take up very little ground room, so you can easily fit them in around other plants, and they look great popping up through lower-growing companions. Whether you're planting spring-blooming bulbs in fall or fall-blooming bulbs in late summer, the basics are the same: Prepare the soil well, and they'll reward you with year after year of beauty.

**Setting out individual bulbs.** When you're tucking bulbs around existing plants, it's usually best to dig one hole per bulb; that reduces the chance of damaging the plants' roots. Follow the recommended planting depth and spacing on the package. Digging shallower holes makes bulbs more vulnerable to animal pests, and they're more likely to sprout too early, so don't be tempted to cheat unless your soil is on the clayey side; in that case, planting an inch or two shallower than suggested may help prevent rotting. Add a bit of slow-release bulb food, dig it into the bottom of the hole, then set in the bulb and cover it with soil.

**Planting bulbs in groups.** If you have plenty of space between your plants, it's usually quicker to dig holes large enough to hold several bulbs. The bulbs will look better growing in groups as well. Follow the same basic advice as for individual bulbs (above). If your soil is high in clay, improve your chance of success by loosening the bottom of the hole with a spading fork before planting, then use a 50:50 mix of compost and topsoil to cover the bulbs and fill the hole. Lay a piece of wire mesh over the soil afterward if squirrels tend to dig up your new plantings (remove it in late winter). If mice and voles are common pests in your garden, you may want to take the added precaution of lining the bottom and sides of the planting holes with ¼-inch wire mesh, or of planting your bulbs in commercially available wire cages.

**Layering bulbs.** Short on time or space to get all your bulbs planted? Try layering several different-sized bulbs in a single spot. Prepare the hole as advised above for group planting, making it deep enough to suit the largest bulbs (such as giant alliums and lilies). Replace enough soil to barely cover them, then add another layer of medium-sized bulbs (such as daffodils and tulips). Repeat once or twice more, finishing with crocuses, squills, or other tiny bulbs before replacing the rest of the soil. It's a great way to enjoy months of beautiful blooms without digging dozens or hundreds of smaller holes.

Planting bulbs in groups.

# FALL-GLORIOUS GRASSES

Who says you shouldn't plant grasses with grasses? Though it's true that they can be very similar in leaf texture, choosing species and cultivars with varying heights, habits, and bloom times can provide more than enough contrast for an effective combination. Masses of warm-season grasses are just about as low-maintenance as you can imagine; simply whack off all the dead top growth in early spring, then stand back and enjoy the show through the rest of the year. This grouping of 'The Blues' little bluestem (*Schizachyrium scoparium*), pink muhly grass (*Muhlenbergia capillaris*), and 'Cassian' fountain grass (*Pennisetum alopecuroides*) backed by taller 'Cloud Nine' switchgrass (*Panicum virgatum*) could thrive in just about any sunny, well-drained site. Don't worry about enriching the soil with compost before planting; the fertile soil that many flowering perennials appreciate can actually cause grasses to grow too fast and fall over. In leaner conditions, their stems will stay strong and upright, and the plants will need division much less often. The only downtime with a combination like this is in spring, but that's easy to fix; simply fill the spaces between the grasses with spring crocus, daffodils, or other early-blooming bulbs.

A  *Schizachyrium scoparium* 'The Blues'
    (little bluestem)
B  *Muhlenbergia capillaris* (pink muhly grass)
C  *Panicum virgatum* 'Cloud Nine' (switchgrass)
D  *Pennisetum alopecuroides* 'Cassian'
    (fountain grass)

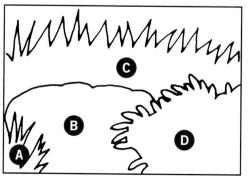

# FALL PLANTING AND TRANSPLANTING

Chances are, looking at photo after photo of beautiful autumn combinations has your brain reeling with new ideas you'd like to try in your own garden. Why put off the fun for months when you can set out new plants or move existing ones right now?

Admittedly, fall planting doesn't provide the immediate gratification of seeing the burst of growth and bloom that typically follows spring planting. But from the plants' perspective, that's a good thing. They have the next several months to develop a strong root system, so by the time warm weather returns, they're primed to produce an abundance of foliage and flowers.

Typical fall weather—mild temperatures and more-regular rainfall—also tends to be gentler than spring on both plants and gardeners. Instead of coping with chilly winds, cool soil, and unpredictable frosts, autumn gardeners usually enjoy comfortably warm days followed by mild nights. And since the plants are already slowing down their growth for the season, they are much less susceptible than tender spring transplants to damage from bright sunshine, drying winds, and sudden cold

An example of frost heaving.

snaps. The more relaxed pace of fall gardening is yet another advantage over spring planting. Early in the year, there are so many things that need to be done, it's hard to find time to simply appreciate being out in the garden. But in fall, it's fun to linger over pleasant tasks without worrying about other jobs that need immediate attention.

It's true, fall planting *can* have a few drawbacks. The main problem, known as "frost heaving," is caused by shifting soil due to alternating periods of freezing and thawing through the colder months. Well-established plants are anchored in place by their roots, but fall plantings may not have rooted firmly enough, and they can end up getting pushed partly or totally out of the soil; once exposed, they're subject to direct damage from cold and drying winds. To avoid this, plant or transplant as early as possible in fall, so your plants will have at least a month or two to get their roots well settled in. Mulching fall plantings is also helpful, because the mulch minimizes the rapid temperature changes that lead to heaving. To learn more about getting plants into the ground, turn to Planting and Transplanting on page 202.

# CLIMBING THE WALLS

Some of the most beautiful annual vines can be a little disappointing for summer color but absolutely fabulous for fall. Although their vigorously twining stems put on plenty of leafy growth in early and midsummer, they often don't bloom or even set buds until August or later. You don't have to wait that long for color, however, if you pair them with earlier-blooming vines, such as spring- and summer-flowering clematis. Annual vines also make fantastic partners for forsythias, weigelas, beautybush (*Kolkwitzia*), and other early shrubs; you get flowers from the shrubs in spring to early summer and a second show of bloom from the vines in late summer and fall. Spanish flag (*Mina lobata*) is a winner if you like your flowers on the bright side, with red new buds that open to orange and age to yellow against lush, lobed, deep green leaves until frost. Cardinal climber (*Ipomoea* × *mul-tifida*) and cypress vine (*I. quamoclit*) have smaller flowers but in a brilliant shade of bright red, while morning glories (*I.* × *nil*) are great for shades of blue, purple, and pink as well as white. Best of all, it's easy to save seeds from all of these vines, so there's no excuse not to grow them year after year!

A   *Mina lobata* (Spanish flag)
B   *Pennisetum alopecuroides* 'Cassian' (fountain grass)
C   *Muhlenbergia capillaris* (pink muhly grass)
D   *Panicum virgatum* 'Cloud Nine' (switchgrass)

For the avid seed collector, fall offers an embarrassment of riches—there are seeds everywhere you look. For those new to this enjoyable activity, though, the bounty can be bewildering. The trick is to go ahead and collect many different kinds of seeds, so you can learn by trial and error. Fortunately, the actual collection process is quick—you can easily gather more than a dozen kinds of seeds in less than an hour. And you don't need any special tools: just a pair of scissors or garden shears, a handful of regular letter envelopes, a pen or pencil to label them with, and a dry, sunny day.

**Collecting exposed seeds.** Seeds that form with no special covering, such as those of asters, coneflowers (*Echinacea* and *Rudbeckia*), zinnias, and other daisy-type flowers, are a snap to harvest; simply pull them off by hand or rub them off into an open envelope. The challenge is to catch them at the right time: after they ripen but before they fall off on their own or get eaten by birds. Start watching them three or four weeks after they bloom. When mature, they typically turn from green to dark brown; then you can collect them. Afraid you'll miss them? Tie a small paper bag over a few seed heads to catch the seeds if they do loosen before you get around to harvesting them.

**Picking individual seedpods.** Some seeds, such as those of morning glories (*Ipomoea*), hollyhocks (*Alcea*), and irises, ripen within an outer covering, called a seedpod. Typically, these pods split along the sides, or develop some other kind of opening, once the seeds are mature. The seeds are somewhat protected from wind, rain, and birds, but you still need to watch the pods daily when they start to turn from green to brown. If the pods are fully brown but haven't opened yet, snip them off into an envelope. If splits or holes *are* visible, you may be able to shake or pour the seeds right out of the pod and into your collecting envelope.

**Gathering from small seed heads.** Plants that produce small blooms—such as catmints (*Nepeta*) and veronicas—also tend to produce small seeds, usually within a covering that may be thin and papery or thick and hard. These seed capsules are usually too tiny to snip off individually. One option is to snip off the entire cluster when most of the capsules have turned brown; another is to hold the clusters over an envelope and rub them with your fingers to release the seeds.

Rubbing exposed seeds into an envelope.

Snipping off a clustered seed head.

# AMAZING CONTAINERS

It's easy to get excited about container plantings early in the growing season, but if you're a little lax in keeping up with regular watering, fertilizing, and grooming, they can look rather ratty by late summer and downright dismal by fall. One way around that is to base your plantings on plants with fascinating foliage, such as this study in tans and browns: spiky, upright *Carex buchananii* with bushy, fine-textured *Haloragis erecta* 'Wellington Bronze' and trailing 'Sweet Caroline Bronze' sweet potato vine (*Ipomoea batatas*). Even without flowers, it provides terrific textural interest all through the growing season. Another option is to pull out the tired-looking annuals in late summer and replace them with cool-season annuals, late sowings of warm-season annuals, or good-looking flowering or foliage perennials to see you through the fall season. Or, pot up some containers specifically for summer interest and some just for fall, then swap them when the summer combo starts to lose its good looks.

A  *Haloragis erecta* 'Wellington Bronze' (haloragis)
B  *Carex buchananii* (New Zealand sedge)
C  *Ipomoea batatas* 'Sweet Caroline Bronze' (sweet potato vine)

# PREPARING POTS FOR WINTER

PERFECT PARTNERS FOR FALL

For most of us, the start of frosty weather marks the end of our container-gardening season. While you may be able to get most of your potted plants through a few light frosts by draping sheets over them, a hard freeze will kill the annuals and tender perennials and significantly slow down or stop the growth of hardy plants. Tidying up the dead or dormant plants, then taking steps to protect the containers they've been growing in, will leave their area looking neat all winter and make replanting in spring a whole lot easier as well.

**Taking apart tender plantings.** If your container plantings include tropicals or tender perennials that you want to bring indoors, plan on dismantling them before the first frost; otherwise, wait until after frost so you can enjoy them for as long as possible. Pot up the keepers, water them well, and set them in a shady, protected spot for a few days. Check carefully for signs of pest problems and treat them with insecticidal soap if necessary before bringing the plants indoors. (For more information, see Preparing Tender Plants for Winter on page 169.) If you've let the plants get nipped by frost, simply pull them out and toss them in your compost pile.

Emptying a clay pot.

**Handling potted perennials.** If you're growing hardy plants in frost-tolerant containers and don't mind taking the chance of losing them to unexpected or extended winter cold, just snip off any dead top growth, if desired, then water lightly and let them be. To provide extra protection, you could move them to a sheltered spot (next to a building, for example), then cover them with several inches of mulch or a layer of evergreen boughs. Or, wrap containers that are too large to move with old blankets or bubble wrap to help insulate the roots. The most dependable option is to remove the plants altogether and put them in a holding bed, or else to bring them into an unheated garage or porch, where they'll stay cool but not frozen.

**Clean 'em out.** Empty containers—especially if they are made out of clay or ceramic—will last longest if you store them inside for the winter. If they are light enough to move, dump the used potting soil into your compost pile or holding bed, scrub them out with a stiff brush, and store them in a garage, basement, or other frost-free place. If you choose to leave weatherproof containers outside, removing the potting soil and turning them upside down for the winter will help minimize damage from freezing. If that's not an option, at least try setting them up on bricks or strips of wood to make sure the drainage holes don't get clogged.

# DON'T GIVE UP!

Ah, the colorful leaves, the crisp air—there's just nothing like taking the time to enjoy your garden in autumn. Compared to the frenzy of spring and early summer, the pace of fall gardening is by far more relaxed. That doesn't mean, though, that you can completely ignore the routine care chores that are part of gardening all through the growing season.

**Keep ahead of watering.** Rainfall is typically more dependable in fall, but if the weather is unusually dry, it's smart to water your established plantings so they are not stressed going into wintertime. You should also continue regular watering for gardens that you installed in spring or summer of the current year, as well as for new fall plantings and fall divisions. As you would in other seasons, try to make sure your fall watering sessions wet the soil, not the plants themselves. Besides reducing the amount of water lost to evaporation, using soaker hoses for multiple plants or spot watering for individual clumps keeps leaves and stems dry, reducing the development and spread of some diseases.

**Keep ahead of plant disease.** Speaking of diseases—and pests, too—these problems generally don't seem as serious in fall as they do earlier in the growing season. While they probably won't seriously spoil your plants' beauty this late in the year, they can weaken your plants at a time when strong growth is important for winter survival. Good general care—including matching the plants to your available growing conditions, building your soil with organic matter, and watering only when

needed—will go a long way toward having a healthy, beautiful fall garden. And by this time of year, beneficial insects have had plenty of time to get established, so they'll take care of many pests before you even notice any damage. But if problems do appear, you'll want to take steps to control them immediately, either by removing the affected parts or by using the appropriate organic sprays.

**Weed duty.** Weeding, too, is a key part of keeping your gardens looking good all through autumn. As temperatures decline, cool-season weeds like chickweed can crop up quickly. Besides detracting from the looks of your garden, these weeds can provide a good winter hiding place for pests. Luckily, fall beds and borders that are packed with flowers and foliage don't leave much room for weeds to get started, so a few quick weeding sessions should stop these pesky plants before they cause a problem.

**The fertilizer issue.** One task you *don't* need to think much about in fall is fertilizing. At this time of year, you want your hardy perennials, shrubs, and trees to slow down in preparation for winter, not to produce lush new top growth that's likely to get nipped by cold weather. It *can* be worthwhile to keep feeding annuals and tender perennials—especially those growing in containers—so they'll keep blooming and producing lush foliage well into autumn. Use liquid fertilizers at this time of year, so plants can get the benefits right away; mix them according to package directions and apply every 10 to 14 days through early fall.

Keeping ahead of weeds.

# FALL FOLIAGE AT GROUND LEVEL

Even if you don't have enough room to plant lots of trees and shrubs in your yard, you can enjoy an abundance of fall color; you just need to think on a slightly smaller scale. Shrubs that can tolerate severe pruning, such as smokebush (*Cotinus coggygria*), are a treasure for adding height without unmanageable bulk; if they get too big for their space, you can cut them back partway or even close to the ground in early spring. Roses aren't a plant that immediately comes to mind for fall impact, but many hybrids — such as the small-flowered but intensely red 'Red Cascade' — can put on a good show of richly colored blooms during the cooler days of autumn. Then there are the perennials and bulbs with colorful fall foliage, such as the bright yellow leaves of Siberian iris (*Iris sibirica*) and hybrid lilies. And don't overlook the value of "borrowed landscape" when you're siting your beds and borders: Larger trees and shrubs growing in your neighbors' yards can provide a beautiful background for your own plantings — especially if they, too, offer colorful fall leaves.

A  *Cotinus coggygria* 'Velvet Cloak' (smokebush)
B  *Rosa* 'Red Cascade' (rose)
C  *Iris sibirica* (Siberian iris)
D  *Lilium* hybrid (lily)

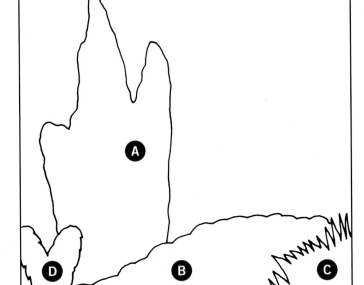

# LEAVES ALONE

Plants with great-looking foliage are a joy for gardeners all through the growing sea-son — and often all year-round. A planting based entirely on evergreens can get a little monotonous, though, so why not mix it up a bit? Pairing evergreen ground covers with deciduous shrubs is a terrific designer's trick for getting both all-year interest and seasonal changes all wrapped up in one dependable, easy-care package. This combination of Tiger Eyes sumac (*Rhus typhina* 'Bailtiger') underplanted with a ground cover of bergenia is an excellent example of what you can do with only two different plants. In spring, the bright yellow sumac foliage shows off beautifully against the bergenia's red-tinged foliage and its pink flowers as well; from summer to early fall, the pairing of rich yellow over intense green is guaranteed to catch the eye. The later-autumn display is absolutely spectacular, as the sumac often turns shades of red and orange to contrast dramatically with its still-green companion. And even after the sumac drops its leaves, its thick, fuzzy stems look striking rising out of the carpet of bergenia, which gradually takes on a reddish tinge for the winter. Who'd guess that just two plants could do so much?

A  *Rhus typhina* 'Bailtiger' (Tiger Eyes sumac)
B  *Bergenia cordifolia* (bergenia)

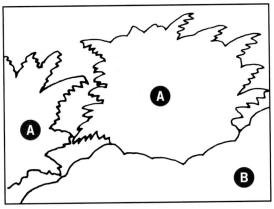

# MAKING THE MOST OF HOLDING BEDS

It's a curious fact: The inspiration for an amazing plant combination and the desire to buy the plants to create it strikes far more often than the urge to actually get those plants in the ground. So if you're like most gardeners, fall probably finds you with a collection of potted plants that you haven't yet found homes for. Instead of stuffing them into any old space you can find or leaving them unplanted all winter, why not create a temporary home for them? Usually called "holding beds" or "nursery beds," these short-term spaces are an ideal place for plants to live until you find the perfect permanent spot for them.

**Size.** Holding beds can be as large or as small as you like; available space is the only limitation. It's best to keep the width at 4 to 5 feet if you can reach into the bed from both sides; 3 feet is better if the bed is set directly against a wall or outbuilding. That way, you can easily reach all of the plants without having to step into the bed. A holding bed that's 4 feet wide and 8 feet long will provide a good starting point for most gardeners. You can always add more beds later if needed, or reduce the size of the one you have in the unlikely event that you haven't used all of the space.

**Site.** Ideally, your holding bed should experience the same light levels as the rest of your gardens. (If most of your property is sunny, for instance, place these beds in the sun too.) Most gardeners site holding beds in an out-of-the-way spot; anywhere near an outdoor faucet for easy watering is great.

**Raised beds.** Holding beds can be right at ground level, but raised beds offer several advantages: There's little or no digging involved in making them, and the loose, rich soil you fill them with encourages great root growth. To hold the soil in place, you'll need some kind of "frame": as simple as dry-stacked rocks, cinder blocks, or rough timbers or as stylish as a low mortared-brick wall. Keep in mind that raised beds typically provide excellent drainage, and the higher they are above ground level, the quicker they'll dry out; 6 inches high is about right for most climates. Filling the frame with a blend of equal parts screened topsoil, sand, and compost provides great growing conditions for a wide variety of plants; in dry areas, using a larger proportion of compost or topsoil or both in the mix will help reduce watering chores.

**Arrangement.** If you like, you can organize your plants into rows when you put them into a new holding bed. Over the years, though, this sort of careful arrangement usually disappears as you remove some of the faster-growing plants and leave others in place for an extra season or two. You might choose to create separate holding beds for different purposes or for different plant types, if you have the room; however, the plants themselves don't seem to mind being mixed up. In fact, young trees and shrubs can provide a perfect amount of shade and shelter for smaller plants growing among them.

131

PERFECT PARTNERS FOR FALL

# CLASSY SEED HEADS

Regularly snipping the dead flowers off your plants — a technique that gardeners usually refer to as "deadheading" — can be a super way to extend the bloom season on many annuals and perennials and even some shrubs. But if you're looking to get the most possible interest from your fall garden, you might want to hold off a little on deadheading, at least from mid- to late summer onward. Otherwise, you may lose one of the least appreciated aspects of the autumn garden: the showy seed heads that provide a wealth of fascinating forms long after the flowers have gone. This late-season combination, for example, highlights two of the classics for excellent seed heads: the flat-topped form of an upright sedum and the small, dark domes of orange coneflowers (*Rudbeckia fulgida*). The multicolored fall foliage of 'Chameleon' euphorbia (*Euphorbia dulcis*) is just about done for the year, but the lacy gray foliage of 'Powis Castle' artemisia will stay along with the seed heads for winter interest. Keep in mind that leaving the seed heads on your plants can mean that they'll produce some (or many) seedlings next spring. Be prepared to transplant the youngsters to other parts of your garden, or weed out those you don't need.

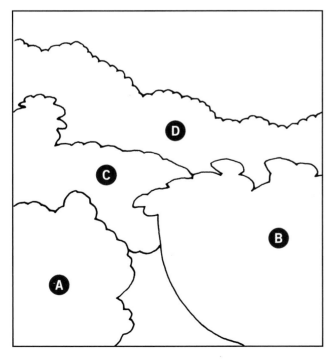

A *Euphorbia dulcis* 'Chameleon' (euphorbia)
B *Sedum spectabile* (showy sedum)
C *Artemisia* 'Powis Castle' (artemisia)
D *Rudbeckia fulgida* (orange coneflower)

To cut or not to cut? That is the question for gardeners getting their plantings ready for winter. Should you leave everything up until spring, cut it all down now, or cut some and leave some? The only right answer is: There's no one right answer.

On the one hand, there are plenty of good reasons to hold off on fall cleanup. Leaving the top growth of your perennials gives some height and structure to your garden throughout the winter, so you aren't just looking at bare earth with a few shrubs scattered around. While they don't show the same rich hues of summer, these winter skeletons have their own color palette, including shades of silver, bronze, copper, tan, brown, and black. And without the distraction of flowers and foliage, you can admire the subtle beauty of their stems, branches, and seed heads— particularly when they are traced with frost or dusted with snow. Wildlife, too, will appreciate your not being too tidy; birds will feast on the remaining seeds, while butterflies and beneficial insects can find ample shelter to overwinter safely.

There are also a number of practical reasons to put off your garden cleanup until spring. The remaining top growth helps to

Kale 'Lacinato'

*Euphorbia dulcis* 'Chameleon'

trap leaves and snow, which provides extra insulation for the crowns and roots; this is especially helpful for plants that might not be fully winter-hardy in your area otherwise. It also reminds you that a plant is growing in a particular spot, so you're not tempted to try to dig there if you're doing some last-minute fall or early-spring planting.

To complicate matters, though, there are also a number of good reasons *to* clean up your gardens thoroughly in fall. While the dead leaves and stems provide good winter quarters for beneficial insects, they can also harbor pests and disease spores, which will then have an easy time finding their favorite plants again next year. Leafy debris makes a great hiding place for critters such as mice and voles as well, which may spend the winter feeding on the roots of your perennials (and the bark of shrubs and trees, too). Also, keep in mind that the same seed heads that feed winter birds will also drop seeds onto the ground below, possibly leaving you with many unwanted seedlings to weed out next year. Besides preventing that problem, fall cleanup will save you time in spring, so you can be planting and digging then instead of dealing with the debris. From an aesthetic standpoint, some people think the dead plants make a garden look messy, and to be fair, some of them do.

So, what's a gardener to do? There is no right answer: only what works best for your particular circumstances. Besides cutting everything in fall or leaving it all until spring, here are some compromises to consider:

♠ Do a thorough fall cleanup in highly visible front-yard gardens, but wait until spring to cut down your backyard beds and borders so you can enjoy them over the winter.

♠ Cut back the plants with soft or floppy stems in fall and leave those that have sturdy, good-looking stems and/or seed heads until spring.

♠ Cut down plants that self-sow prolifically as soon as possible and leave the rest until spring.

♠ Leave the top growth on marginally hardy plants until spring, but cut back everything else in fall.

♠ If you've had problems with pests, diseases, or rodents in the past, cut down the top growth in fall and rake out all the debris from the affected gardens to remove hiding places.

♠ If you can count on having snow on the ground most of the winter, cut back all of the plants that are usually under the snow and leave only the taller ones for spring.

Still can't decide whether a fall or spring cleanup is better? Why not spread out the job through the winter? It gives you a good reason to get out in the garden on mild days and spreads out the workload, so cleanup is more of a pleasure than a chore. You'll also learn which plants hold up well and for how long, so you can adjust your cleanup schedule next year as needed.

# VERY BERRIED

Brightly colored berries are a joy in any autumn garden, but they're especially welcome in shady sites, where late-season color is often rather scarce. This combination is based mostly on foliage, including the slender green, yellow-rimmed blades of 'Oehme' palm sedge (*Carex muskingumensis*), which look good from spring through fall (turning tan for winter), and black mondo grass (*Ophiopogon planiscapus* 'Nigrescens'), which is present all year long. But the real star in this grouping is the Italian arum (*Arum italicum* var. *pictum*), with hooded, greenish white flowers in spring, spikes of orange-red berries in fall, and cream-marbled green leaves from fall through spring. Italian arum can self-sow freely and is considered invasive in some regions; if you're concerned about that in your area, you could get a similar berry effect from Jack-in-the-pulpits (*Arisaema*). Be aware that young Jack-in-the-pulpit plants usually produce male flowers only, while mature plants are typically female, and you need both for pollination and berry production. Planting several of the corms in one clump and waiting a few years will usually produce the desired results. Stinking iris (*Iris foetidissima*), with clusters of bright red seeds, is another option for fall interest in shade.

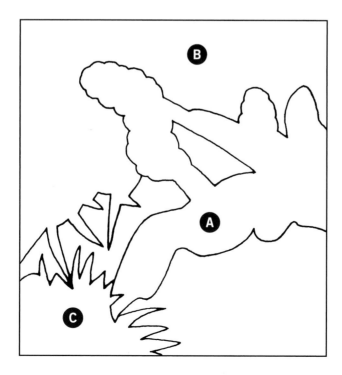

A  *Arum italicum* var. *pictum* (Italian arum)
B  *Carex muskingumensis* 'Oehme' (palm sedge)
C  *Ophiopogon planiscapus* 'Nigrescens'
   (black mondo grass)

# DEALING WITH DEBRIS

Whether you garden in sun or shade, you won't much enjoy your carefully planned fall combinations if all those beautiful berries are buried in dropped leaves or hidden by dead stems. Raking up leaves and cutting down plants are the easy parts of fall cleanup: The real challenge is figuring out what to do with all of the debris you're left with. Those of you with large properties have the luxury of creating brush piles to hide this unwanted material (with the added benefit of creating shelter for birds and other wildlife). But if space is limited, you'll need to come up with some other alternatives so your valuable gardening room isn't taken up with mounds of dead leaves, broken stems, and the like.

Actually, calling these garden by-products "debris" isn't quite fair, because it implies that they're useless and unwanted. When you know what to do with them, though, you'll find that this couldn't be further from the truth! These plant-derived materials are invaluable for adding organic matter to your garden soil, either dug in before planting or as a mulch afterward. You can chop them up and use them immediately or pile them up and let them decompose somewhat before using them in spring. Either way, the more "homemade" organic matter you have, the less packaged material (such as dried manure, peat moss, or commercial compost) you'll have to buy and haul home for the same purpose. When you take that into consideration, it's easy to see that investing a little time in properly handling your garden waste can save you money in the long run.

You can make the whole process much easier on yourself if you keep the different types of debris separated at cleanup time. The softer the material, the faster it'll break down and the sooner it'll be ready to use in the garden; keeping leaves, end-of-the-season grass clippings, and thin stems in one area will give you a supply of practically ready-to-use mulch. Branches and tough, woody stems will need further processing before you can use them, so put them in another area until you're ready to chip them or trim them into stakes.

If the debris produced by your beds and borders exceeds the space you have to store it, you have two options. One is to do your garden cleanup all at one time (either in fall or early spring), then use a chipper/shredder to chop it all up — that immediately reduces the volume and gives you a perfect supply of material for end-of-the-season mulching or composting. Or, spread out your cleanup sessions through the colder months, so you don't have a massive amount of debris to deal with all at one time.

Clean up with a chipper/shredder.

# EXTERIOR DECORATING

Even in the most carefully planned gardens, empty spaces can appear as the growing season goes on. Plants may not grow quite as fast or as large as you expected; heat or drought may cause some to die or go dormant weeks sooner than you expected. Some gardeners resort to popping potted mums into the gaps; container-raised annuals are another option. But if you haven't grown your own and don't feel like spending the money for just a few weeks of extra color, why not make do with items you already have around your home? A pretty pot (with or without plants in it) or even an empty watering can would serve the purpose; small pieces of statuary, gazing balls, baskets, or other ornaments (such as this heavy glass jug) work great too. Or, for something really different, consider tucking pumpkins, squash, and gourds into those empty spaces. There's no better way to celebrate the bounty of fall!

A *Ipomoea batatas* 'Margarita' (sweet potato vine)

B *Salvia coccinea* 'Lady in Red' (scarlet sage)

C *Dahlia* 'Bishop of Llandaff' (dahlia)

D *Tagetes* hybrid (marigold)

E *Tropaeolum majus* (nasturtium)

F *Zinnia* 'Profusion Orange' (zinnia)

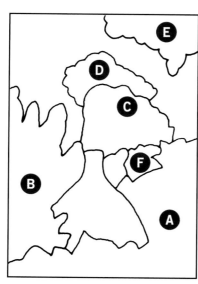

When it's time to tidy up your yard and garden for winter, don't forget about the various accessories that made your beds and borders more beautiful during the growing season. Even if you choose to leave them outdoors for the winter, a little care now will help prolong the life of your favorite ornaments and furniture. And don't forget to take care of those hand tools; they'll last a lot longer that if you tend to them as well.

Removing rust from metal.

Before freezing weather returns, bring in any knickknacks, signs, and other garden accessories that might get damaged by wet or cold, such as ceramic items, twig trellises, and hand-painted ornaments. Move wooden furniture into a sheltered spot, if possible; if not, at least set the feet up on bricks so they aren't sitting directly on wet ground. Empty garden buckets and watering cans and drain the water out of your hoses, then bring them indoors or into a shed. Repair any leaks in the hoses, replace worn or cracked washers, then coil and hang up the hoses so they won't get kinked.

Although most aspects of tool care are simple enough for anyone to do, sharpening cutting and digging tools can be a little daunting. If you look at the edge of these tools, you'll usually see that it's cut at an angle, called the bevel. If you sharpen your tools yourself, you'll want to match the existing bevel. (Digging tools may not have a bevel when you buy them; in this case, sharpen to a 45 degree angle.) Avoid the temptation to hone to a razor-sharp edge because the thinner metal will be more prone to chip or bend. An electric drill with a coarse grinding disk attachment can do a great job for sharpening digging tools, but be careful; it can remove a lot of metal quickly! A handheld mill file takes longer but gives you much closer control over the angle. A medium-grit sharpening stone is the best choice for maintaining the blades of fine cutting tools, such as pruning shears and loppers.

Not sure you want to do the job yourself? Then treat your tools to a professional sharpening once a year. Late fall is a great time to have them done because shops aren't very busy then; delay until spring, when everyone remembers that their tools are dull, and you may have to wait weeks to get them back.

After sharpening but before storage, it's important to protect all the metal parts of your tools from rust. Ideally, use a *penetrating* oil, which contains alcohol and other solvents that displace water and help the oil get into any tiny cracks or pits in the metal. Once the solvents evaporate, they leave behind a very light coating of oil. That's usually enough to provide a light amount of lubrication for moving parts, but you may choose to use a few drops of *lubricating* oil to provide extra protection for springs and pivot points.

For more tips on cleaning, maintaining, and storing hand tools (and power equipment), turn to Caring for Tools on page 224.

# IT'S FOR THE BIRDS

Glorious autumn gardens aren't just a treat for people to look at — they're also an all-you-can-eat buffet for hungry birds and other wildlife. Asters, boltonia, coneflowers (*Echinacea* and *Rudbeckia*), and many other classic daisy-form flowers provide lots of nectar for migrating butterflies and pollen for beneficial insects, then turn into seed-rich heads that feed hungry birds well into the winter months. Goldenrods (*Solidago*) and Joe-Pye weeds (*Eupatorium*) are also excellent end-of-the-season food sources for bees and beneficials, and 'Purple Majesty' millet (*Pennisetum glaucum*) and other grasses with lots of fall seeds are sure to bring birds to your garden. Need other ideas? Berry-bearing shrubs and trees can also be bird magnets, especially those with energy-rich fruits, such as spicebush (*Lindera benzoin*), dogwoods (*Cornus*), and sassafras (*Sassafras albidum*).

A  *Rudbeckia fulgida* var. *fulgida* (orange coneflower)
B  *Aster laevis* 'Bluebird' (smooth aster)
C  *Pennisetum glaucum* 'Purple Majesty' (millet)
D  *Solidago rugosa* 'Fireworks' (goldenrod)
E  *Eupatorium maculatum* 'Gateway' (Joe-Pye weed)

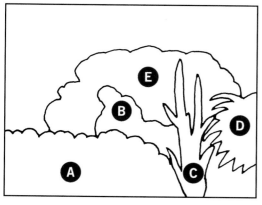

# READY, SET, FEED!

Well-planned autumn gardens supply lots of seeds and berries for our feathered friends, but many of us still like to provide supplemental food throughout the colder months at least, in the form of seed and suet feeders. To increase the odds of attracting birds—and keeping them around—don't forget that they also need water and shelter. Evergreen shrubs and trees are excellent sources of shelter; densely branched deciduous shrubs and trees can also provide some protection. Complete your backyard habitat by providing nesting boxes and other places for wildlife to raise their young.

**Clean your feeders.** Whether you put away your bird feeders for the summer or you leave them out all year, fall is a good time to give them a thorough cleaning. Fill a large tub with hot water and liquid dish soap, then scrub your feeders thoroughly (wear gloves while you do this) and rinse with water. To make sure all traces of soap are gone, soak in fresh water with several cups of vinegar added, then rinse again. Or, for extra disinfectant action, soak them in a 10-percent bleach solution (1 part household bleach to 9 parts water) for several minutes, then let air-dry. Make sure your feeders are thoroughly dry before filling them with seed. Cleaning them once or twice a month through the feeding season will help prevent the spread of diseases among visiting birds. If you haven't done so already, clean out any birdhouses too, and rinse them with the bleach solution.

**Don't forget drinking water.** When you set up your feeders, be sure to provide a water source for your birds too. Ceramic and concrete baths are prone to damage from freezing, so you're better off cleaning and putting them away in fall. For winter birds, a ground-level bath may be a better choice than an aboveground bath, because the ground-level bath will stay unfrozen longer. Siting the bath on the south side of a building, fence, or hedge can help too. You'll probably still need an electric heater to keep the water open; if that's not an option, floating a piece of Styrofoam on the surface will help insulate the surface (allow just an inch or two of water to be uncovered around the edge). In an uncovered bath, adding a few stones that stick up above the water level will allow the birds to rest and drink without getting wet.

Clean feeders before hanging in fall.

PERFECT PARTNERS FOR FALL

# HANDLING CONTAINER PLANTINGS

After a summer of watering, fertilizing, pinching, and primping, it can be tempting to take a break when fall arrives and let your container plants fend for themselves. Just like in-ground gardens, though, potted plantings benefit from a little attention at the end of the season.

The decisions you made back at spring planting time have a major impact on the fall care your containers will need. For example, clay and ceramic pots tend to crack in freezing weather, so if you used them for summer displays, you'll have to remove all of the plants and bring the pots indoors. Cement, fiberglass, and wooden planters can usually survive winters outdoors. Plastic pots left outdoors may crack in extreme cold but have the advantage of being relatively inexpensive to replace.

If you're growing only annuals or tender perennials, any container with drainage holes is suitable, because you can dump out the soil and bring the planter indoors for winter storage. But if you want to leave hardy plants in containers through the winter, the planters must be sturdy enough to withstand freezing. It's also wise to take some precautions at planting time to give protection to the roots. Lining the containers with sheets of Styrofoam or bubble wrap before adding the growing mix will provide extra insulation against winter cold (and against strong summer sun). An alternative way to get a similar insulating effect is to put a smaller pot inside of a large one, then fill the space between the two with Styrofoam "peanuts," peat moss, or some other material.

Another way to make your fall container cleanup easier is to keep "temporary" plants (annuals and tender perennials) separate from "permanent" ones (hardy perennials, shrubs, vines, small trees, and the like). That way, you won't have to disturb the permanent plantings when you remove the temporary ones before or after frost.

In any season, grouping your container plantings makes for much easier maintenance, whether it's spring frost protection, summer watering, fall cleanup, or winter protection. If they are already in a sheltered spot, winter protection is that much easier; if not, try to make sure that the planters that you'll be leaving outdoors are small enough to carry or wheel to a protected place. When moving the containers isn't an option, go ahead and use extra-large pots; at least they'll be slower to freeze than small pots will.

Keep tender plants together for easy fall cleanup.

# UP CLOSE AND PERSONAL

In spring and summer, it seems like there's always so much to do outdoors and so little time to get it all done. By fall, though, the pressure's off; oh sure, there are still plenty of projects you could tackle, but somehow things just don't seem as hectic. This is the ideal chance to relax a bit and spend some time simply soaking in all the beauty you've worked so hard all season to create. Converting an unused corner of a deck, porch, or patio into a small sanctuary, complete with a comfy seat and pots of your favorite flowers and foliage, is the perfect way to reward yourself for a job well done. Use the leftover containers of annuals that you didn't need as fillers in your beds and borders, or let the space do double-duty as a holding area for the annuals and tender perennials that you've potted up in preparation for bringing indoors before frost. Along with good-looking flowers and foliage, remember to include something for fragrance, such as purple basil or another good-looking herb that releases its scent when you rub its leaves. Talk about a scent-sual treat!

A *Zinnia angustifolia* (narrowleaf zinnia)
B *Solenostemon scutellarioides* 'Sedona' (coleus)
C *Dahlia* hybrid (dahlia)
D *Ocimum basilicum* (purple basil)
E *Carex buchananii* (New Zealand sedge)

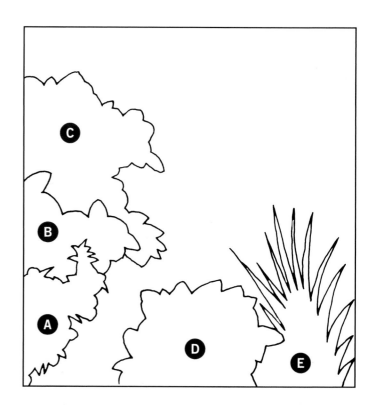

# PUTTING IT ALL TOGETHER

**W**ITH SO MANY FANTASTIC FLOWERING, FRUITING, AND FOLIAGE plants to choose from for fall interest, it can be tempting to plan a whole landscape around them, and the results could be simply spectacular. Of course, most of us want gardens that look great in spring and summer, too — and we can have them, if we're willing to put a little extra care into selecting our plants and combining them effectively.

In the following pages, you'll find ten examples of gardens that can grace your yard in autumn as well as one or more of the other seasons. Use the plans as they are, modify them to fit your particular needs, or take the design suggestions as a jumping-off point for your unique planting plans. Once you start looking at gardens with an eye toward autumn interest, you're likely to find lots of ways to extend the beauty of your existing plantings as well. Checking out other gardens and getting inspiration from pre-made plans are valuable ways to get ideas, but the best way to explore the glories of the fall garden is to just get out there and get planting!

**What's your style?** Perhaps you enjoy the free-for-all extravagance of this combo, featuring variegated giant reed (*Arundo donax* 'Variegata'), dahlias, crocosmia, cannas, and other fall-bloomers, or maybe you'd prefer something a bit more restrained.

# STUNNING SUNNY GARDENS

Sunny sites offer an abundance of exciting options for all seasons, but they're particularly pleasing for fall gardens because they support the widest variety of flowering and fruiting plants. Ample sunlight also tends to bring out the brightest hues in leaves that change color in autumn, adding even more plants to the designer's palette. While there are sun-lovers for all parts of the border, bright sites are a real boon for gardeners who like *big* plants. Some fall perennials use the summer sun's energy to shoot up 6 to 10 feet tall before their flowers even think about opening — perfect for filling big spaces or for providing seasonal screening for a deck, pool, or other outdoor living space. Luckily for space-challenged gardeners, there are also plenty of more-compact cultivars of these substantial perennials to bring bright blooms down to a more manageable size.

## A Sunny Street-side Border

An expanse of lawn is an easy way to fill a sun-drenched front yard, but it doesn't add much in the way of ever-changing color and texture. You don't want to replace that useless turf with just *any* plants, though. In such a visible spot, they need to look great both *before* and *after* their bloom season, not just while they are in full flower. A street-side border should also be low-maintenance, so you're not stuck spending a lot of time kneeling or bending over out there in full view of neighbors and passersby.

This design is packed with hardworking, easy-care, non-fussy plants that provide an abundance of color and texture from foliage, flowers, and seed heads from mid-spring through fall — and well into winter too. All it needs is a bit of grooming once or twice a year (prune out any deadwood on the rose and trim back the caryopteris to about 1 foot tall in early spring; cut the rest of the perennials back to the ground in either late fall or early spring). After the chance of frost has passed, pop in a six-pack of 'Profusion Orange' zinnias along the front, then stand back and enjoy your sunny border as it gets better and better through the growing season!

A  *Caryopteris incana* 'Jason' (3 plants)
B  *Geranium* 'Brookside' (3 plants)
C  *Lonicera × brownii* 'Dropmore Scarlet'
   (2 plants)
D  *Panicum virgatum* 'Northwind' (3 plants)
E  *Rosa* 'Radrazz' (1 plant)
F  *Salvia* 'Caradonna' (3 plants)
G  *Sedum* 'Black Jack' (3 plants)
H  *Solidago rugosa* 'Fireworks' (3 plants)
I  *Zinnia* 'Profusion Orange' (6 plants)

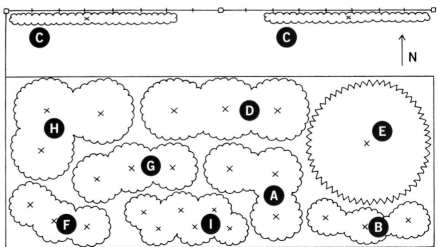

PUTTING IT ALL TOGETHER

***Caryopteris incana* 'Jason'**
SUNSHINE BLUE CARYOPTERIS
Small, bright yellow leaves from spring through fall; bright blue flowers in early to mid-fall. 2'–3' tall × 1'–2' wide. Full sun (in cooler areas) to partial shade; average, well-drained soil. Zones 5–9.
Suggested alternative : *C.* × *clandonensis* 'Worcester Gold' (blooms a few weeks earlier and is not quite as bright yellow in leaf).

***Geranium* 'Brookside'**
'BROOKSIDE' GERANIUM
Deeply lobed green foliage turns bright red in fall; blue flowers from late spring to mid- or late summer. About 30" tall and wide. Zones 5–8.
Suggested alternative: 'Rozanne' (more spreading than upright and starts blooming later, but continues well into fall and has reddish fall leaf color).

***Lonicera* × *brownii* 'Dropmore Scarlet'**
'DROPMORE SCARLET' HONEYSUCKLE
Oblong green leaves turn shades of yellow, orange, and red in fall; reddish orange flowers from early or midsummer well into fall, often followed by red berries. Can grow 10'–15' tall (size depends on the size of the support structure). Full sun to light shade; average, well-drained soil. Zones 4–8.
Suggested alternative: *L.* × *heckrottii* (goldflame honeysuckle; flowers are deep pink outside and peachy yellow inside).

***Panicum virgatum* 'Northwind'**
'NORTHWIND' SWITCHGRASS
Slender, olive green blades that turn shades of yellow in fall and then tan through the winter; airy greenish to tan

flower heads appear in late summer and last through winter. 5'–6' tall × 1'–2' wide. Full sun; average, well-drained soil. Zones 4–9.
Suggested alternative: 'Heavy Metal' (not quite as strongly upright and slightly shorter, with blue-green foliage).

Rosa 'Radrazz'

***Rosa* 'Radrazz'**
KNOCK OUT ROSE
Roughly oval, deep green leaves may turn deep purple in fall; bright reddish pink, semi-double flowers from early summer well into fall, followed by orange hips. 3'–4' tall and wide. Full sun to light shade; average to moist but well-drained soil. Zones 4–9.
Suggested alternative: 'Radtko' (Double Knock Out; with double flowers).

***Salvia* 'Caradonna'**
'CARADONNA' SALVIA
Small, medium to deep green leaves on purple stems through the growing season; spikes of deep purple-blue flowers from midsummer into fall with deadheading. About 2' tall × 18" wide. Full sun; average, well-drained soil. Zones 4–8.
Suggested alternative: *S.* 'Blue Hills', 'East Friesland', or 'May Night' (about 18" tall); *Veronica* 'Goodness Grows' (even shorter and more mat-forming, with bright blue flowers).

***Sedum* 'Black Jack'**
'BLACK JACK' SEDUM
Oblong, deep purple leaves all through the growing season; broad heads of tiny, rosy pink flowers open in early fall and hold their form well into winter. About 2' tall × 1' wide. Full sun to light shade; average, well-drained soil. Zones 3–8.
Suggested alternative: 'Purple Emperor', or another dark-leaved, upright sedum.

Solidago rugosa 'Fireworks'

***Solidago rugosa* 'Fireworks'**
'FIREWORKS' GOLDENROD
Slender, deep green leaves all season; sprays of bright yellow flowers from late summer into fall. 3'–4' tall × about 2' across. Full sun to light shade; average, well-drained soil. Zones 5–9.
Suggested alternative: *Rudbeckia fulgida* var. *fulgida* (shorter, with dark-centered, bright yellow daisies).

***Zinnia* 'Profusion Orange'**
'PROFUSION ORANGE' ZINNIA
Small green leaves from spring to frost; bright orange, single blooms from early summer until frost. 12"–18" tall and wide. Full sun; average, well-drained soil. Annual.
Suggested alternative: *Gaillardia* × *grandiflora* 'Oranges and Lemons' (perennial, with larger but lighter orange-and-yellow flowers).

# GROOMING YOUR GARDENS FOR WINTER

Regardless of whether you decide to do your main garden cleanup in fall or spring, there's still plenty to do to get your yard ready for winter. Here's a tip that will make any cleanup job go a bit easier: Instead of using a bucket or wheelbarrow to gather the debris, spread out a tarp right next to the area you're working on and toss all the clippings onto it as you cut. When you're done, simply pick up the four corners and drag it over to your compost pile. That'll save you the separate step of raking up the debris and stuffing it into a cart or wheelbarrow, and you won't need to make endless trips back and forth to pick up everything.

**Handling annuals.** Generally, it's a good idea to remove the annuals from your gardens in fall. Most of them don't add much in the way of winter interest, and many look downright ugly once they've been zapped by cold. Lots of annuals can bloom until a light or hard frost, so wait until they've been blackened to remove them. (Impatiens and begonias are two exceptions; if they get frosted, they turn slimy and are unpleasant to handle, so remove them soon *before* frost.) Pull out the plants, roots and all, or clip the stems right at ground level and leave the roots to decompose and thereby add organic matter to the soil.

**Cutting down perennials.** If you've decided to cut down some or all of your perennials now, wait until they are fully dormant—in late fall or even early winter. If you cut too early and the weather stays mild, they might decide to resprout and use up their stored energy in the process, reducing the chance they'll overwinter successfully. Use hand shears to snip individual stems, or try hedge shears or even a string trimmer to make quick work of multiple plants. Don't cut too close to the ground or you might damage the crowns; about 3 inches above the ground is fine for most plants.

**Cleaning up leaves.** Before you count your cleanup chores as done, take a little time to inspect the rest of your yard. If any ground covers are buried in fall leaves, rake them off. (It's fine to leave *some* of the leaves, because they'll act as a good organic mulch; you just don't want a lot of leaves sitting on top or they'll smother the ground cover.) If any of your shrubs or trees showed signs of leaf diseases this past growing season, it's a good idea to rake up their dropped leaves, along with the top layer of mulch. Then give them another inch or two of fresh mulch to cover any remaining spores and reduce the chance of disease problems next year.

Removing leaves from ground cover.

# SHADY CHARACTERS FOR AUTUMN

It's easy to create a flower-filled shade garden for spring: Sunlight is abundant before the trees leaf out, and many woodland wildflowers take advantage of this opportunity by putting on their bloom display early in the growing season. Once the spring show of flowers is over, foliage tends to take center stage, but that doesn't mean you have to settle for solid shades of green. Choosing plants with distinctive leaf textures and colors ensures that your shady garden is as appealing in autumn as it is in spring. Tuck in a few shade-loving fall-bloomers too, and you'll enjoy some seasonal surprises to complement the long-lasting display of beautiful leaves.

## A Shady Deck Border

This foliage-based, multiseason mixed border offers a veritable rainbow of colors from spring through fall, along with winter interest from some ever-present leaves (including the autumn ferns, heucheras, Lenten roses, and wild gingers). Flowers aren't lacking, either, from the late-winter blooms of Lenten roses to the fragrant white blossoms of fothergilla in spring; the heucheras and foamy bells in early summer; and the hydrangea, black snakeroots, toad lilies, and yellow waxbells in late summer and fall.

From a practical standpoint, this design focuses on dependable plants that don't demand a lot of fussing, trimming, or deadheading. After all, you want to be able to *relax* on your deck — not feel guilty about a garden that needs endless mainte-

nance. An hour or so in late winter should suffice for cutting down any remaining winter-killed top growth on the perennials, trimming the old leaves off the Lenten roses, and adding some fresh mulch if needed; beyond that, the plants pretty much look after themselves.

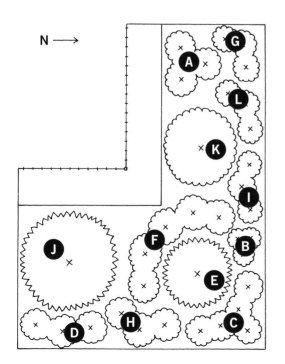

N →

A    *Actaea simplex* 'James Compton' (3 plants)

B    *Asarum europaeum* (3 plants)

C    *Carex siderosticha* 'Lemon Zest' (5 plants)

D    *Dryopteris erythrosora* 'Brilliance' (3 plants)

E    *Fothergilla* 'Blue Shadow' (1 plant)

F    *Helleborus* × *hybridus* (5 plants)

G    *Heuchera* 'Lime Rickey' (3 plants)

H    *Heuchera* 'Peach Flambé' (3 plants)

I    × *Heucherella* 'Stoplight' (3 plants)

J    *Hydrangea quercifolia* 'Little Honey' (1 plant)

K    *Kirengeshoma palmata* (1 plant)

L    *Tricyrtis formosana* 'Gilt Edge' (3 plants)

### *Actaea simplex* 'James Compton'
'JAMES COMPTON' BLACK SNAKEROOT

Lacy, deep purple-brown foliage; brushy white flower spikes in late summer to early fall. 3'–4' tall × 2' wide. Partial shade; moist, well-drained soil. Zones 4–8. Suggested alternative: *Actaea simplex* 'Black Negligee' (usually 4'–5' tall).

### *Asarum europaeum*
EUROPEAN WILD GINGER

Kidney-shaped, glossy deep green leaves effective all year; small, brown ground-level flowers in spring. About 4" tall × 6"–12" wide. Partial to full shade; average, well-drained soil. Zones 4–9. Suggested alternative: *Hexastylis shuttleworthii*.

### *Carex siderosticha* 'Lemon Zest'
'LEMON ZEST' SEDGE

Broad, spiky, bright yellow blades turn greenish yellow in summer; last through fall. About 10" tall and wide. Full sun to partial shade; evenly moist but well-drained soil. Zones 5–9. Suggested alternative: *Carex* 'Banana Boat'.

### *Dryopteris erythrosora* 'Brilliance'
'BRILLIANCE' AUTUMN FERN

Lacy fronds are coppery orange when new, maturing to deep green and lasting through much or all of the winter. About 2' tall and wide. Partial shade; average, well-drained soil. Zones 5–9. Suggested alternative: *Dryopteris erythrosora*.

### *Fothergilla* 'Blue Shadow'
'BLUE SHADOW' FOTHERGILLA

Rounded blue-gray to blue-green leaves in spring/summer turn red, orange, and yellow in fall; brushy clusters of white flowers in spring. 5'–6' tall and wide. Full sun to partial shade; slightly acidic, average to moist, well-drained soil. Zones 5–8. Suggested alternative: *F. gardenii* 'Blue Mist'.

### *Helleborus* × *hybridus*
HYBRID LENTEN ROSE

Deep green foliage is present year-round; saucer-shaped white, pink, or deep red flowers from late winter to mid-spring. 12"–18" tall and about as wide. Partial to full shade; average, well-drained soil. Zones 5–9. Suggested alternative: *H. foetidus*.

*Heuchera* 'Dolce Key Lime Pie'

### *Heuchera* 'Lime Rickey'
'LIME RICKEY' HEUCHERA

Bright yellow new foliage ages to green-tinged yellow and is effective into winter; airy clusters of tiny white flowers in summer. About 1' tall and wide in leaf; to 18" tall in bloom. Light shade; average, well-drained soil. Zones 4–8. Suggested alternative: 'Dolce Key Lime Pie' heuchera.

### *Heuchera* 'Peach Flambé'
'PEACH FLAMBÉ' HEUCHERA

Orange-pink to orange-brown foliage is present year-round; airy clusters of tiny white flowers in summer. About 1' tall and wide in leaf; to 18" tall in bloom. Light shade; average, well-drained soil. Zones 4–8.

Suggested alternative: 'Mardi Gras' or another orange- or purple-leaved heuchera.

### × *Heucherella* 'Stoplight'
'STOPLIGHT' FOAMY BELLS

Bright yellow foliage with red center markings, especially in spring (may go summer-dormant but looks good again in fall); white flowers in spring. About 6" tall × 1' wide in leaf; 12"–18" tall in bloom. Partial shade; average, well-drained soil. Zones 4–8. Suggested alternative: 'Sunspot'.

### *Hydrangea quercifolia* 'Little Honey'
'LITTLE HONEY' OAKLEAF HYDRANGEA

Lobed yellow leaves turn red in fall; large-clustered white flowers in late summer. About 3' tall and wide. Partial shade; average to moist, well-drained soil. Zones 5–9. Suggested alternative: 'Pee Wee.'

### *Kirengeshoma palmata*
YELLOW WAXBELLS

Large, lobed green leaves all through the growing season; yellow, bell-shaped blooms in late summer to early fall. Usually 3'–4' tall and wide. Partial shade; slightly acidic, evenly moist but well-drained soil. Zones 5–8. Suggested alternative: *Hosta* 'Great Expectations'.

### *Tricyrtis formosana* 'Gilt Edge'
'GILT EDGE' TOAD LILY

Glossy green leaves edged with yellow are present all season; purple-spotted white flowers start in summer and continue into fall. 1'–2' tall × about 2' wide. Partial shade; average to moist but well-drained soil. Zones 6–9. Suggested alternative: *T. hirta* 'Miyazaki Gold' or *T. formosana* 'Samurai'.

# HANDLING GARDEN DEBRIS

Both shady and sunny gardens present you with the same challenge at the end of the growing season: What are you going to do with all the dead leaves and trimmings? The 3 R's (reduce, reuse, and recycle) are finally becoming commonplace for household trash, and they're just as effective for handling yard and garden waste. With a little know-how, you can turn even a large pile of debris into a welcome source of soil-building material. If you have enough temporary storage space, gather up the leaves, stems, and other trimmings in fall, then pile them up to deal with later; it's a great reason to get outdoors for a few hours on a mild winter day! Or, take care of them as part of each day's cleanup, and you won't be stuck looking at unsightly debris piles in your backyard.

**Mulching on the spot.** For the ultimate in time savings, go ahead and chop up dead stems right in the garden. Simply cut them off just above the base, hold them in one hand, and use your pruning shears to snip them into small pieces so they fall right back into the garden. No hauling away, no piles of debris—just an instant mulch. This works best when you're dealing with small beds, lots of fairly soft or thin stems, or fairly short cleanup sessions; after a while, your hands can get rather tired! Keep a bucket nearby to hold the small bits you don't want to return to the garden, including seed-filled seed heads and diseased leaves.

**Leave some leaves.** Instead of raking up all of the leaves from your trees and shrubs, let at least some of them stay where they fall. This works best in beds, borders, ground covers, and foundation plantings, where the leaves can decompose and release nutrients and organic matter right where they're needed. If the leaves are so large or so numerous that they cover the plants or grass, then rake them up so they don't smother your garden or lawn. Add them to your compost bin, pile them up to make leaf mold, or shred them with your lawn mower and dig them into your soil or use them for winter mulch.

**Handling the hard stuff.** The most challenging type of garden waste to deal with is tough stems and woody branches. If you have a small amount of this durable debris, you could either chop it up manually with loppers or smash it with a hammer and add it to your compost pile. (Smashing exposes more surface area for quicker decomposition, but it will still take awhile to break down.) For large amounts of woody brush, it's worth buying or renting a chipper/shredder to reduce that material to useful mulch. Or, use your creativity and turn those unwanted prunings into useful garden items, such as stakes and rustic trellises.

Chopping tender stems into the garden.

# HIGH AND DRY

A hot, dry site doesn't have to be a desert of rocks and cacti! It can offer a bounty of beautiful blooms and pleasant scents as well, if you choose your plants wisely. Dry-soil autumn gardens tend to need a lot less pinching and staking than do those in average to moist soils, because the lack of moisture naturally keeps the plants lower and encourages much sturdier stems. On flat sites, drought-tolerant perennials and grasses sail through the worst summer heat with little or no watering, then put on a glorious display once the temperatures become a bit more moderate in autumn. On dry, sun-baked slopes, you might instead choose low-growing ground covers, which need even less maintenance, then tuck in patches of fall-flowering crocus and other autumn-blooming bulbs to finish the growing season on a high note.

## A Delightful Doorway Garden

This welcoming entry garden is filled with color all through the growing season, thanks to a carefully chosen combination of long-blooming flowers and green, yellow, blue, silver, and variegated foliage. (By the way, incorporating bloom and leaf colors that repeat those on the outside of your home — on the trim or shutters, for example — is a great way to visually link your garden to the house.) Sheltered nooks, like the L-shaped site here, are particularly useful for showcasing scented flowers because the air gets stirred less and fragrances tend to linger.

Doorway gardens depend on plants that look good even when not in flower, with features such as handsome foliage (on the corkscrew chives, feather reed grass, lavender, pinks, and sedum, for instance) and attractive seed heads (on the coneflowers, feather reed grass, and Russian sage). For additional interest, you could plant some spring bulbs for extra-early color; white 'Thalia' daffodils are one great choice for both beauty and fragrance. Maintenance here is minimal. Trim the coneflowers and feather reed grass close to the ground in late winter or early spring, prune back the lavenders by about half once the first flush of blooms fades, and shear the faded flowers off the pinks once or twice during the summer to promote rebloom.

A   *Abelia × grandiflora* 'Little Richard' (1 plant)
B   *Allium* 'Blue Twister' (3 plants)
C   *Calamagrostis × acutiflora* 'Avalanche' (3 plants)
D   *Dianthus* 'Firewitch' (3 plants)
E   *Echinacea* 'Fragrant Angel' (3 plants)
F   *Echinacea* 'Matthew Saul' (3 plants)
G   *Lavandula angustifolia* 'Buena Vista' (3 plants)
H   *Perovskia* 'Filigran' (1 plant)
I    *Sedum rupestre* 'Angelina' (3 plants)

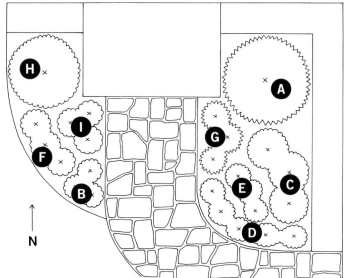

### *Abelia* × *grandiflora* 'Little Richard'

'LITTLE RICHARD' GLOSSY ABELIA

Tiny, glossy leaves are reddish when new, turning rich green in summer and then deep purple-red in fall and lasting well into winter; fragrant white flowers and pink calyces from late spring into early fall. About 3' tall × 3'–4' wide. Full sun to partial shade; average, well-drained soil. Zones 6–9.

Suggested alternative: 'Rose Creek'.

### *Allium* 'Blue Twister'

'BLUE TWISTER' CORKSCREW CHIVES

Slender, blue-green twisted foliage through the growing season; clusters of pink flowers in mid- to late summer (into early fall with deadheading). About 1' tall and wide. Full sun to light shade; average, well-drained soil. Zones 3–8.

Suggested alternative: *Allium senescens* var. *glaucum* (intensity of blue leaf color can vary).

### *Calamagrostis* × *acutiflora* 'Avalanche'

*Calamagrostis* × *acutiflora* 'Karl Foerster'

'AVALANCHE' FEATHER REED GRASS

Very slender, white-centered, green-edged blades through the growing season, turning tan in winter; pinkish green flower plumes appear in midsummer, turning tan

and lasting into winter. 4'–5' tall × 2'–3' wide. Full sun to light shade; average, well-drained soil. Zones 4–8.

Suggested alternative: 'Overdam' (green leaves with white edges) or 'Karl Foerster' (solid green leaves).

### *Dianthus* 'Firewitch'

'FIREWITCH' PINK

Slender, blue-gray leaves look good all year long; deep pink flowers bloom most abundantly in late spring to early summer; can repeat through rest of growing season if deadheaded. About 8" tall × 18" wide. Full sun; average, well-drained soil. Zones 3–8.

Suggested alternative: 'Bath's Pink' (lighter pink flowers).

### *Echinacea* 'Fragrant Angel'

'FRAGRANT ANGEL' CONEFLOWER

Deep green foliage through the growing season; fragrant, daisylike blooms with golden orange centers and white petals from early summer to early fall, developing into dark seed heads that last well into winter. 30"–40" tall × about 18" wide. Full sun to light shade; average, well-drained soil. Zones 3–9.

Suggested alternative: 'Primadonna White'.

### *Echinacea* 'Matthew Saul'

HARVEST MOON CONEFLOWER

Deep green foliage through the growing season; scented, daisy-form flowers with golden orange centers and golden yellow petals from early summer to early fall, followed by long-lasting dark seed heads that add interest well into winter. About 3' tall × about 18" wide. Full sun; average, well-drained soil. Zones 4–9.

Suggested alternative: Another coneflower in same color range, such as 'Sunrise' (paler yellow) or 'Sunset' (more distinctly orange).

### *Lavandula angustifolia* 'Buena Vista'

'BUENA VISTA' ENGLISH LAVENDER

Narrow, fragrant, grayish green leaves; spikes of purple-blue flowers mostly in late spring to early summer but often again in fall. 18"–24" tall and wide. Full sun; average, well-drained soil. Zones 5–9.

Suggested alternative: Another cultivar of English lavender, such as 'Hidcote Superior' or 'Royal Velvet' (although neither is as likely to bloom again in fall).

### *Perovskia* 'Filigran'

'FILIGRAN' RUSSIAN SAGE

Lacy gray leaves through the growing season; airy clusters of small blue flowers from mid- or late summer into fall on whitish stems that remain attractive through the winter. About 3' tall and wide. Full sun; average, well-drained soil. Zones 4–9.

Suggested alternative: 'Little Spire'.

### *Sedum rupestre* 'Angelina'

*Sedum rupestre* 'Angelina'

'ANGELINA' SEDUM

Ever-present bright yellow foliage that takes on orange tones in winter sun; yellow summer flowers. About 6" tall × 12"–18" wide. Full sun to partial shade; average, well-drained soil. Zones 3–9.

Suggested alternative: *S. spurium* 'John Creech' (green foliage and pink flowers).

# PLANTING BULBS IN POTS

When you're planning a garden around an entryway, keep in mind that pumpkins, gourds, and other seasonal accents can help bring the autumn show right up to your doorstep. In other seasons, you might use container plantings instead: heat-loving annuals for summer and potted bulbs for early color. Sure, you could *buy* pots of already-in-bloom bulbs in spring, but it's easy to start them yourself in autumn. Simply add some extra bulbs to your order for fall planting, then pot them up when you plant the rest in the ground. Plastic pots work well, because you don't have to worry about them cracking during cold weather. You can always slip them into prettier-looking pots for display in spring.

**Starting single-layer pots.** For the best show, start with large, firm bulbs that are uniform in size, so they'll bloom all at the same time. Pots that are 6 to 8 inches in diameter will hold about a dozen small bulbs or six larger bulbs; 10- to 12-inch-diameter pots can hold around 18 small bulbs or about a dozen daffodils or tulips. Add at least 1 inch of moistened potting mix to the bottom of the pot, then set in your bulbs so they are almost touching. Fill in with more potting mix to within ½ to ¼ inch of the top.

**Layering bulbs in a pot.** For an extended show in a limited space, combine two or more types of spring bulbs in each pot. Start as you would for single-layer pots above, then set in the largest bulbs, covering them with just enough potting mix to cover. Repeat with smaller bulbs, such as dwarf daffodils, and finally with squills, reticulated iris (*Iris reticulata*), or other tiny bulbs if there is enough room. Make sure you can cover the top layer with at least 1 inch of potting mix.

Layering bulbs in a pot.

**Post-planting care for potted bulbs.** Water thoroughly, then set the potted bulbs into a cool spot (ideally 33° to 40°F). Indoors, use a refrigerator or unheated porch or garage; outside, group them against the house foundation or bury them in the ground. For your outdoor display, move them to their decorative porch containers in late winter or early spring. (For earlier indoor bloom, bring them into a warmer, bright area after 10 to 12 weeks.) After bloom, move the pots to a less visible place, keep watering, and feed every two weeks with liquid fertilizer until the leaves start to turn brown. Plant the dormant bulbs in your garden for rebloom next year.

# WET AND WILD

Do you have a low spot in your yard where water tends to puddle for a day or two after a heavy rain or a frequently soggy site where water flows out of a downspout from your home's gutters? While these sites can stay distinctly wet during the rainy seasons, they may dry out quickly when rainfall is less abundant: a tough combination for many traditional border flowers, but no problem for a number of tougher perennials and grasses. Many of these no-nonsense plants have evolved to deal with these very conditions in their natural habitats, so they easily make the transition to similar sites in our home landscapes.

## A Bed for the Birds

If you're going to invest time and energy in designing and planting a garden, it just makes sense to make your plants work as hard as you do! This design is based on perennials that can readily adapt to alternating wet and dry conditions, contribute significant interest for a good part of the growing season, and supply an abundance of nectar and seeds to attract a bounty of songbirds, butterflies, and maybe even hummingbirds. Many of the plants tend to either spread out by creeping roots or fill a lot of aboveground space with their bushy top growth, so we've included just a few favorites in this design. Other options abound, including many other fall-flowering ornamental grasses, asters and other daisy-form flowers, along with fruiting shrubs, such as viburnums and deciduous hollies (*Ilex*).

This planting plan is designed to fit in the corner of a yard, but you could easily change the shape or dimensions to fit your site. Even though these plants can tolerate dry spells once they've had a few years to get their roots established, it's a good idea to water them regularly during dry spells through at least their first growing season. Once they're established, maintenance is mostly a matter of cutting down all of the plants to ground level in early spring. Keep in mind that the birds are likely to miss at least some of the seeds as they feed, so you'll also want to watch for self-sown seedlings and remove them to prevent the plants from getting too crowded.

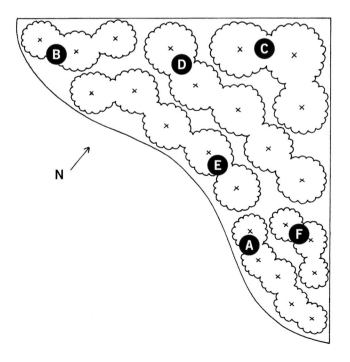

A   *Chelone lyonii* 'Hot Lips' (5 plants)
B   *Eupatorium dubium* 'Little Joe' (3 plants)
C   *Helianthus* 'Lemon Queen' (3 plants)
D   *Panicum virgatum* 'Shenandoah' (5 plants)
E   *Rudbeckia fulgida* var. *fulgida* (5 plants)
F   *Vernonia noveboracensis*  (3 plants)

N

### *Chelone lyonii* 'Hot Lips'
'HOT LIPS' TURTLEHEAD

Bronzy new growth that turns deep green for summer and fall; spikes of rosy pink flowers in late summer and early fall. 2'–3' tall and wide. Full sun to partial shade; evenly moist soil. Zones 5–8.
Suggested alternative: *C. lyonii* or *C. obliqua*; *Physostegia virginiana* 'Vivid' (spreads even more quickly by creeping roots).

### *Eupatorium dubium* 'Little Joe'
'LITTLE JOE' JOE-PYE WEED

Narrow, deep green leaves in spring and summer, darkening to reddish purple in mid- to late fall; domed clusters of rosy pink flowers in late summer to early fall, holding their form into winter. 4'–5' tall × 12"–18" wide. Full sun to partial shade; moist but well-drained soil. Zones 4–8.
Suggested alternative: *E. purpureum* 'Little Red'; *E. maculatum* 'Purple Bush'.

*Helianthus* 'Lemon Queen'

### *Helianthus* 'Lemon Queen'
'LEMON QUEEN' PERENNIAL SUNFLOWER

Deep green spring and summer foliage, turning shades of deep red or yellow in autumn; clear yellow daisies in late summer and early fall. 6'–8' tall × 2'–3' wide. Full sun to light shade; average to moist but well-drained soil. Zones 4–9.

Suggested alternative: *H. angustifolius* 'Mellow Yellow' (lighter yellow flowers on 8'–10'-foot-tall plants).

*Panicum virgatum* 'Shenandoah'

### *Panicum virgatum* 'Shenandoah'
'SHENANDOAH' SWITCHGRASS

Slender green blades tipped with red by early summer, turning solid burgundy in fall before drying to tan; stands through the winter; airy red-tinged flower plumes in fall that also last into winter. About 4' tall × 18"–24" wide. Full sun to light shade; average to moist but well-drained soil. Zones 4–9.
Suggested alternative: 'Rotstrahlbusch' (similar in height but doesn't take on reddish tones until late summer).

### *Rudbeckia fulgida* var. *fulgida*
ORANGE CONEFLOWER

Deep green leaves through the growing season (basal clumps are usually ever-green); dark-centered, golden yellow daisies in late summer and early fall, aging into dark seed heads that last through most of the winter. About 30" tall × 18"–24" wide. Full sun to light shade; average to moist but well-drained soil. Zones 4–9.
Suggested alternative: *R. fulgida* var. *sullivantii* 'Goldsturm' (blooms earlier—from mid- to late summer—but has similar seed heads).

### *Vernonia noveboracensis*
NEW YORK IRONWEED

Narrow, deep green leaves from spring through fall; airy clusters of deep reddish purple flowers in late summer to early or mid-fall. Usually 5'–7' tall (shorter if cut back by half in midsummer) × 18"–24" wide. Full sun to light shade; average to moist but well-drained soil. Zones 5–9.
Suggested alternative: Another species of ironweed, such as *V. altissima* or *V. fasciculata*; another *Eupatorium purpureum* or *E. maculatum* selection.

Vernonia noveboracensis

# PROVIDING TEMPORARY SUPPORT

Tall-growing fall flowers are great for in-your-face color, but they're no fun if their stems end up flopping into the mud. You might plan ahead and stake or cut back clumps earlier in the season, or you might take the chance that they make it into fall without sprawling. If you try the latter approach and lose the gamble, all is not lost; there are a couple of propping-up options to consider. Whichever you choose, try to get them in place before the plants fall over completely, because it's far easier to prop up a leaner than it is to straighten up fully sprawled stems. (The results will look more natural, too.)

**Stake 'em up!** The traditional pairing of stakes and string is one solution for supporting sprawlers—particularly those with tall stems. The stakes need to be very sturdy, since full-grown stems can be very heavy: ½- to 1-inch-wide wooden stakes that are about three-quarters of the plant's height should do the trick. Pound three to five stakes into the ground around the clump a few inches away from the crown, until they are 8 to 12 inches deep. Use twine or yarn to corral the stems between the stakes, running it loosely around the outside of the clump as well as back and forth among the stems. Here's a hint: If you paint the stakes black or dark brown and use yarn of the same color, you'll hardly notice them!

**Brush for bushy plants.** When lower, bushy plants flop open, you can often save the day by propping them up with twiggy branches. Raid your brush pile for short but well-branched shoots left over from last fall's or spring's pruning; pieces about 18 inches long are usually ideal. Carefully push several of them 6 to 8 inches into the ground around the clump. Lift up the perennial's stems with your fingers, then let them go a few at a time so the leaves and flowers are caught by the twigs. With some primping, you should be able to get all the stems supported in a fairly natural-looking mound. Trim off any twiggy tips that stick up over the blooms.

Using metal trellising as a prop.

**Make the most of your mis-stakes.** Sometimes, the best solution for supporting flopping stems is the most obvious one—literally! Instead of trying to stake subtly, use some decorative object to prop up leaning stems. Wooden obelisks, short sections of picket or ironwork fencing, and even interesting bits of rusted metal can serve as attractive garden accents and functional support systems at the same time. You might even decide you like the effect and leave them in place permanently. Or, stockpile a few of these mobile "props" as you find them, then move them around your garden as needed when leaners threaten to become sprawlers.

# HEATING THINGS UP

Bright shades of red, orange, yellow, and purple are the basis of nature's fall color palette, and they're a natural choice for celebrating autumn in a garden setting, too. These rich colors are useful for adding drama to small spaces, but they're particularly striking in larger spaces, especially when you place them against a background of bright or dark greens, such as an evergreen hedge. If you're not sure you'd enjoy such color intensity all through the growing season, you can base your plantings on softer shades for spring and summer, then toss in some bright blooms and colorful fall foliage to end the show with a bang.

## A Spectacular Side-yard Garden

Side yards are an ideal place to experiment with color schemes that you're not sure you want to try in a more highly visible spot. Adding a fence and gate helps to create a sense of enclosure and privacy for your backyard while providing several exciting garden opportunities: You can plant on the side facing the street, the side facing the backyard, or both sides. Including an arbor over the gate provides a perfect support for a colorful vine, too.

This design is packed with a variety of hot-colored tender perennials and annuals for shocking summer and fall color. You won't want to set out these heat-loving plants until all chance of frost has passed, but you can get a jump on the growing season by starting the annuals and bulbs indoors a few weeks earlier. They'll take several weeks to fill in after planting, but with plenty of heat and water, they'll soon create a lush display of colorful flowers and foliage. After frost, you can dig up the cannas and dahlias for indoor storage in a frost-free place, then pull out the rest of the frost-killed plants.

A   *Canna* 'Minerva' (3 plants)

B   *Canna* 'Pretoria' (3 plants)

C   *Capsicum annuum* 'Black Pearl' (5 plants)

D   *Celosia argentea* var. *cristata* Plumosa Group 'Fresh Look Orange' (5 plants)

E   *Celosia argentea* var. *cristata* Plumosa Group 'Fresh Look Red' (5 plants)

F   *Dahlia* 'Bishop of Llandaff' (3 plants)

G   *Lablab purpureus* 'Ruby Moon' (1 plant)

H   *Gomphrena globosa* 'Rainbow Purple' (5 plants)

I   *Hibiscus acetosella* 'Maple Sugar' (1 plant)

J   *Ipomoea batatas* 'Margarita' (1 plant)

K   *Lantana* 'New Gold' (3 plants)

L   *Mina lobata* (1 plant)

M   *Nicotiana* 'Perfume Deep Purple' (5 plants)

N   *Nicotiana langsdorffii* (5 plants)

O   *Pennisetum glaucum* 'Purple Majesty' (3 plants)

P   *Pennisetum setaceum* 'Rubrum' (1 plant)

Q   *Ricinus communis* 'Carmencita' (3 plants)

R   *Salvia* 'Purple Majesty' (2 plants)

S   *Tithonia rotundifolia* 'Fiesta del Sol' (5 plants)

T   *Zinnia elegans* 'Benary's Giant Purple' (5 plants)

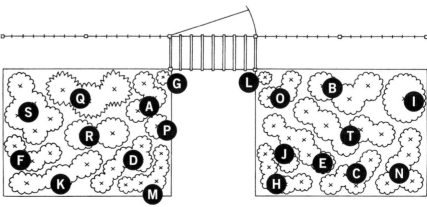

Canna Tropicanna

### Canna 'Minerva'
'MINERVA' CANNA

Large, broad green leaves with creamy white pinstripes through the growing season; yellow flowers from midsummer to frost. 4'–6' tall × 12"–18" wide. Full sun to light shade; average to moist but well-drained soil. Zones 8–10; grow as an annual elsewhere. Also sold as 'Nirvana' or 'Striped Beauty'.

Suggested alternative: Another variegated canna, such as 'Pretoria' or Tropicanna ('Phaison').

Canna 'Pretoria'

### Canna 'Pretoria'
'PRETORIA' CANNA

Large, broad green leaves striped with yellow and rimmed with red through the growing season; large orange flowers from midsummer to frost. About 6' tall × 12"–18" wide. Full sun to light shade; average to moist but well-drained soil. Zones 8–10;

grow as an annual elsewhere. Also sold as 'Bengal Tiger'.

Suggested alternative: Another variegated canna with orange flowers, such as the slightly shorter Tropicanna Gold ('Mactro').

Capsicum annuum 'Black Pearl'

### Capsicum annuum 'Black Pearl'
'BLACK PEARL' PEPPER

Oblong, near-black leaves through the frost-free season; small purple flowers through summer, followed by rounded near-black fruits that ripen to bright red in late summer and fall. 18"–24" tall × about 1' wide. Full sun; average, well-drained soil. Zones 9–11; grow as an annual elsewhere.

Suggested alternative: Other purple-leaved peppers in the same height range, such as 'Little Nubian', 'Peruvian Purple', and 'Pretty in Purple'.

### Celosia argentea var. cristata Plumosa Group 'Fresh Look Orange'
'FRESH LOOK ORANGE' CELOSIA

Medium-sized, medium green leaves through the growing season; dense plumes of bright orange flowers from midsummer to frost. 12"–18" tall × about 8" wide. Full sun; average, well-drained soil. Annual.

Suggested alternative: Another celosia with orange plumes, such as 'Apricot Brandy' or 'Castle Orange'.

### Celosia argentea var. cristata Plumosa Group 'Fresh Look Red'
'FRESH LOOK RED' CELOSIA

Medium-sized, medium green leaves through the growing season; dense plumes of rich red flowers from midsummer to frost. 12"–18" tall × about 8" wide. Full sun; average, well-drained soil. Annual.

Suggested alternative: Another celosia with red plumes, such as 'Castle Scarlet'.

Dahlia 'Bishop of Llandaff'

### Dahlia 'Bishop of Llandaff'
'BISHOP OF LLANDAFF' DAHLIA

Lacy, deep purple to near-black foliage through the growing season; single to semi-double scarlet flowers from midsummer to frost. About 3' tall × about 1' wide. Full sun to light shade; average, well-drained soil. Zones 8–10; grow as an annual elsewhere.

Suggested alternative: Another dark-leaved dahlia in the 2'- to 3'-tall range, such as deep red 'Bishop of Auckland' or 'Bednall Beauty'.

### Gomphrena globosa 'Rainbow Purple'
'RAINBOW PURPLE' GLOBE AMARANTH

Small, oblong green leaves through the growing season; globelike, magenta-purple flower heads from early summer to frost. About 18" tall × 8"–12" wide. Full sun; average, well-drained soil. Annual.

Suggested alternative: 'Buddy Purple'

(about 8" tall) or another purple-flowered globe amaranth.

Hibiscus acetosella 'Maple Sugar'

### Hibiscus acetosella 'Maple Sugar'
'MAPLE SUGAR' AFRICAN ROSE MALLOW

Deeply lobed, deep red leaves through the growing season; red to pink flowers in late fall to winter where the plants are hardy. Usually 4'–6' tall × about 2' wide. Full sun to light shade; average to moist but well-drained soil. Zones 8–11; grow as an annual elsewhere. Also sold as 'Jungle Red'.
Suggested alternative: *H. acetosella* 'Red Shield' (also known as 'Coppertone'); a red-leaved annual amaranth (Amaranthus), such as 'Hopi Red Dye'.

### Ipomoea batatas 'Margarita'
'MARGARITA' SWEET POTATO VINE

Heart-shaped, bright yellow leaves on long, trailing stems through the growing season. About 6" tall × 6'–8' wide. Full sun to light shade; average to moist but well-drained soil. Zones 10–11; grow as an annual elsewhere.
Suggested alternative: 'Sweet Caroline Light Green' (same color but with lobed leaves on less-vigorous vines).

Ipomoea batatas 'Margarita'

### Lablab purpureus 'Ruby Moon'
HYACINTH BEAN

Three-part, deep green leaves on twining stems through the growing season; clusters of bright purplish pink flowers from midsummer to frost, followed by deep reddish purple pods in late summer and fall. 10'–20' tall (depending on the size of the support). Full sun; average, well-drained soil. Zones 10–11; grow as an annual elsewhere. Also sold as *Dolichos lablab*.
Suggested alternative: *L. purpureus* (the species may have lighter pink or even whitish flowers).

### Lantana 'New Gold'
'NEW GOLD' LANTANA

Rough, rich green leaves through the growing season; clusters of bright yellow flowers from late spring or early summer to frost. 1'–2' tall × 2'–3' wide. Full sun; average, well-drained soil. Zones 8–11; grow as an annual elsewhere.
Suggested alternative: Another compact, bright yellow lantana, such as 'Landmark Gold' or 'Lucky Pot of Gold'; melampodium (*Melampodium paludosum*).

### Mina lobata
SPANISH FLAG

Lobed, deep green leaves on twining stems through the growing season; one-sided spikes of red buds that open to orange and fade to yellow from midsummer to frost. 8'–12' tall (depending on the height of the support). Full sun to light shade; average, well-drained soil. Annual. Also sold as *Ipomoea lobata*.
Suggested alternative: Chilean glory vine (*Eccremocarpus scaber*); cardinal climber (*Ipomoea × multifida*).

### Nicotiana 'Perfume Deep Purple'
'PERFUME DEEP PURPLE' FLOWERING TOBACCO

Bright green, roughly spoon-shaped leaves through the growing season; trumpet-shaped, deep purple, fragrant flowers from early summer to frost. 12"–18" tall × about 8" wide. Full sun to light shade; average to moist but well-drained soil. Zones 10 and 11; grow as an annual elsewhere.
Suggested alternative: A purple-flowered angelonia, such as 'AngelMist Purple Improved'.

### Nicotiana langsdorffii
FLOWERING TOBACCO

Bright green, roughly spoon-shaped leaves through the growing season; bell-shaped, bright yellowish green flowers from midsummer to frost. 2'–4' tall × 8"–12" wide. Full sun to light shade; average to moist but well-drained soil. Grow as an annual.
Suggested alternative: *N. alata* 'Lime Green' (larger, lighter green flowers).

### *Pennisetum glaucum* 'Purple Majesty'
'PURPLE MAJESTY' MILLET

Long, straplike, deep purple leaves through the frost-free season; dense, spikelike clusters of cream-colored flowers in mid- to late summer mature into deep purple seed heads in late summer and fall. 4'–5' tall × 12"–18" wide. Full sun; average, well-drained soil. Zones 9–11; grow as an annual elsewhere.

Suggested alternative: *P. glaucum* 'Purple Baron' or 'Jester' (3–4' tall); *P. macrostachyum* 'Burgundy Giant' (about 6' tall).

*Pennisetum setaceum* 'Rubrum'

### *Pennisetum setaceum* 'Rubrum'
PURPLE FOUNTAIN GRASS

Slender, glossy, deep purplish red blades all through the frost-free season; brushy tan flower spikes heavily blushed with pink to burgundy from mid- or late summer to frost. 4'–5' tall × 12"–18" wide. Full sun; average to moist but well-drained soil. Zones 10 and 11; grow as an annual elsewhere.

Suggested alternative: *P. macrostachyum* 'Burgundy Giant'; a dark-leaved *Phormium* selection, such as 'Platt's Black' or 'Dark Delight'.

*Ricinus communis* 'Carmencita'

### *Ricinus communis* 'Carmencita'
'CARMENCITA' CASTOR BEAN

Large, lobed, deep red leaves through the frost-free season; clusters of pinkish female flowers over cream-colored male flowers from midsummer into fall, with the females maturing into bright red, spiny seed capsules from late summer to frost. 6'–8' tall × about 2' wide. Full sun to light shade; average to moist but well-drained soil. Zones 9–11; grow as an annual elsewhere.

Suggested alternative: Another dark-leaved castor bean, such as 'Carmencita Pink' (with bright pink seedpods) or 'Dwarf Red Spire' (slightly shorter).

### *Salvia* 'Purple Majesty'
'PURPLE MAJESTY' SALVIA

Deeply veined, bright green leaves through the growing season; spikes of rich purple flowers from early or midsummer to frost. 4'–6' tall × about 3' wide. Full sun to light shade; average, well-drained soil. Zones 7–10; grow as an annual elsewhere.

Suggested alternative: *S. guaranitica* 'Black and Blue' (blue flowers) or *S.* 'Indigo Spires' (deep purple-blue flowers).

*Salvia guaranitica* 'Black and Blue'

### *Tithonia rotundifolia* 'Fiesta del Sol'
'FIESTA DEL SOL' MEXICAN SUNFLOWER

Lobed, velvety, deep green leaves through the growing season; bright orange daisies from midsummer to frost. 3'–4' tall × 2'–3' wide. Full sun; average, well-drained soil. Annual.

Suggested alternative: *T. rotundifolia* 'Torch' (4'–6' tall); an orange-flowered zinnia, such as 'Benary's Giant Orange' (about 4' tall).

# PREPARING TENDER PLANTS FOR WINTER

When you create gardens that include perennials not hardy in your area, figuring out exactly when to bring those tender plants indoors is always a tough call. You don't want them exposed to too much cold, but you also don't want to cut short your outdoor display by bringing them in earlier than is necessary. Planning can make the whole process go more smoothly, so in early fall, make a list of what you want to bring inside. Start digging up a few of those plants at a time when nighttime temperatures start dipping into the 40s, or wait until frost is predicted and spend a whole day gathering all the plants on your list and hauling them indoors. The choice is yours!

**Planning at planting time.** The way you planted your tender perennials in spring has an influence on how easy your fall digging-up sessions will be. Scattering the plants throughout your beds and borders means that when you remove them in fall, the remaining annuals and hardy perennials will still be there to carry on the show until at least the first frost. On the downside, it's easy to overlook the tenders when they're mixed in with other plants, and you might forget to dig some until it's too late. Combining them into "blocks" within a border, or keeping them in only one part of your yard, makes them much easier to find when it's time to bring them indoors (a big plus when you've waited until the last minute to dig them).

**Post-digging options.** Once you dig them up, what do you do with them? It depends on whether they'll keep growing through the winter or instead stay dormant until spring. Those that grow from specialized structures such as rhizomes, tuberous roots, bulbs, and corms—including cannas, dahlias, and gladiolus—typically survive winter in the dormant state; lift them from the soil with a spading fork, cut back the top growth, and place them into labeled bags or boxes for winter storage. To overwinter other plants, you'll need to either take cuttings or dig and pot up the clumps. If the plants are very large, cut them back by half or more before bringing their pots indoors; they'll take up less space and look better when they resprout.

**Going mobile.** Of course, the easiest way to bring tender plants indoors is to keep them in individual pots, so you simply carry them indoors when cool nights threaten. In return for this convenience, though, you'll have to water and fertilize them much more often during the growing season than you would if they were growing in the ground. Before bringing potted plants indoors for the winter, check them carefully for signs of aphids and other pests and spray with insecticidal soap if needed. And don't be surprised if the plants drop some of their leaves when you bring them in; that's a common reaction as they adapt to the warmer, drier air and lower light levels inside your home.

Digging up tender perennials for overwintering.

# KEEPING YOUR COOL

If your color preferences run more toward soft pinks and blues than brilliant reds and oranges, there are plenty of terrific fall plants for you to choose from. In fact, autumn tends to bring out the best in pastel-colored flowers: The less-intense light shows off their delicate hues, and the cooler temperatures help them last far longer than they would under scorching summer sun. To complement the abundance of light-colored blooms, look for companions that have pink, white, or yellow fall fruits — such as snowberries (*Symphoricarpos*) and some deciduous hollies (like *Ilex verticillata* 'Winter Gold') — and softer shades of the usual bright fall foliage colors.

## Pretty in Pastel

In any season, light-colored flowers show off beautifully in small spaces, but their pale hues often don't make much of a visual impact when you see them at a distance, particularly if the blooms themselves are on the small side. Planting them in masses is a great way to give them more of a presence, and has the added benefit of making maintenance much easier.

Based on a very simple combination of lines and arcs, this relatively small island bed design would fit well into a fairly narrow space, such as a side yard. By increasing the size of each planting area within the design, it would be easy to expand this into a substantial bed to fill a much larger space. Although this design provides some color interest in early summer from

the Bowman's root and catmint, it's really at its best from late summer through fall for bloom and foliage color. As a bonus, it includes many attractive seed heads that last through most or all of the winter. Give the whole garden a thorough cleanup by cutting everything just above ground level in early spring, and shear back the catmint by about half in midsummer, to enjoy a beautiful show of late-season pastels every year.

A   *Anemone × hybrida* 'Party Dress' (3 plants)
B   *Aster* 'Wood's Pink' (6 plants)
C   *Aster laevis* 'Bluebird' (5 plants)
D   *Gillenia trifoliata* (5 plants)
E   *Nepeta* 'Six Hills Giant' (5 plants)
F   *Pennisetum orientale* 'Karley Rose' (6 plants)
G   *Physostegia virginiana* 'Miss Manners' (5 plants)

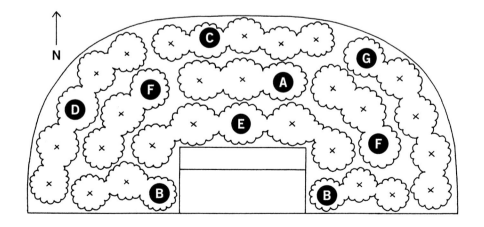

### *Anemone* × *hybrida* 'Party Dress'
'PARTY DRESS' JAPANESE ANEMONE

Deep green, three-part, lobed leaves from spring through fall; large, double pink flowers with yellow centers in late summer and early fall. 3'–4' tall × 2'–3' wide. Full sun to partial shade; average to moist but well-drained soil. Zones 4–8.

Suggested alternative: Another pink-flowered Japanese anemone, such as semi-double 'Bressingham Glow', 'Lady Gilmore', or 'Queen Charlotte'.

### *Aster* 'Wood's Pink'
'WOOD'S PINK' ASTER

Short, narrow green leaves from spring through fall; small, clear pink, yellow-centered daisies from late summer to mid-fall. 12"–18" tall and wide. Full sun; average to moist but well-drained soil. Zones 4–8.

Suggested alternative: Another compact, pastel-flowered aster, such as 'Wood's Light Blue' or purple-blue 'Professor Kippenburg'.

### *Aster laevis* 'Bluebird'
'BLUEBIRD' SMOOTH ASTER

Short, narrow green leaves from spring through fall; small, purple-blue, yellow-centered daisies from early to mid-fall. 3'–4' tall × about 18" wide. Full sun; average, well-drained soil. Zones 3–8.

Suggested alternative: Another purple-blue aster in the same height range, such as *A. oblongifolius* 'October Skies' or 'Raydon's Favorite'.

### *Gillenia trifoliata*
BOWMAN'S ROOT

Toothed, three-part, green leaves in spring and summer, turning maroon in fall; tiny white flowers in late spring and early summer, maturing into deep red seed capsules that provide fall and winter interest. About 3' tall and wide. Full sun to partial shade; average to moist but well-drained soil. Zones 4–8. Also sold as *Porteranthus trifoliatus*.

Suggested alternative: *Gillenia stipulatus*; *Gaura lindheimeri*.

### *Nepeta* 'Six Hills Giant'
'SIX HILLS GIANT' CATMINT

Small, aromatic, gray-green leaves from early spring through fall; loose spikes of small purple-blue flowers in spring into summer, with repeat bloom in late summer and fall if sheared back by about half in midsummer. About 3' tall × 2'–3' wide. Full sun to partial shade; average, well-drained soil. Zones 4–8.

Suggested alternative: Another blue-flowered catmint, such as 'Walker's Low' or *N. sibirica* 'Souvenir d'Andre Chaudron'; 'Little Spire' Russian sage (*Perovskia*).

### *Pennisetum orientale* 'Karley Rose'
'KARLEY ROSE' FOUNTAIN GRASS

Long, slender green leaves from spring through fall; fuzzy, rosy pink flower spikes from early or midsummer through fall. 3' tall × 1' wide. Full sun; average, well-drained soil. Zones 5–8.

Suggested alternative: *P. orientale* 'Tall Tails' (about 4' tall); 'Heavy Metal' switchgrass (*Panicum virgatum*); frost grass (*Spodiopogon sibiricus*).

### *Physostegia virginiana* 'Miss Manners'
'MISS MANNERS' OBEDIENT PLANT

Short, narrow, deep green leaves through spring and summer, turning yellowish in fall; spikes of white flowers from midsummer to early fall with regular deadheading. 2'–3' tall × 12"–18" wide. Full sun to partial shade; average to moist but well-drained soil. Zones 3–9.

Suggested alternative: 'Whirling Butterflies' gaura (*Gaura lindheimeri*).

*Aster laevis* 'Bluebird'

# OFF WITH THEIR HEADS!

Removing faded flowers—a technique that gardeners commonly call deadheading—isn't much of an issue with most plants that wait until fall to bloom because you deal with the spent flower stems when you do your routine late-fall or early-spring cleanup. But if you're trying to get summer-bloomers, such as catmints (*Nepeta*) and obedient plant (*Physostegia virginiana*), to extend their display into autumn, deadheading can be a very handy trick to try.

So, how does it work? Basically, deadheading stops a plant from producing seeds. Besides eliminating the problem of unwanted seedlings, interfering with seed production can also encourage the plant to send out more flowers in an effort to make seed from *those* blooms. By removing individual blossoms or clusters, you may extend the bloom season for several weeks. Or, you can shear off all the spent flowers at once and perhaps get a whole new crop of flowers in return. That means two or even three bloom cycles each year instead of just one! Granted, the blossoms often aren't quite as abundant in these later flushes, and their stems are usually shorter, but they're still welcome in the fall garden. Even if the plant doesn't flower again, it will likely produce a clump of fresh, great-looking foliage that adds interest to your autumn beds and borders.

Despite all of the benefits that deadheading can provide, there are some times when you *don't* want to use it. If you hope to collect the seeds from a particular plant, for instance, removing the spent flowers is counterproductive. Deadheading also eliminates the many wonderful seed heads and berries that can extend your garden's beauty well into the winter months. So if you're growing perennials with interesting winter silhouettes, such as bee balms (*Monarda*) and asters, or if you want lots of seeds and berries to attract winter birds, it's smart to think twice about what you are deadheading, and why. To get the best of both worlds (long bloom season *and* showy seed heads), experiment with deadheading for just a few weeks, then leave the rest of the flowers to mature on the plants.

Removing entire flower stem to encourage rebloom.

# HAVING IT ALL

Fall gardens aren't just about showy flowers and colorful foliage, of course; they can be quite productive, too. The combination of warm soil and cool air provides ideal growing conditions for many cool-season flowers, vegetables, and herbs, as well as for late-summer sowings of fast-maturing flowers and veggie crops. Basil, peppers, and other traditional summer edibles continue into fall; kales, chard, and other cold-tolerant leafy crops extend the harvest into winter, so you can enjoy a wide range of flavors over a long period even in a small garden space.

## A Taste of Fall

Mixing vegetables, herbs, and flowers together is a great way to create plantings as useful as they are pretty. With careful planning, you can enjoy two harvests a year from the same amount of space by pulling out tired spring crops, such as dill and lettuce, in midsummer and sowing again for a fall harvest.

This design features two small, narrow borders that flank a path leading out from a kitchen door. To increase your yields, consider adding a few container plantings by the door, too. Paving the area right outside the door, as well as the path between the beds, ensures firm, clean footing, so you can easily pop out for quick harvests without even having to slip on your shoes. While this garden is planned more for production than good looks, it does provide a

significant amount of color all through the growing season, thanks to the attractive foliage as well as the abundance of brightly hued blooms that are both edible and useful for cutting. Harvest the spring-sown plants often to encourage them to keep growing and flowering, then pull out the annuals when they stop producing to make room for a new sowing in summer.

Most of these plants will keep producing through a few light frosts. The basil and peppers hate cold temperatures, but if you pot up a few plants and bring them indoors before the first frost, you can extend their production by at least several weeks. Remember: Avoid using pesticides on or near flowers, vegetables, and herbs that you plan to use for eating.

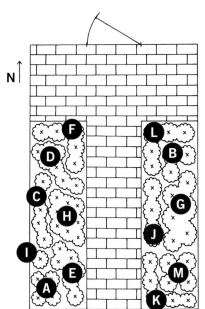

A   *Anethum graveolens* 'Fernleaf' (5 plants)

B   *Beta vulgaris* Cicla Group 'Bright Yellow' (3 plants)

C   *Brassica oleracea* Acephala Group 'Redbor' (5 plants)

D   *Calendula officinalis* (7 plants)

E   *Capsicum annuum* 'Sweet Pickle' (6 plants)

F   *Fragaria vesca* (5 plants)

G   *Helianthus annuus* 'Sundance Kid' (6 plants)

H   *Lactuca sativa* 'Merlot' (9 plants)

I   *Ocimum* 'Pesto Perpetuo' (1 plant)

J   *Ocimum basilicum* 'Red Rubin' (3 plants)

K   *Petroselinum crispum* 'Triple Curled' (5 plants)

L   *Tropaeolum majus* 'Alaska Mix' (5 plants)

M   *Viola* hybrids (5 plants)

### *Anethum graveolens* 'Fernleaf'
'FERNLEAF' DILL

Lacy, bright green, fragrant, and flavorful foliage for several weeks (in fall from an early to midsummer sowing); lacy clusters of tiny yellow flowers (in fall from an early to midsummer sowing). About 2' tall × 6"–8" wide. Full sun to light shade; average, well-drained soil. Annual.
Suggested alternative: Another dill, such as 'Dukat' (3' tall); cilantro (*Coriandrum sativum*).

### *Beta vulgaris* Cicla Group 'Bright Yellow'
'BRIGHT YELLOW' SWISS CHARD

Broad, bright green leaves on thick bright yellow stalks through the growing season. 18"–24" tall × about 1' wide. Full sun to light shade; average to moist but well-drained soil. Annual.
Suggested alternative: Another Swiss chard, such as red 'Rhubarb' or mixed-color 'Bright Lights'.

*Brassica oleracea*
Acephala Group 'Redbor'

*Calendula officinalis*

### *Brassica oleracea* Acephala Group 'Redbor'
'REDBOR' KALE

Frilly edged, grayish to greenish purple leaves in spring and summer, turning deep purple in fall and lasting well into winter. 2'–3' tall × 12"–18" wide. Full sun to light shade; average to moist but well-drained soil. Annual.
Suggested alternative: Another kale, such as pink-stemmed, blue-leaved 'Ragged Jack' or blue-green 'Lacinato'.

### *Calendula officinalis*
POT MARIGOLD

Bright green, roughly oval to lance-shaped leaves from spring through fall; single to double orange daisies from spring through fall with regular deadheading. 1'–2' tall × 6"–9" wide. Full sun; average, well-drained soil. Annual.
Suggested alternative: Signet marigold (*Tagetes tenuifolia;* also sold as *T. signata*).

### *Capsicum annuum* 'Sweet Pickle'
'SWEET PICKLE' PEPPER

Small, bright green leaves through the frost-free season; small, sweet, upright fruits that ripen through shades of yellow, orange, purple, and red from midsummer to frost. 12"–18" tall and wide. Full sun; average to moist but well-drained soil. Zone 10; grow as an annual elsewhere.
Suggested alternative: Another compact, small-fruited pepper, such as sweet 'Jingle Bells' or medium-hot 'Marbles'.

*Capsicum annuum* 'Chilly Chili'

### *Fragaria vesca*
ALPINE STRAWBERRY

Toothed, three-part, green leaves from spring through fall (and through most or all of the winter in mild areas); small white flowers from late spring into fall, ripening into small, sweet, bright red fruits from early summer through fall. About 6" tall and wide. Full sun to partial shade; average to moist but well-drained soil. Zones 5–8.

Suggested alternative: Musk strawberry (*F. moschata*)—equally flavorful, but a creeper instead of a clump-former.

## *Helianthus annuus* 'Sundance Kid'
'SUNDANCE KID' SUNFLOWER
Rough, heart-shaped green leaves in summer and fall; semi-double flowers with dark centers and bright yellow outer petals in fall from mid- to late-summer sowing. About 2' tall × 6"−8" wide. Full sun; average, well-drained soil. Annual.
Suggested alternative: Another dwarf sunflower, such as reddish 'Double Dandy' or mixed-color 'Music Box'.

## *Lactuca sativa* 'Merlot'
'MERLOT' LETTUCE
Crinkled, wavy-edged, deep red leaves in late summer and fall (from mid- to late-summer sowing). About 6" tall and wide. Full sun to partial shade; average to moist but well-drained soil. Annual.
Suggested alternative: Another red or green-leaved lettuce, such as 'Outredgeous' or 'Oakleaf'.

## *Ocimum* 'Pesto Perpetuo'
'PESTO PERPETUO' BASIL
Aromatic and flavorful, light green leaves edged with white through the frost-free season. 2'−3' tall × 1' wide. Full sun; average to moist but well-drained soil. Zone 10; grow as an annual elsewhere.
Suggested alternative: Another kind of basil, such as lime, licorice, or cinnamon; rosemary (*Rosmarinus officinalis*).

## *Ocimum basilicum* 'Red Rubin'
'RED RUBIN' BASIL
Aromatic and flavorful, deep reddish purple leaves through the frost-free season; spikes of small pink flowers in summer and fall. 1'−2' tall × about 1' wide. Full sun; average to moist but well-drained soil. Annual.
Suggested alternative: Another purple- or green-leaved basil, such as dark 'Osmin' or tiny-leaved green bush basil.

## *Petroselinum crispum* 'Triple Curled'
'TRIPLE CURLED' PARSLEY
Deeply crinkled, bright green leaves from spring through fall, often lasting through the winter in mild areas. About 8" tall and wide. Full sun to partial shade; average to moist but well-drained soil. Grow as an annual.
Suggested alternative: Another curled-leaf parsley or flat-leaved Italian parsley.

## *Tropaeolum majus* 'Alaska Mix'
'ALASKA MIX' NASTURTIUM
Circular, light green leaves randomly splashed with creamy white through the growing season; red, orange, or yellow flowers from summer to frost. 8"−12" tall and about as wide. Full sun to light shade; average to moist but well-drained soil. Annual.
Suggested alternative: Another nasturtium cultivar, such as 'Tip Top Mahogany' (with chartreuse leaves and deep red flowers) or 'Empress of India' (with red flowers and blue-green foliage).

*Viola x wittrockiana* 'Baby Bingo'

## *Viola* hybrids
PANSIES
Small, bright green leaves through most of the year; flat-faced flowers in a wide range of colors and bicolors in fall and spring (and during mild winter weather too). 6"−8" tall and about as wide. Full sun to partial shade; average to moist but well-drained soil. Zones 4−9, but usually grown as an annual.
Suggested alternative: Another cool-season color accent sold in fall, such as edible or ornamental cabbage or kale (*Brassica oleracea*) or a chrysanthemum.

PUTTING IT ALL TOGETHER

Whether you're growing vegetables or flowers, frost isn't exactly the life-or-death issue in fall that it is early in the growing season. In spring, it's imperative to protect tender transplants when frost threatens; otherwise they can get damaged or killed outright, spoiling your display for the entire growing season. But by fall, many of those same plants are tough enough to withstand the identical amount of frost. And even if they don't survive, at least you've had all season to enjoy them. Still, it's natural to want to get the longest possible show from your beds and borders, so why not take a few minutes to protect frost-sensitive annuals and perennials when cold weather threatens? If you can get them through the first frost or two, you can often get at least another week or two of bloom—and maybe longer.

**Collect your protectors.** Often, you don't get much warning when the first frost comes calling, so it's smart to do some advance planning. First, keep in mind that moist soil will hold heat better, so keep your garden well watered. Pulling the mulch away from your tender plants can help, too; otherwise, the covering will prevent heat from radiating out of the soil and warming the air

Temporary protection.

around the leaves and stems. Also, make a list of the plants you want to protect, then gather enough sheets, boxes, stakes, and other materials to cover them all, so you won't have to hunt for them at the last minute. Plastic milk jugs and soda bottles are good to have on hand, too. (Filled with warm water and set out on chilly nights, they're great for protecting special plants!)

**Swing into action.** When frost is imminent, start covering plants in mid- to late afternoon, when the soil is as warm as it's going to get. Give top priority to gardens that are out in the open, particularly if they are on the top of a hill or at the bottom of a slope; save more sheltered spots for last. To protect individual plants, use upside-down boxes, pots, baskets, and buckets. To shield groups or large single plants, use old sheets, shower curtains, tarps, or floating row cover. If possible, keep the coverings from resting directly on the plants by draping them over stakes or ropes. Make sure they go completely to the ground and don't gather them around the base of the plants; you want to include as much soil surface as you can underneath to trap the radiating heat. Move containers of tender plants next to walls, or set them under a bench or deck.

**The day after.** Ideally, you should wait until the frost has thawed the next morning, then remove the covers. What if you won't be home then? If it's still dark when you leave for work, it's probably best to leave the covers in place until you get home; one day in the dark

shouldn't hurt the plants. If the sun is coming up when you leave, you can usually get away with removing the covers even if the frost hasn't melted yet. Don't despair if you forgot to cover a favorite plant; you may be able to save it by spraying it thoroughly with water before the sun hits the leaves. If it looks like only the outer tips have gotten frosted, trim off any damaged parts, and new growth may appear from the remaining stems.

Some cold-hardy annuals, like this kale, can survive (and even thrive) after a touch of frost.

# TAKING IT EASY

For many gardeners, one of the best aspects of fall gardening is the lack of stress. By this time of the year, the big projects are basically done, and daily maintenance isn't nearly as critical, so there's time to actually sit down and appreciate the beauty of the season. If you enjoy the laid-back mood of autumn, you'll be happy to know that it's possible to capture that feeling all through the gardening season. The secret is to concentrate on low-maintenance ground covers, perennials, and shrubs that thrive with practically no input from you.

## A Fuss-free Foundation Border

Plantings that hug house foundations are traditionally a collection of evergreen shrubs and ground covers — functional, perhaps, but not especially interesting. Replacing them with well-chosen deciduous shrubs and herbaceous plants that have multiseason interest gives you an ever-changing display of flowers, foliage, and fruits without making any more work for yourself in the process.

This design incorporates a number of other easy-care features as well, such as an access path between the back of the border and the house. (Besides preventing the plants from crowding too close to the house, reducing the need for pruning, it also keeps them out of the bone-dry zone that commonly forms under a roof overhang, thus minimizing the need for watering.) Within the border, using compact shrub cultivars practically eliminates pruning chores, while the low-growing, spreading perennials act like a living mulch to help to crowd out weeds. All that's really needed is to trim the dead perennial stems close to the ground in spring; you might also choose to give the spirea a light trim after its first bloom to promote rebloom.

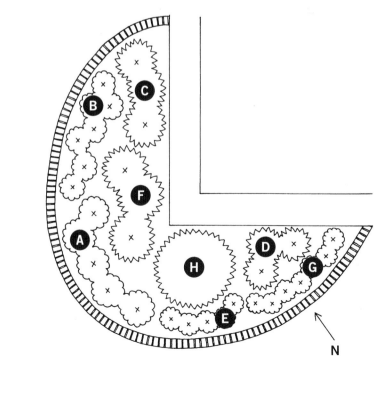

A   *Amsonia* 'Blue Ice' (5 plants)

B   *Ceratostigma plumbaginoides* (7 plants)

C   *Clethra alnifolia* 'Sixteen Candles' (3 plants)

D   *Itea virginica* 'Merlot' (3 plants)

E   *Sedum spurium* 'Voodoo' (5 plants)

F   *Spiraea betulifolia* 'Tor' (3 plants)

G   *Veronica* 'Aztec Gold' (7 plants)

H   *Viburnum opulus* var. *americanum*
    'Bailey Compact' (1 plant)

### Amsonia 'Blue Ice'
'BLUE ICE' BLUESTAR

Slender, rich green leaves in spring and summer, turning bright yellow in fall; small, medium blue flowers in early summer. 12"–18" tall × 18"–24" wide. Full sun to light shade; average to moist but well-drained soil. Zones 4–9.
Suggested alternative: *A. tabernaemontana var. montana;* fall-flowering 'Sheffield Pink' chrysanthemum.

Ceratostigma plumbaginoides

### Ceratostigma plumbaginoides
LEADWORT

Oval to oblong, bright green leaves in late spring and summer, turning deep red in fall and lasting well into winter in mild areas; small, bright blue flowers from mid- or late summer through fall. 6"–12" tall × 1'–2' wide. Full sun to light shade; average, well-drained soil. Zones 5–9.
Suggested alternative: Pink-flowered 'Herrenhausen' oregano (*Origanum laevigatum*).

### Clethra alnifolia 'Sixteen Candles'
'SIXTEEN CANDLES' SUMMERSWEET

Lightly toothed, deep green leaves in spring and summer, turning bright yellow in fall; upright spikes of fragrant white flowers in mid- to late summer. About 3' tall and wide. Full sun to partial shade; moist but well-drained soil. Zones 3–9.
Suggested alternative: Another compact summersweet, such as 'Sweet Suzanne' or 'White Dove'.

### Itea virginica 'Merlot'
'MERLOT' SWEETSPIRE

Elliptical, deep green leaves in spring and summer, turning rich shades of red (sometimes with orange and yellow too) in fall and often lasting into early winter; arching spikes of fragrant white flowers in early summer. About 3' tall and wide. Full sun to light shade; average to moist but well-drained soil. Zones 5–9.
Suggested alternative: Another compact sweetspire, such as Little Henry ('Sprich').

### Sedum spurium 'Voodoo'
'VOODOO' TWO-ROW SEDUM

Small, succulent, deep red foliage throughout the year; clusters of reddish pink flowers in summer. 3"–6" tall × 1' wide. Full sun to light shade; average, well-drained soil. Zones 3–10.
Suggested alternative: Another reddish-leaved two-row sedum, such as 'Fuldaglut' or 'Dragon's Blood'; a dark-leaved ajuga, such as Chocolate Chip ('Valfredda') or 'Mahogany'.

### Spiraea betulifolia 'Tor'
'TOR' BIRCHLEAF SPIREA

Small, deep green leaves in spring and summer, turning shades of purple, red, orange, and yellow in fall; clusters of small white flowers in late spring (with possible rebloom if sheared lightly after flowering). 3'–4' tall and wide. Full sun to light shade; average, well-drained soil. Zones 4–8.
Suggested alternative: A compact blueberry (*Vaccinium*) cultivar, such as 'Northland', 'North Sky', or 'Ornablue'.

### Veronica 'Aztec Gold'
'AZTEC GOLD' VERONICA

Small, bright yellow leaves from early spring through fall; clusters of purple-blue flowers in late spring and early summer. 6"–8" tall × 12"–18" wide. Full sun to light shade; average to moist but well-drained soil. Zones 3–8.
Suggested alternative: 'Trehane' (not quite as bright yellow in leaf).

Viburnum opulus var. americanum

### Viburnum opulus var. americanum 'Bailey's Compact'
'BAILEY'S COMPACT' VIBURNUM

Three-lobed, deep green leaves in spring and summer, turning shades of red and purple in fall; clusters of white flowers in early summer, followed by clusters of bright red berries in fall. About 6' tall and wide. Full sun to partial shade; average to moist but well-drained soil. Zones 2–7.
Suggested alternative: Another viburnum that's about the same size with good fall color, such as *V.* × *carlcephalum* 'Cayuga' or *V. dilatatum* 'Catskill'.

# ADDING EDGING STRIPS

A key part of creating a low-maintenance transition between any garden and adjoining lawn areas is planning and installing an easy-care edge. A smooth curve along the outer edge of the border, in combination with a ground-level edging strip, lets you mow easily and trim the perimeter at the same time. Edgings can be as simple as a plastic or metal strip, as elegant as a carefully laid pattern of bricks, or somewhere in between.

**Choosing the material.** You'll often see rolls or sections of plastic edging sold at garden and home centers. While these are inexpensive and easy to install, they tend to get pushed out of the ground during the winter and need frequent resetting. Steel or aluminum edging strips cost more and are longer lasting. They aren't especially attractive, but like plastic, they work well on curved edges. Landscape timbers are fine for straight edges but not practical for curves. Edgings made from pavers or bricks take the most time and money to install, but they are both durable and decorative. Consider choosing a material that complements the color or style of your home; if your house is brick, for instance, using a brick edging for your gardens creates a visual link between your home and the yard.

**Installing a raised edge.** An elevated edging strip helps to hold garden soil in place, but it also requires an extra trimming step, because your mower won't be able to get close to the edge. To install, use a sharp spade to dig a shallow trench. For a plastic or metal strip, a trench that's 3 to 4 inches wide and half the height of the strip is fine. For thicker edgings, make the trench just as wide as your chosen material and about 2 inches deeper than half of its height (if the timbers are 6 inches high, for example, dig the trench 5 inches deep); then add a 2-inch layer of sand to the trench. Set your edging into the trench, tap it in place with a hammer or mallet if needed, and make sure it is level. Replace the soil on the garden side of the edging.

**Making a mowing strip.** An edging strip that's set flush with the soil is also called a mowing strip, because you can run a mower's wheels right along it, neatly trimming the grass along that edge while you're doing your regular mowing. As with a raised edging, you install a flat edging by digging a shallow trench that's as wide as the strip you want to make; in this case, though, make the trench 2 inches deeper than the total height of the edging material. (If you're using pavers that are 2 inches high, for instance, make the trench 4 inches deep.) Spread a 2-inch layer of sand in the trench, lay the edging materials in place, and make sure they are level.

Flat edging for easy mowing.

# AUTUMN ABUNDANCE FOR SUNNY CONTAINERS

Wise plant choices can make the difference between container combinations that fizzle out by midsummer and those that look better and better as the growing season goes on. Instead of depending on transplants that are filled with flowers at spring shopping time, put more emphasis on tender perennials and tropicals. They may not look all that exciting at first, but as soon as the temperatures start to rise, so does their wow factor! Hardy perennials with colorful foliage, ornamental grasses, and even small shrubs are also good candidates for adding multiseason interest to your container combinations.

## Tropical Explosion

Sun-drenched sites can support an exciting array of eye-catching flowers and foliage plants that look glorious in autumn containers. Containers can dry out quickly in sunny conditions, however, so plantings may need frequent watering to stay lush throughout the growing season. Use large planters that can hold several plants to minimize watering chores (they dry out more slowly than small pots). Self-watering containers are also a blessing if you can't deal with daily watering during dry spells.

This collection of square and rectangular planters provides a sense of enclosure around a patio without blocking the view beyond. Tropicals and tender perennials, with a few hardier perennials for long-lasting foliage interest, bloom in bright colors that hold up well even in strong summer sun. At its best from late summer to frost, when cooler temperatures and less-intense sunlight allow blooms and leaves to develop their richest colors, it needs little care: Keep soil as evenly moist as possible (but not waterlogged), and use liquid fertilizer every 2 or 3 weeks to encourage lush growth. Pinch off flower spikes on coleus, and deadhead heliotrope and gloriosa daisy to encourage bloom for months. To save for next year, pot up cold-tenders and bring them indoors before frost. In many areas, heuchera and yucca can stay outdoors, but for extra protection, transplant them into an empty space in your garden over the winter.

A   *Alternanthera dentata* 'Purple Knight' (1 plant)

B   *Angelonia* 'Angelface Blue' (1 plant)

C   *Catharanthus roseus* 'First Kiss Blueberry' (2 plants)

D   *Heliotropium arborescens* 'Fragrant Delight'
    (2 plants)

E   *Heuchera* 'Tnheu041' (1 plant)

F   *Ipomoea batatas* 'Sweet Caroline Light Green'
    (2 plants)

G   *Ipomoea batatas* 'Sweet Heart Red' (2 plants)

H   *Lysimachia congestiflora* 'Outback Sunset' (1 plant)

I   *Lysimachia congestiflora* 'Persian Chocolate'
    (1 plant)

J   *Pennisetum setaceum* 'Eaton Canyon' (1 plant)

K   *Rudbeckia hirta* 'Prairie Sun' (1 plant)

L   *Salvia coccinea* 'Lady in Red' (3 plants)

M   *Solenostemon scutellarioides* 'Blackberry Waffles'
    (1 plant)

N   *Solenostemon scutellarioides* 'Sedona' (1 plant)

O   *Verbena tenuisecta* 'Imagination' (4 plants)

P   *Yucca* 'Gold Sword' (2 plants)

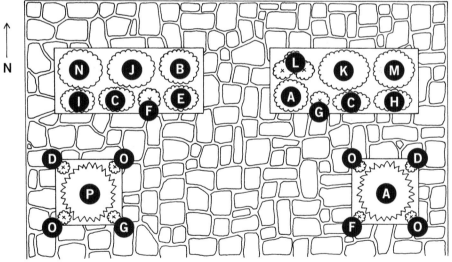

*Alternanthera dentata* 'Purple Knight'

### *Alternanthera dentata* 'Purple Knight'

'PURPLE KNIGHT'
ALTERNANTHERA

Glossy, deep maroon leaves all through the frost-free season. 18"–24" tall and wide. Full sun to partial shade; average to evenly moist but well-drained soil. Zones 9–11; grow as an annual elsewhere.
Suggested alternative: 'Gail's Choice' (very similar) or 'Rubiginosa', also known as 'Ruby' or 'Wave Hill' (also similar-looking but usually 24"–30" tall and wide).

### *Angelonia* 'Angelface Blue'

'ANGELFACE BLUE' ANGELONIA

Narrow, deep green leaves through the growing season; loose, spikelike clusters of fragrant, deep purple-blue blooms with white centers from late spring or early summer to frost. About 18" tall × 12"–18" wide. Full sun; average, well-drained soil. Zones 9–11; grow as an annual elsewhere.
Suggested alternative: 'AngelMist Purple Improved' (may be slightly taller).

### *Catharanthus roseus* 'First Kiss Blueberry'

'FIRST KISS BLUEBERRY' ROSE PERIWINKLE

Oblong, glossy, bright green leaves through the growing season; flat-faced, rich purple flowers with darker centers from early summer to frost. About 1' tall and wide. Full sun; average, well-drained soil. Zones 9–11; grow as an annual elsewhere.
Suggested alternative: *Verbena tenuisecta* 'Illumination' or another purple verbena.

### *Heliotropium arborescens* 'Fragrant Delight'

'FRAGRANT DELIGHT'
HELIOTROPE

Deeply veined, deep green leaves through the growing season; clusters of richly fragrant, medium to light purple flowers from early summer to frost. 12"–18" tall and wide. Full sun; average to moist but well-drained soil. Zones 9–11; grow as an annual elsewhere.
Suggested alternative: 'Iowa' or another fragrant, purple-flowered cultivar.

*Heuchera* 'Tnheu041'

### *Heuchera* 'Tnheu041'

'DOLCE CRÈME BRÛLÉE'
HEUCHERA

Peachy orange foliage is present year-round (coloring is most intense in spring and fall); airy clusters of tiny white flowers in summer. About 1' tall and wide in leaf; to 18" tall in bloom. Full sun to light shade; average, well-drained soil. Zones 4–8.
Suggested alternative: *Impatiens* 'Tango' (green foliage, deep orange flowers).

### *Ipomoea batatas* 'Sweet Caroline Light Green'

'SWEET CAROLINE LIGHT GREEN' SWEET POTATO VINE

Deeply lobed, bright yellow to greenish yellow foliage on trailing stems through the frost-free season. About 6" tall × 3' or more in length. Full sun to partial shade; average to moist but well-drained soil. Zones 10–11; grow as an annual elsewhere.
Suggested alternative: 'Sweet Heart Light Green' (similar color but with heart-shaped foliage).

### *Ipomoea batatas* 'Sweet Heart Red'

'SWEET HEART RED' SWEET POTATO VINE

Heart-shaped, reddish brown to pinkish orange foliage on trailing stems through the frost-free season. About 6" tall and 3' or more in length. Full sun to partial shade; average to moist but well-drained soil. Zones 10–11; grow as an annual elsewhere.
Suggested alternative: 'Sweet Caroline Bronze' (somewhat similar colors but with lobed leaves).

### *Lysimachia congestiflora* 'Outback Sunset'

'OUTBACK SUNSET' LOOSESTRIFE

Bright yellow to greenish yellow leaves with green markings through the growing season; clustered yellow flowers in spring and summer. About 4" tall × 8"–12" wide. Full sun to full shade; average to moist but well-drained soil. Zones 8–10; grow as an annual elsewhere.
Suggested alternative: *L. congestiflora* 'Golden Harvest' (solid yellow leaves); *L. nummularia* 'Aurea' (smaller, bright yellow foliage).

## Lysimachia congestiflora 'Persian Chocolate'
'PERSIAN CHOCOLATE' LOOSESTRIFE

Deep purple to purple-green leaves through the growing season; clustered yellow flowers in spring and summer. About 4" tall and 8"–12" wide. Full sun to full shade; average to moist but well-drained soil. Zones 8–10; grow as an annual elsewhere.

Suggested alternative: *L. congestiflora* 'Persian Carpet' (purple-centered green leaves); *Tradescantia pallida* (larger, rich purple leaves).

*Pennisetum setaceum* 'Rubrum'

## Pennisetum setaceum 'Eaton Canyon'
'EATON CANYON' RED FOUNTAIN GRASS

Slender, glossy, deep purplish red blades all through the frost-free season; brushy tan flower spikes heavily blushed with pink to burgundy from mid- or late summer to frost. 2'– 3' tall × about 1' wide. Full sun; average to moist but well-drained soil. Zones 10–11; grow as an annual elsewhere. Also sold as 'Dwarf Rubrum' or 'Red Riding Hood'.

Suggested alternative: A compact, dark-leaved *Phormium*, such as 'Tom Thumb'; a dark-leaved *Cordyline*, such as 'Red Sensation', 'Red Star', or *C. baueri*.

## Rudbeckia hirta 'Prairie Sun'
'PRAIRIE SUN' GLORIOSA DAISY

Hairy, medium green leaves from spring through fall (basal clumps may be evergreen); large, daisylike blooms with green centers and yellow-tipped orange petals from late spring or early summer through fall (with deadheading). About 2' tall × 1' wide. Full sun; average, well-drained soil. Zones 4–8 (may be short-lived).

Suggested alternative: Any *R. hirta* selection in the same height range.

## Salvia coccinea 'Lady in Red'
'LADY IN RED' SALVIA

Bright green leaves through the growing season; spikes of bright red flowers from early summer to frost. 18"–24" tall × about 1' wide. Full sun to light shade; average, well-drained soil. Zones 9–11; grow as an annual elsewhere.

Suggested alternative: *S. roemeriana* (about 1' tall); a red-flowered cultivar of autumn sage (*S. greggii*), such as 'Cherry Chief' or 'Maraschino', or of scarlet sage (*S. splendens*), such as 'Flare'.

## Solenostemon scutellarioides 'Blackberry Waffles'
'BLACKBERRY WAFFLES' COLEUS

Large, deeply veined, deep purple leaves through the frost-free season. 24"–30" tall × about 1' wide. Full sun to partial shade; average to moist but well-drained soil. Zones 10–11; grow as an annual elsewhere.

Suggested alternative: Another dark-leaved, such as 'Mars' ('Purple Duckfoot').

## Solenostemon scutellarioides 'Sedona'
'SEDONA' COLEUS

Clear orange to brick red foliage through the frost-free season. 1'–2' tall × about 1' wide. Full sun to partial shade; average to moist but well-drained soil. Zones 10–11; grow as an annual elsewhere.

Suggested alternative: Another coleus in the same color range, such as 'Copper Glow', 'Klondike', or 'Rustic Orange'.

## Verbena tenuisecta 'Imagination'
'IMAGINATION' MOSS VERBENA

Lacy, bright green leaves from spring through fall; clustered, violet-purple flowers from late spring through light frost. About 1' tall × 18"–24" wide. Full sun; average to moist but well-drained soil. Zones 7–10; grow as an annual elsewhere.

Suggested alternative: Another low-growing purple verbena, such as 'Babylon Purple'.

*Yucca* 'Gold Sword'

## Yucca 'Gold Sword'
'GOLD SWORD' YUCCA

Slender, spiky green leaves with wide yellow centers all year long; tall stalks of creamy white bells on older plants in summer. 18"–24" tall and wide. Full sun to light shade; average, well-drained soil. Zones 5–9.

Suggested alternative: Another yellow-variegated yucca in the same size range, such as *Y. filamentosa* 'Color Guard' or 'Bright Edge'.

# HANDLING TENDER PLANTS INDOORS

Bringing tender plants inside in fall is only half of the challenge—the other half is figuring out where to put them! Some need warmth and light to keep growing actively, others prefer to rest in a cool, dark place; a few can get by with either treatment. Experiment with the plants you have under the conditions you have available; over time, you'll learn the perfect spot for each of your favorites. Check all indoor plants every week or two for signs of pest problems, and spray with insecticidal soap if needed. Keep all dead leaves and flowers picked off too, and dust lightly to keep the leaves clean and healthy.

**Warm thoughts.** The conditions within the average home can keep many tender plants—including begonias, dracaenas, and hibiscus, to name just a few—growing and even flowering all through the winter. Keep the nighttime temperatures at least 55°F, and provide as much light as possible; if sunny window space is limited, set them under fluorescent plant lights. Indoor air tends to be very dry, but you can increase humidity around plants by setting them on shallow trays of pebbles with enough water to almost cover the stones. Water and fertilize regularly to support vigorous growth, and pinch off shoots as needed to encourage dense, bushy growth.

**Cool and bright's all right.** A number of tender plants—among them, flowering maples (*Abutilon*), fuchsias, impatiens, and geraniums (*Pelargonium*)—can overwinter happily in a bright but cool spot indoors (about 50°F during the day and 35° to 40°F at night). A sunny, closed-off spare room or an enclosed but unheated porch is ideal. Boost humidity as explained above. They won't grow as fast as those in warm conditions, so they don't need water or fertilizer quite as often.

**Keep these in the dark.** Some tender plants can survive the cold months without any light at all; these include caladiums, cannas, dahlias, and other plants that grow from bulbs, corms, rhizomes, and tuberous roots. After digging, let them dry for a week or two in an airy, frost-free place. Gladiolus bulbs usually store best when dry; other bulbs are usually buried in a bag or box of barely moist peat moss, vermiculite, or sawdust. Sprinkle with additional water as needed through winter: Keep them moist enough to prevent shriveling, but not so wet that they rot. Most bulbs do well when stored at 40° to 50°F; caladiums are better at 55° to 60°F.

Overwintering tender plants indoors.

# DECORATING POTS FOR LATE-SEASON INTEREST

Vibrant and versatile, container gardens are invaluable for adding seasonal interest to decks, porches, patios, and a variety of other settings. They really shine in summer and fall, but with some advance planning—and some extra attention in autumn—potted plantings can provide beauty through the colder months as well. Whether you leave the plants in place year-round or pop them in after you remove your summer annuals, they'll add a welcome cheerful splash of color. Just remember to keep them watered—they can dry out even in wintertime. A few inches of mulch will also help keep container plants in prime form, just as it does for those growing in the ground.

**Berry nice ideas.** Whether grown alone or paired with evergreen foliage, berry-producing shrubs are a perfect off-season addition to outdoor containers. Compact female selections of evergreen or deciduous hollies (*Ilex*), such as 'Red Sprite' winterberry, are excellent choices; remember, though, that you'll need a compatible male holly nearby during the summer bloom season to get the berries. The bright, clustered fruits of pyracantha are also superb for winter color. For best results with potted shrubs, look for cultivars that are rated at least one—and ideally two—hardiness zones colder than yours (if you live in Zone 6, for instance, look for those reported to be hardy in Zone 4). While most berry-bearing shrubs prefer sun during the growing season, they can survive just fine with shade to partial shade all winter.

**Winter foliage and flowers.** A wide variety of foliage plants are great candidates for winter containers. Evergreen conifers are excellent for height and color, and they come in a range of colors, including dark to light green, purplish, silver-blue, and yellow-gold. Yuccas, too, have a dramatic winter presence—especially those with variegated foliage, such as 'Gold Sword' and 'Color Guard'. Boxwoods can be left to grow naturally or trimmed into a variety of shapes. Evergreen ground covers, such as pachysandra, thymes, liriope, and vinca, work well as fillers around taller-growing companions. You can even enjoy winter flowers in mild climates; try camellias, heaths (*Erica*), pansies, and primroses.

**Make outdoor arrangements.** If you live in a very cold climate, or if you simply don't want to fuss with live plants in pots, there are plenty of other fun ways to dress up containers for winter. Cut pine, spruce, cedar, or other evergreen branches and push them directly into the potting soil. Or make a tripod with bamboo stakes, and wire evergreen branches to them. Dress containers up with natural "ornaments" such as pinecones, berries, grasses, and seed heads. For extra color, use cut branches of shrubs with colorful stems. Shrubby dogwoods (selections of *Cornus alba* and *C. stolonifera*) are superb—'Cardinal' has bright red bark; 'Bud's Yellow' and 'Silver and Gold' have yellow stems; and 'Midwinter Fire' is orange, red, and yellow.

189

A winter-themed window box.

# CONTAINERS MADE FOR THE SHADE

Container-planting options for shady sites sure don't get the same attention that sunny pots and planters do — and that's a pity. Containers that are in shade for at least part of the day tend to hold moisture longer, so you don't need to water them nearly as often. Besides saving you time, that gives you more design flexibility, since you can mix smaller individual pots with larger, multiplant containers without worrying about watering every single day. Even wind-exposed containers such as window boxes and hanging baskets are often much easier to maintain in shady areas than in full sun.

## Lovely Leaves for Fall

Just like shaded ground-level gardens, autumn container plantings rely primarily on foliage features, such as distinctive textures and out-of-the-ordinary colors. Once you've chosen a few particularly good foliage plants for spring-through-fall interest, you can tuck in a few shade-tolerant late-bloomers for accents. Perennials are especially pleasing for shady containers, because they provide the seasonal variety that common shade annuals simply can't match. From a practical standpoint, they save you money, too! You can buy very small starter pots of the perennials, use them in your containers for a season, then plant the filled-out clumps in your garden at the end of the growing season.

This design features a collection of half-barrel planters and window boxes to accent a shaded garden shed. The display is surprisingly flower-filled early in the season, thanks to the ajuga, bergenia, foamflowers, Solomon's seal, and spotted deadnettle. Some bloom continues into summer with the foamy bells and hosta, followed by the lilyturf and toad lily in late summer and fall. Besides the dependable spring and summer foliage interest from all of the plants, several of them — including the bergenias, foamflowers, and Solomon's seal — also contribute a striking color change in autumn. Lots of them will look good through most or all of the winter as well.

During the growing season, simply water as needed, fertilize a few times, and occasionally snip off any spent blooms or discolored leaves.

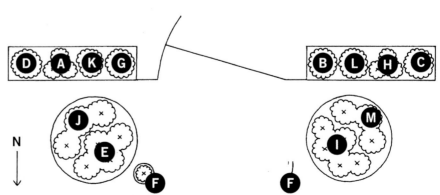

A   *Ajuga reptans* 'Mahogany' (1 plant)

B   *Athyrium* 'Burgundy Lace' (1 plant)

C   *Bergenia* 'Pink Dragonfly' (1 plant)

D   *Hakonechloa macra* 'All Gold' (1 plant)

E   × *Heucherella* 'Burnished Bronze' (3 plants)

F   *Hexastylis shuttleworthii* 'Callaway' (2 plants)

G   *Hosta* 'Little Sunspot' (1 plant)

H   *Lamium maculatum* 'Pink Chablis' (1 plant)

I   *Liriope muscari* 'Pee Dee Gold Ingot' (3 plants)

J   *Polygonatum falcatum* 'Variegatum' (3 plants)

K   *Tiarella* 'Sugar and Spice' (2 plants)

L   *Tiarella* 'Tiger Stripe' (2 plants)

M   *Tricyrtis hirta* 'Miyazaki Gold' (3 plants)

### *Ajuga reptans* 'Mahogany'

'MAHOGANY' AJUGA

Glossy, deep purple-black leaves through the growing season and lasting through much or all of the winter; short spikes of blue flowers in spring. 4"–6" tall × 8"–12" wide. Partial shade; average, well-drained soil. Zones 4–8.

Suggested alternative: Another dark-leaved ajuga, such as 'Black Scallop', 'Bronze Beauty', or 'Purple Brocade'.

### *Athyrium* 'Burgundy Lace'

'BURGUNDY LACE' PAINTED FERN

Lacy, silvery gray fronds with a deep gray-green to purplish gray center stripe through the growing season. About 1' tall × 1'–2' wide. Partial shade; evenly moist but well-drained soil. Zones 4–8.

Suggested alternative: Another painted fern, such as 'Pewter Lace' or 'Ursula's Red'.

### *Bergenia* 'Pink Dragonfly'

'PINK DRAGONFLY' BERGENIA

Oblong, rich green leaves through the growing season, turning deep reddish purple in winter; clustered pink flowers in spring. 6" tall and wide × about 1' tall in bloom. Full sun to partial shade; average to moist but well-drained soil. Zones 4–8.

Suggested alternative: Another bergenia, such as 'Bressingham Ruby' or 'Winter Glow'.

### *Hakonechloa macra* 'All Gold'

'ALL GOLD' HAKONE GRASS

Slender blades of bright yellow to greenish yellow foliage that turn shades of orange to red in fall. About 1' tall and 18" wide. Partial to full shade; evenly moist but well-drained soil. Zones 5–8.

Suggested alternative: 'Aureola' (green-and-yellow-striped blades).

### × *Heucherella* 'Burnished Bronze'

'BURNISHED BRONZE' FOAMY BELLS

Lobed, deep red new leaves age to glossy, dark chocolate brown and are usually attractive through the growing season; airy clusters of pink flowers in late spring to early summer and sometimes again later in the season. About 8" tall and wide in leaf; 12"–18" tall in bloom. Full sun to partial shade; average to moist but well-drained soil. Zones 4–8.

Suggested alternative: Another dark-leaved foamy bells, such as 'Birthday Cake' (more compact, with creamy white flowers) or 'Chocolate Lace' (with reddish purple foliage).

### *Hexastylis shuttleworthii* 'Callaway'

'CALLAWAY' WILD GINGER

Glossy, deep green, heart-shaped leaves veined with silvery gray all year long (semievergreen in cold winters); small brown flowers at ground level in spring. About 3" tall × 6"–12" wide. Partial to full shade; average, well-drained soil. Zones 5–8.

Suggested alternative: Another evergreen wild ginger, such as *H. naniflorum*, *H. splendens*, or *H. speciosa*.

### *Hosta* 'Little Sunspot'

'LITTLE SUNSPOT' HOSTA

Deep green leaves with large yellow centers and yellow fall color; pale purple flowers in midsummer. About 10" tall × 1'–2' wide in leaf; 12"–18" tall in bloom. Full sun to partial shade; average to moist but well-drained soil. Zones 3–8.

Suggested alternative: Another small hosta, such as 'Chartreuse Wiggles' (narrower greenish yellow leaves) or 'Cracker Crumbs' (bright yellow to yellow-green leaves with thinner green margins).

*Hakonechloa macra* 'Aureola'

### *Lamium maculatum* 'Pink Chablis'

'PINK CHABLIS' SPOTTED
DEADNETTLE

Small green leaves heavily splashed with
silver through the growing season and
often through most or all of the winter
as well; pink flowers mostly in spring but
sporadically to frost. About 6" tall × 1'
wide. Partial to full shade; average to moist
but well-drained soil. Zones 4–9.
Suggested alternative: Another spotted
deadnettle, such as 'Pink Pewter' or 'Shell
Pink'.

### *Liriope muscari* 'Pee Dee Gold Ingot'

'PEE DEE GOLD INGOT' BLUE
LILYTURF

Narrow, arching, bright yellow to light yellow foliage is effective year-round; purple-
blue blooms in mid- to late summer. About
1' tall and wide. Full sun to partial shade;
average to moist but well-drained soil.
Zones 6–10.
Suggested alternative: *L. muscari* 'Variegata'
(yellow-edged green leaves); *Carex
siderosticha* 'Lemon Zest' (broader, solid
yellow blades).

### *Polygonatum falcatum* 'Variegatum'

VARIEGATED SOLOMON'S SEAL

Reddish stems carry cream-edged green
leaves that turn bright yellow in fall; white
flowers in late spring to early summer.
2'–3' tall and about 2' across. Partial to full
shade; average, well-drained soil. Zones
5–8.
Suggested alternative: A Solomon's seal
with solid green leaves, such as *P. odoratum*
'Chollipo'; Solomon's plume (*Smilacina
racemosa*).

*Polygonatum falcatum* 'Variegatum'

### *Tiarella* 'Sugar and Spice'

'SUGAR AND SPICE' FOAMFLOWER

Deeply cut, glossy green leaves with deep
purple centers through the growing season, often turning bronzy in fall and lasting well into winter; brushy spikes of fragrant, pink-tinged white flowers mostly in
spring but sometimes again in fall. About
6" tall and wide in leaf; to about 1' tall in
bloom. Partial shade; average to moist but
well-drained soil. Zones 4–8.
Suggested alternative: Another foamflower
with lacy, dark-centered green leaves, such as
'Iron Butterfly' or 'Mint Chocolate'.

### *Tiarella* 'Tiger Stripe'

'TIGER STRIPE' FOAMFLOWER

Lobed, light green leaves with some purplish markings in spring and summer,
often turning deep red to reddish purple in
fall and winter; brushy spikes of fragrant
pinkish white flowers mostly in spring.
About 6" tall in leaf and 12" tall in bloom;
1'–2' wide. Partial shade; average to moist

but well-drained soil. Zones 4–8.
Suggested alternative: Another foamflower
with lobed, dark-marked green leaves, such
as 'Inkblot' or 'Pirate's Patch'.

### *Tricyrtis hirta* 'Miyazaki Gold'

'MIYAZAKI GOLD' TOAD LILY

Yellow-rimmed green leaves all season;
purple-spotted white flowers in fall. About
30" tall and 12"–18" wide. Partial to full
shade; evenly moist but well-drained soil.
Zones 4–8.
Suggested alternative: *T. formosana* 'Gilt
Edge' (with wider yellow leaf edges) or
'Samurai' (also with wider edges but more
compact).

# FALL GARDEN CARE PRIMER

T O MANY PEOPLE, AUTUMN SEEMS LIKE AN ENDING: GROWTH SLOWS, colors fade, and summer fun is just a memory. But for gardeners in the know, fall is a time to look ahead to next spring, while the successes and disappointments of the current season are still fresh in our mind. It's prime time for setting out new plants, moving those that are out of place, and planting bulbs to brighten our gardens next year. It's also a super opportunity for stocking up on new plants by shopping at clearance sales, dividing overgrown clumps, taking cuttings, and sowing seeds. The more we can accomplish in fall, the less hectic things will be in the garden next spring.

So, if you find yourself with some free time on a beautiful autumn weekend, take the opportunity to simply enjoy the beauty of your yard for a bit. Then, get busy! Fall is a fantastic time to tackle those garden tasks you've been putting off, while the days are still productively long and the cooler weather makes outdoor work a pleasure instead of an endurance trial. From creating new gardens and rejuvenating older ones to sprucing up a lawn that's seen better days, there are plenty of projects to keep you busy *and* improve the look of your yard.

**Pause to admire.** While you're busy catching up with yard work, make sure you take the time to admire the splendid fall combinations all around you. This shady-site grouping features a carpet of bigroot geranium (*Geranium macrorrhizum*), with bright green, aromatic foliage, flanked by a fall-red Japanese maple (*Acer palmatum*) and deep green Siberian cypress (*Microbiota decussata*).

# EVALUATING YOUR GARDEN

Great-looking fall gardens rarely "just happen": They're the result of work and planning on the part of their caretakers. Taking time to really *look* around your yard at some point during the growing season can really help you fine-tune the areas that already work well and identify those that could use some serious attention. Sometimes a little "tweaking" — such as adding a few different plants or dividing older

Make notes of things you'd like to change.

clumps — is enough to turn a tired old planting into a dramatic landscape accent. But if you've inherited a weedy, overgrown garden from your home's former owner, or if you've neglected a certain area for a season or two, a complete overhaul might be more practical.

## Take notes
### SPRING THROUGH FALL

If a particular garden looks all right but seems to be missing a little "oomph" in any season, it might just need a little design help. Making notes of what looks good each week through a whole growing season can show you when interest is lacking; adding a few plants to cover the down times may be enough. Or, if you aren't pleased with the mix of colors, choose one color scheme to go through the whole season, or let it change for different seasons. Don't forget to look at the foliage as well. Having too much grasslike foliage, or too many plants with small leaves, can throw off the visual balance. Replacing some of them with large, broad leaves is often enough to add just the right amount of zip.

## Watch for overcrowding
### EARLY TO MID-FALL, OR EARLY SPRING

It's natural for plants to grow at different rates, so over time, it's not unusual for the vigorous ones to crowd out the slower-growers. Dividing the fast-spreading ones every year or two will keep them in check; so can regularly removing the faded flowers to prevent self-sowing.

But if a garden has been neglected for more than a year or two, it may be more practical to remove some or all of the plants and start over. When you replant, try to match your plants more carefully; let the fast-spreading thugs fight it out in a "free-for-all" bed and combine more-restrained plants in another area.

## Assess your foundation plantings
### FALL OR SPRING

One area that just about any home can use some help with is the foundation planting — that narrow strip of ground that runs along the whole front of the house. Around new homes, this area is usually filled with assorted of small, builder-supplied shrubs surrounded by an expanse of mulch; around older homes, it's often a tangle of overgrown, out-of-scale evergreens.

If you have a new planting, it's smart to carefully evaluate the shrubs that are there to make sure they are suited to the growing conditions and that they won't get too big for the space. (Those cute little conifers can get quite large in just a few years, unless you're inclined to prune them often.) Replacing some

Renovate overgrown foundation plantings.

or all of them with dwarf flowering or foliage shrubs can drastically reduce future maintenance and add changing seasonal interest, too. In established foundation plantings, you might want to remove seriously overgrown shrubs altogether and try heavy pruning to reduce the size of the rest.

To spruce up foundation plantings of any age, consider filling in around the shrubs with ground covers and spring bulbs. Or, widen the bed, if possible, and let the shrubs serve as a background for a colorful planting of perennials.

# IMPROVING YOUR SOIL

Soil building may not be the most glamorous fall gardening project, but when you see the results it'll give you next year, you'll be glad you took the time now. Whether you're starting a new garden or want to keep an existing planting at peak performance, evaluating your existing soil and adding organic matter are two important steps in creating a beautiful and healthy display of flowers and foliage all through the growing season.

Check pH with a simple test.

## *Take a soil test*

LATE SUMMER TO EARLY FALL

Sure, it's possible to garden successfully without ever taking a soil test — but why not try it at least once? If you're creating your first garden on a new property, finding out the soil's pH (in other words, whether it is acidic or alkaline) can help you choose the plants best suited to the natural conditions. That means fewer plant failures, so you'll save money and have a better-looking yard, too. In established landscapes, a soil test can be helpful for evaluating the pH and nutrient balance in trouble spots, where plants aren't performing as well as you think they should.

Kits sold through garden centers are adequate for getting a basic idea of pH; test kits available through your local Cooperative Extension office will give you a much more detailed analysis. (The Internet or your local phone book contains listings of Cooperative Extension offices.) Whichever method you choose, testing your soil in late summer to early fall gives you plenty of time to add any amendments your soil needs, so your gardens will be in prime form to start growing in spring.

## Start a compost pile

### EARLY TO MID-FALL

If you have a garden, you need a compost pile. This is a great time to get one started, because there are plenty of ingredients around to work with: both "greens" (nitrogen-rich materials), such as grass clippings and fresh garden trimmings, and "browns" (materials that are mostly carbon), such as dried leaves and dead stems. When you mix greens and browns, keep them evenly moist, create a large enough pile, and turn it every few weeks to mix in plenty of air, the composting process will go quickly. It's harder to build an ideal compost pile later in the season, when greens are less abundant, but the materials will still break down — just at a slower rate.

♣ *Pile it on.* In its simplest form, a compost pile is just that: an uncontained heap of organic material. A site that gets plenty of sun in fall and winter will help keep your pile warm and promote faster breakdown. To allow good air circulation all around the pile, build it on a wooden pallet or a base of crisscrossed poles or timbers. (If you're composting near a tree, this will also help to keep roots from creeping up into the pile.) Ideally, the heap

Fall cleanup provides an abundance of compost ingredients.

should be at least 3 feet on each side, so it's large enough to heat up and decompose quickly. Chopping up the material before you add it to the pile will also dramatically speed up the process and make the final product a lot less lumpy.

♣ *Get wired.* Besides making your composting area look neater, a cage or bin helps to keep the material evenly moist, promoting faster decomposition. Enclosures also prevent loose materials from blowing away. It's easy to make a basic cage from wire rabbit fencing or a similar sturdy fencing with narrow openings: Simply fasten the two ends together with wire or heavy twine to create a broad cylinder, then stand it on end. When you're ready to turn the pile, just unhook the fasteners

and pull off the cage; set it up again next to the first pile and turn the materials into the reassembled cage. If the wire you've used isn't heavy enough to support itself, pound a few metal fence posts into the ground around the cage and fasten the wire to them.

♣ *Bin there, done that.* Compost bins are more solid than cages and tend to be more permanent. Buy a commercially produced bin — they're usually made out of wood or plastic — or build your own from cement blocks, lumber, or wooden pallets. Remember to leave one side open or hinged in such a way that you can easily reach the compost for turning or shoveling. If possible, set up at least two enclosures. That way, you can fill one side while you are using the finished compost in the other side. A roof is a nice touch for protecting the pile from wind, sun, and rain; a tarp isn't as attractive but will serve the same purpose.

### *Make the most of compost*

LATE SUMMER TO EARLY WINTER

Don't be fooled by the pictures of fine, crumblike compost you see in advertisements; unless you sift it through a screen, homemade compost is typically on the lumpy side, and that's okay. Chunky compost makes a great topdressing for flower beds and shrub plantings. Applied in late summer or early fall, a 4-inch layer will probably break down before winter; applied in late fall or early winter, it'll act like a protective winter mulch and then decompose in spring. Either

way, the compost provides plenty of organic matter to feed earthworms and other helpful soil organisms, which in turn will help provide great growing conditions for your plants.

### *Make leaf mold*

EARLY FALL TO EARLY WINTER

Inundated with dropped leaves every autumn? Can't resist the urge to bring home your neighbors' bagged leaves on fall trash days? When Mother Nature gives you lots of leaves, make leaf mold! This dark, crumbly material is black gold for gardens, whether you use it as a soil amendment, a mulch, or a topdressing for outdoor seedbeds. Unlike compost, there's no fuss about balancing the ingredients, no turning, and no weed seeds.

Topdress borders with chunky compost.

Making leaf mold can be as simple as piling up a bunch of leaves and waiting for them to decompose. In windy sites, though, uncontained leaves are likely to blow away, so many gardeners prefer to corral their leaves in wire bins and cover them with a tarp, or else stuff them into plastic bags with a few slits for air. It generally takes a year or more until leaf mold is ready to use, but if you start a new batch in fall, you'll have a steady supply every year.

For faster results, shred the leaves first. A lawn mower with a bagging attachment is ideal, because it chops the leaves and then gathers them for easy handling, but even a regular mower will do: Just rake the leaves into rows and run the mower over them, then rake up the remains.

Making sure that the leaves are evenly moist when you pile them up is also important, especially if

## DON'T KEEP THESE!

While it's smart to make good use of as much garden waste as you can, some of it simply isn't safe to compost or use as mulch. Here are a few items that you're better off bagging for disposal:

- Diseased stems, leaves, buds, and blooms
- Seed heads of garden plants that self-sow too freely
- Stolons and rhizomes (creeping stems and roots) of weeds and fast-spreading garden plants
- Thorny stems and leaves
- Weeds that have gone to seed

they'll be in a covered pile or bag. So as you add layers of leaves, mist them with a hose, then tamp them down; you want them to be damp but not waterlogged. Whenever they turn dark, with a loose, crumbly feel, they're ready to use.

### Stock up on livestock manure

EARLY FALL TO LATE WINTER

If you have access to livestock manure but are worried about its high nitrogen content "burning" your plants, autumn is a great time to stockpile it in preparation for spring. It's fine to spread fresh manure right on new garden areas you won't be planting until spring; otherwise, simply pile it up in your composting area and let it sit over the winter, then spread it on established plantings in spring. Either way, winter rains will help leach out the excess nitrogen, and the decomposed manure will be a great source of organic matter. As a bonus, the manure won't smell as much in cold weather as it would in the summertime — and you'll be indoors for most of the winter, anyway.

# STARTING NEW GARDENS

Fall is a fantastic time to get new garden areas ready for spring planting. You have plenty of time to figure out the perfect size and shape now, and the site will have an opportunity to settle over the winter. Once spring arrives, you can get your plants in the ground as soon as they're delivered or you bring them home. To get started, you have a decision to make: To dig or not to dig?

### Build a bed by layering

ANY SEASON

Creating a new planting area by layering topsoil or organic matter or a combination of the two over the site may sound too easy to be effective, but it does work. You can start a bed any time it's convenient: no need to worry about whether the soil is too wet or too dry, or even if it's frozen. Unlike digging, layering won't bring new weed seeds up to the surface, and the layers won't crust over like heavily cultivated soil can, so water and air can easily move through them. If you have plenty of layering material on hand, you can easily complete a new bed or border in a single afternoon. Or, you could just use what you have on hand for the first layer, then add more layers as you gather materials throughout the fall.

♠ *Preparing the site.* When you're ready to start your no-dig garden, begin by removing large weeds and surface debris and then mowing the site as low as possible. To improve the look of the area — and to help hold the layers in place — you might choose to build a "frame" around the edge of the bed-to-be, using rocks, landscape timbers, or some other decorative material. An edging that's 4 to 6 inches high may look too short after you first add the layers, but it should be just about right by springtime, once the layers have settled. It's not absolutely necessary to build a frame, though.

♠ *Gathering the materials.* The most labor-intensive part of creating a layered bed is gathering the layering materials themselves. If you're buying topsoil, livestock manure, or compost in bulk, keep in mind that you'll need a spot to dump it in and a way to move it to the garden site. (And if you're dealing with "aromatic" materials such as manure and mushroom soil, you'll want to

Create a new garden by layering.

move that stuff away from your house *fast!*) You can also scrounge up organic matter in your own yard, including homemade compost, grass clippings, and fall leaves. Other possibilities are peat moss, straw, coffee grounds, and kitchen scraps (not including meat, bones, or fat).

♠ *Pile it on!* If you plan to cover the site first with at least 4 inches of topsoil, you can probably get away with spreading it directly on the surface; usually, though, it's better to cover the site with a layer of wet newspapers (about 10 sheets thick to smother average lawn grass; 20 or more for very vigorous turf or weeds). Now, start spreading out your ingredients in layers: roughly 3 to 6 inches deep for heavy material like soil or manure, 6 to 8 inches for chopped leaves, and 8 to 12 for straw and other lightweight materials. If possible, alternate layers of heavy

and lighter materials. Three or four layers should be enough. The more lightweight materials you use, the higher the "finished" bed will look; remember that they'll flatten out as they break down over the winter.

## Dig in
### EARLY TO MID-FALL

Digging is the traditional way to start a new garden. First, you'll need to remove all the existing vegetation, then till or dig the site. If your soil is on the clayey (heavy) side, fall is a particularly good season for

digging, because it tends to be drier now; plus, winter freezes will do a good job breaking up any clods left on the soil surface. And no matter what kind of soil you have, digging a new garden certainly provides lots of exercise! To learn more about hand-digging, turn to Creating a New Garden Site, on page 110.

## Try a compromise
### EARLY TO LATE FALL

Not sure which way to go — digging or layering? Why not try installing one bed each way, then judge

## GETTING RID OF EXISTING WEEDS

One drawback to the layering technique is that it may not stop existing perennial weeds from popping up. If you have serious weed woes where your dream garden's going to go, consider these options:

♠ Carefully hand-weed the area *before* adding the layers. This is most practical if you have just a few taprooted weeds, such as dock and dandelions.

♠ Use thick layers to smother what's underneath. A layer of topsoil about 6 inches thick should prevent all but the most vigorous weeds from re-emerging. If you use lighter materials, such as compost and chopped leaves, make the layers at least 8 inches thick.

♠ Create a heavy-duty weed barrier with cardboard or thick layers of newspapers (roughly 20 sheets, depending on how bad the weeds are), then add your soil or organic-matter layers. The cardboard or papers will smother just about any weed problem, then gradually break down into soil-improving humus.

for yourself which one works better? Or try a combination of both techniques. If there's only sparse grass or annual weeds where the new garden will go, simply dig or till the area lightly, then cover it with a few inches of mulch or compost for the winter. That takes a bit more physical effort than layering by itself, but it doesn't require nearly as much layering material — an important point if you have to haul the stuff from some distance.

Plant large bulbs in individual holes.

# PLANTING AND TRANSPLANTING

The simple act of putting plants into the ground and watching them grow is one of the most gratifying parts of the whole gardening experience. We spend months looking forward to the ritual of buying or raising new plants, then getting our hands dirty during the frenzy of spring planting. But don't limit the fun to just a few weeks in spring, when fall is another super time to indulge in this enjoyable activity.

## *Plant hardy bulbs*

LATE SUMMER TO EARLY WINTER

Sure, everyone thinks about bulbs when they're blooming in the spring — but the real action comes later in the season. Late summer is the time to get fall-flowering bulbs in the ground, and fall (or even early winter) is fine for planting spring-bloomers.

♣ *Fall planting for spring garden color.* Not sure about exactly *when* to plant spring-flowering bulbs? In most climates, it's best to get them in the ground as soon as they're delivered, or as soon as they show up in local outlets. The longer they sit

around, the more prone they are to drying out and the less time they'll have to get settled in before winter. It's also far easier on your knees and hands to plant before the soil gets cold. If you find yourself with leftover bulbs in late fall, however, go ahead and plant them unless the ground is frozen solid; they'll stand a far better chance of surviving in the ground than sitting in a bag or box all winter.

One exception to the early-planting ideal is in southern gardens. Here, you may want to wait to as late as December or even early January so your bulbs don't come up too early and get nipped by freezing air. (Tulips seem particularly prone to early rising, even in cooler climates, so they are good candidates for late planting just about anywhere.) If you need to hold bulbs for more than a week or two before planting, keep them in a ventilated mesh or paper bag in the refrigerator, away from any ripening produce (which releases a gas that can harm bulbs) and out of reach of children (as some bulbs are poisonous if eaten).

For specific tips to simplify bulb-planting in any season, see Growing Bulbs in Grass on page 22

Pot up extra bulbs for spring.

and Planting Bulbs in Beds and Borders on page 120.

♣ **Container bulb plantings.** Spring bulbs make great fillers for year-round pots and planters, but handling them before and after bloom can be a little tricky. If you plant them directly in the containers in fall, the soil may freeze before the bulbs have enough time to develop a root system, and they may be damaged by the cold. If they do grow and bloom, you have to look at the yellowing foliage as it matures, then take the chance of digging into them when you add your plants for the summer display.

Fortunately, there's an easy way to solve all of these challenges. Simply plant the bulbs in plastic nursery pots in fall, then sink them in a holding bed or put them in a sheltered spot outdoors and cover them with several inches of mulch for the cold months. Lift the pots in late winter, then set them into the soil in the display containers. When they're finished flowering, lift out the pots again and put them in an out-of-the-way spot to finish ripening. In the meantime, your display containers will be all ready for their summer plants!

While you're potting up bulbs for yourself, why not plant up some additional containers; they make great holiday gifts that the recipients can enjoy for months after they receive them. For more details on planting bulbs for container displays, see Planting Bulbs in Pots on page 159.

## Get hardy plants in the ground

LATE SUMMER TO MID-FALL

This time is prime time to plant hardy perennials, ground covers, shrubs, vines, and trees. For complete details, check out "Let's Get Planting!" on page 56.

## Pay attention to new plantings

EARLY FALL THROUGH WINTER

Most plants aren't producing tender new top growth at this time of year, so they don't need as much post-planting pampering now as they would in spring. They'll sail through frosts, and their mature leaves are sturdy enough to stand up to sun and wind. The important thing is to provide ideal conditions for good *root* growth, so your plants will be well settled in before winter arrives.

♣ **Water wisely.** Rainfall tends to be more dependable in fall than in summer, but if it's lacking, regularly water

Shop fall nursery sales.

new plantings (perennials and bulbs as well as shrubs and trees) to keep soil evenly moist. It's especially important for plants with evergreen foliage, because their roots need access to water all winter to replace moisture lost through leaves. Keep watering during dry spells until ground freezes.

♠ ***Manage the mulch.*** Spreading a 2- to 4-inch-deep layer of shredded bark, chopped leaves, or other organic mulch over the soil will keep the soil warm for longer after planting, encouraging root growth. Then, once the soil cools, it will keep it evenly cold until spring, minimizing possible damage from rapid freeze—thaw cycles. Make the mulch ring as wide as the planting hole. Cover the crowns of perennials with no top

growth (remove the mulch in spring), but leave evergreen perennials uncovered. Avoid piling mulch right around the base of woody-stemmed plants; leave at least an inch of mulch-free space around them.

♠ ***Watch through the winter.*** If snow blankets the ground all through winter, the job is done until spring. Otherwise, stroll through your garden once a week or so (especially during warm spells). If any of your new fall plantings has been pushed out of the ground, gently push it back into the soil. If you can't, pile more mulch around it to keep the roots from drying out until you can replant it properly in spring. Also, keep watering during dry spells if the soil is unfrozen.

## TIMING IS EVERYTHING

If you've had bad luck with fall planting in the past, you may be choosing the wrong plants. Paying extra attention to hardiness zones for potential purchases can make the difference between a successful return in spring and a disappointing waste of time and money. To be safe, stick with plants that are normally cold-hardy to one zone cooler than yours for fall planting. (In Zone 6, for example, choose those that are rated to at least Zone 5.) Planting questionably hardy plants in spring, so they have the whole growing season to settle their roots before cold weather, gives them a *much* better chance to winter over. Spring planting may also be more successful for late-flowering plants, for the same reason.

# MAKING MORE PLANTS

Shopping for new plants has to be one of the most fun parts of gardening — but it's not the only way to fill your gardens. Taking cuttings, dividing clumps, layering stems, and sowing seeds are all easy ways to make more plants, so you'll have plenty to tuck into gaps, create new plantings, fill containers, and share with your friends and family. Autumn is an ideal time for many propagation techniques, so what are you waiting for? Let's get growing!

## *Take softwood cuttings*

SPRING TO EARLY FALL

Knowing how to take softwood cuttings is an invaluable skill for gardeners of all levels. While you can use this technique just about any time, taking cuttings of annuals and tender perennials in late summer to early fall gives you smaller versions of your favorites to overwinter indoors; then in spring, you can take cuttings from *those* plants to fill your gardens again. For details on softwood cuttings, see Taking Cuttings of Tender Treasures on page

## 51.

### *Divide perennials and ground covers*

EARLY TO MID-FALL
OR EARLY TO MID-SPRING

At this time of year, it's easy to see which of your border plants or ground covers would benefit from being divided. Separating large clumps can help rejuvenate mature plants, increasing their vigor and reducing the chance of their stems sprawling; it also gives you new pieces to replant or share. To learn more about the different ways you can divide your plants, turn to Divide to Conquer on page 38 and Dividing Perennials on page 114.

Be aware that long-established clumps of some perennials can be a major chore to dig up, let alone to divide. Large ornamental grasses, in particular, can root so deeply that it practically takes a backhoe to get them out. In cases like this, if you simply want a new piece to plant elsewhere, it's possible to get one without digging up the whole clump: Take a very sharp spade and use it to cut a small wedge out of the outer edge. Dig up the wedge, then refill the hole with compost or a compost/soil mix. Come next year, you won't even notice the piece is missing. Avoid the temptation to do this too often, though; if you repeatedly remove the young, vigorous edge growth each year, only the older growth will be left, and the original clump will be noticeably weakened.

Most perennials recover quickly from being divided and are all the better for it; however, keep in mind that there are some exceptions. Those that generally prefer to be left alone, unless you really need to divide or move them, include baby's breaths (*Gypsophila*), bleeding hearts (*Dicentra*), false indigos (*Baptisia*), gas plants (*Dictamnus*), lupines (*Lupinus*), monkshoods (*Aconitum*), peonies, and poppies (*Papaver*).

### *Layer flexible stems*

EARLY TO LATE FALL

"Layering" is a technique that lets a shoot make roots while it's still attached to its parent plant. Since it has a steady supply of food and moisture during the rooting process, the chances of it dying before it roots are practically nil. Simple layering works with just about any shrub, tree, or vine with a flexible stem growing near the base. Bend the stem to the ground and set a rock on the soil to mark a spot about 1 foot behind the stem tip. Remove the leaves where the stem touches the ground, then use a knife to slice a sliver of bark off the underside of the stem. Loosen the soil in the spot you marked and bend the stem to the ground again. Bury the wounded section about 3 inches deep, using a wire pin or rock to hold the stem in place, and tie the shoot tip to a stake to encourage upright growth. Keep the soil evenly moist. Next fall, snip off the rooted layer where it's attached to the parent plant and transplant it to its new home.

## Save seeds

EARLY FALL TO EARLY WINTER

Fall gardens are loaded with seeds, so why not gather some of the bounty for yourself? You can find out all about it in Saving and Sowing Seeds on page 72 and Gathering Seeds on page 124.

Exposed seeds are easy to collect.

## Take hardwood cuttings

MID- TO LATE FALL

If you have a favorite deciduous shrub or vine you want to propagate in fall, hardwood cuttings are an excellent option. Because the plants aren't actively growing when you take the cuttings, it's not so critical to keep the temperature and humidity levels just right, as it is for softwood cuttings. Mid- to late autumn is a super time to gather and plant hardwood cuttings because

## CUTTING REMARKS

Propagating plants by cuttings is typically a spring or summer project, but it's a fun activity for fall as well. Unlike divisions, which can give you anywhere from two to a dozen or so new plants, cuttings allow you to create many dozens of identical offspring, saving you a bundle if you need to fill a new garden or expand an existing one. Or bring your extras to plant swaps and exchange them for new plants. Taking cuttings also lets you propagate favorite plants without digging them up—a plus if plants don't like having their roots disturbed or are too large or too small to divide.

The general principle is the same however you take the cuttings: Remove part of a plant, then put that piece in the right conditions to promote growth of the missing parts. A shoot, for instance, needs to form roots to be able to grow, while a root section needs to produce stems and leaves. Providing the right amount of moisture and the ideal temperature range for the cutting to regenerate its missing parts is a key to success.

The other important aspect of taking cuttings is matching the correct technique with the plant you want to propagate, and with the time of year. *Softwood cuttings* work best with plants that are actively growing, while *hardwood cuttings* and *root cuttings* work better with plants that have already dropped their leaves. In autumn, you'll use softwood cuttings for annuals and tender perennials that you want to bring indoors for the winter, and hardwood cuttings or root cuttings for many deciduous shrubs, trees, and vines.

To take any kind of cutting, you'll need a clean, sharp tool that will make a neat cut without crushing the stem or root: either a knife or a pair of scissor-type pruning shears. You'll also need something to plant the cuttings in: either pots filled with moistened potting mix or a holding bed (see Building a Holding Bed: Any Season on page 209 for details).A cold frame provides excellent winter protection for potted hardwood or root cuttings. While you're waiting for cuttings to "take" (produce new roots or shoots), check them at least once a week to make sure they haven't dried out. Keep the rooting medium evenly moist, but avoid overwatering, because soggy soil can cause cuttings to rot.

they'll have all winter to form roots before the buds start to grow. This technique works on a wide variety of deciduous shrubs, trees, and vines, but some root more readily than others. If you're new to hardwood cuttings, build your confidence with easy-to-root plants, such as forsythias, grapes (*Vitis*), honeysuckles (*Lonicera*), mock oranges (*Philadelphus*), roses, shrubby dogwoods (*Cornus*), weigelas, and willows (*Salix*).

🍂 *Gathering hardwood cuttings.* Using a sharp pair of scissor-type pruning shears, cut off 6- to 8-inch-long shoot tips, two or three weeks after the leaves have dropped. Vigorous, first-year shoots that are about pencil-thick are ideal if you can find them; avoid distinctly spindly or crowded growth. Snip an inch or two off the tip from each cutting, making a straight cut about ½ inch above a bud. At the other end of the cutting, make an angled cut

Use sharp shears to prepare cuttings.

Remember to label your cuttings!

slightly below a bud. These different cuts will help remind you which end is which at planting time.

🍂 *Planting hardwood cuttings.* When you're ready to "stick" your prepared cuttings, plant them in pots filled with moist potting mix or a 50:50 blend of peat moss and perlite, or directly outdoors in a deeply dug, well-drained nursery bed. If desired, dip the bottom of each cutting into a commercial rooting hormone to promote root formation. (The package directions usually include a list of plants that benefit from this treatment.) Insert each cutting into the mix or soil so the top bud is about 1 inch above the surface. Space the cuttings roughly 2 to 4 inches apart.

🍂 *Caring for hardwood cuttings.* Water thoroughly to settle the mix or soil around the cuttings. Set potted cuttings into a cold frame for

winter protection; check regularly through the winter and water if the mix starts to dry out. Protect your outdoor-planted cuttings with a 6-inch layer of chopped leaves, shredded bark, or other organic mulch to prevent damage from frost heaving; remove the mulch in spring. Leave all hardwood cuttings in place for at least one whole growing season, so they have plenty of time to form roots, and keep the soil evenly moist. Transplant them to larger pots, a holding bed, or your garden in fall.

## Sow seeds for winter chilling

### MID- TO LATE FALL

No need to wait until spring to sow all of your seeds: Planting in mid- to late autumn is an excellent option for a wide variety of perennials, bulbs, vines, shrubs, and trees. You won't need any special equipment — basically just some labels and either pots filled with moistened seed-starting mix or a "nursery" area where you can plant directly in the ground. You don't have to worry about plant lights or heating mats, as you do for indoor sowing, and because the seedlings appear when the weather is right, there's no fussing with hardening off tender young plants.

Want to try your hand at fall seed sowing? Here are just a few of the many plants that are likely to give you great results: columbines (*Aquilegia*), coneflowers (*Echinacea* and *Rudbeckia*), delphiniums, foxgloves (*Digitalis*), hollyhocks (*Alcea*), lupines (*Lupinus*), penstemons, poppies (*Papaver*), and veronicas.

♠ *Putting seeds to bed.* For the ultimate in easy seed-starting, sow your seeds directly in the ground. You need a spot where the seeds won't be disturbed (remember that some can take two or three years to sprout), and good drainage is critical, so a raised bed is ideal. To make sure the seeds don't get washed away by heavy rain, and to keep different kinds separate, you can make 4-inch-high mini-frames from scrap lumber or rings cut from ice-cream tubs and push them halfway into the soil; then sow within the frames.

♠ *Sowing in pots.* If you don't have room for a special seed-sowing bed, or if you're working with very tiny, scarce, or expensive seeds, sowing in pots may be a better idea. Besides giving you more control over the placement of the seeds, planting in a commercial seed-starting mix minimizes the chance of weed seedlings, soilborne diseases, and

Top-dress seed pots with fine gravel.

soil-dwelling insects troubling your seedlings. Sow as you normally would in 4-inch plastic pots (or 6-inch pots, if you have lots of seeds), then set the pots in a sheltered spot or in a cold frame.

♠ *Aftercare for outdoor-sown seeds.* Whether you sow in the ground or in pots, covering sown seeds with a ¼- to ½-inch layer of sand or fine gravel can increase your chance of success. Like any other mulch, the sand or gravel will protect the seeds from drying sun and wind as well as pounding rain, and it will prevent the soil or mix from crusting over, which can interfere with germination. An additional covering of wire mesh will help discourage damage from mice, birds, and curious pets.

## Take root cuttings

LATE FALL OR LATE WINTER
TO EARLY SPRING

If you're interested in expanding your propagation skills, fall can be a good time to get to the "root" of the matter. Taking root cuttings isn't a widely used technique, but it can come in handy for propagating some shrubs, trees, vines, and perennials — particularly those that don't root readily from stem cuttings. While plants are dormant (not actively producing top growth), their roots are full of stored energy. When you take a piece of root and place it in the right conditions, it will use that energy to produce new shoots and roots. Just make sure you gather root cuttings from plants that aren't grafted (as are many hybrid roses and lilacs, for instance); otherwise, you'll be propagating the "understock" and not the desirable top growth you want.

A number of woody and herbaceous plants will "take" from root cuttings closer to springtime, but when you're using this technique in fall, it's best to stick with thick-rooted plants. Some good candidates are bear's breeches (*Acanthus*), flowering quinces (*Chaenomeles*), hops (*Humulus*), non-grafted lilacs

(*Syringa*), "own-root" roses, sea hollies (*Eryngium*), and sumacs (*Rhus*).

♠ ***Collecting your cuttings.*** Late fall — after the plants drop their leaves but before the ground freezes — is a fine time to take autumn root cuttings. If the plant you want to propagate is growing in a container, your job is easy; simply slide it out of the pot. In a bed or border, use a trowel or small shovel to carefully dig around the base of the plant. Once some roots are exposed, look for one that's about pencil-thick, then cut it off as close to the crown (center) of the plant as possible. Taking just one or two roots per clump generally doesn't disturb the parent plant. When you're done, put the plant back in its pot or replace the soil around the remaining roots.

♠ ***Cutting the cuttings.*** Fall-gathered root cuttings need to be fairly large, because it will be awhile before they produce top growth to make

Try your hand at root cuttings.

more food. To prepare them, lay a root on a hard surface, remove any small, fibrous side roots, then snip it into pieces. Make a straight cut at the end that had been closer to the crown, measure back 3 to 6 inches, then make a slanting cut. Make a new, straight cut on the remaining root piece to indicate the top of the next cutting, then repeat the measuring and cutting process as the length of the root allows.

♠ ***Planting and aftercare.*** Plant your root cuttings 2 to 3 inches apart in pots containing a moistened 50:50 mix of peat moss and perlite, or else outdoors in a nursery bed. Insert them vertically into the soil with the slanted end down, so the top (straight-cut) end is 1 to 2 inches below the soil surface. Put potted cuttings in a cold frame for the winter; cover outdoor-planted cuttings with a few inches of mulch (remove the mulch in spring). If they produce good top growth and appear to be well rooted, transplant them to individual pots or your garden in fall; if they are on the weak side, leave them in place for another growing season.

## Build a holding bed

ANY SEASON

A "holding bed" or "nursery bed" — a special area set aside for temporary growing space — is an invaluable addition to a garden of any size. If you can't afford to buy all the plants you need for a new garden at full price, for example, you can shop the sales and frequent local plant swaps, then plant your purchases in holding beds. Over the course of a year or two, you could gather everything you need at the fraction of the price you would have paid for full-size, garden-ready plants.

Holding beds are also handy for providing immediate planting space when you move to a new home or need to relocate plants on your existing property due to house repairs, construction, or garden renovation. Use them as winter quarters for hardy perennials when you dismantle your container plantings in fall, or for outdoor propagation projects such as sowing seeds and taking cuttings. To learn more about the details of building and using these versatile garden spaces, turn to Making the Most of Holding Beds on page 131.

♠ ***Caring for holding beds.*** Holding beds typically need the same care as the rest of your garden, with the exception of somewhat more frequent watering if they include new seedlings or small transplants. Mulch is as beneficial here as it is in permanent plantings, especially if you use a material that breaks down quickly, such as compost or chopped leaves; chunky wood-based mulches will get mixed into the soil when you move plants and may make it too coarse for delicate little seedlings. If pets, rabbit, deer, or other critters are a problem, cover holding beds with netting or floating row cover. For added protection, you could even cover part of all of the beds with portable cold frames.

♠ **Managing plants in holding beds.** Take a good look at your holding beds several times throughout the growing season and make a note of plants that are ready to move to larger quarters. Slow-growers may need to stay in

Don't let shrubs stay in temporary quarters too long.

place several years to reach garden size, whereas others may take only a few weeks to fill out. Try not to leave young trees or shrubs in one place for more than three years; after that, they can be difficult to move without disturbing many of their bedmates in the process. Fill their holes with the same soil mix you started with,

if possible, or else improvise with sifted compost, leftover potting soil, or whatever similar growing mix you have available. Chances are you'll have plenty of young plants on hand waiting to fill those gaps as soon as you move something else out. If not, maybe it's time to go plant shopping again!

# THE BIENNIAL SOLUTION

Biennials—plants that produce only leaves during their first year, then bloom, set seed, and die in their second year—offer some of the most beautiful blooms around; common foxglove (*Digitalis purpurea*), honesty or money plant (*Lunaria annua*), forget-me-nots (*Myosotis*), and sweet William (*Dianthus barbatus*) are just a few examples. Unfortunately, the odd life cycle that these plants share makes them a challenge to use effectively in the garden. Their first-year foliage clumps tend to be low and not particularly interesting; their second-year stems are often tall and dramatic—at least until they set seed and die out in summer, leaving large gaps in late-season beds and borders.

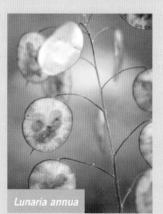
*Lunaria annua*

How can holding beds help? Sow your biennial seeds there in summer, then move the young plants to your garden in fall of their first year or early spring of their second season. By sowing a new batch of seed each summer, you'll always have biennial seedlings coming along, so you don't need to let their garden counterparts go to seed; simply pull them out after they flower, then replace them with the new seedlings for a dependable display next year.

# STAKING, PRUNING, AND GROOMING

There's no denying that good design is an important part of creating a gorgeous garden. Just as important, though, is knowing how to care for your plants, so you can help them grow to their potential and look their very best by the time autumn returns. Some of these small but important tasks you'll actually *do* in fall; others are spring and summer tasks that will pay off as the garden gears up for its final show.

## Plan ahead for support

### EARLY SPRING TO EARLY SUMMER

If you're new to growing a particular plant (or to gardening in general), you have an excellent excuse for not staking in spring. After all, it's a waste of time to support plants that can hold themselves up just fine, and a border bristling with stakes that may be visible well into summer is not a pretty picture. After a year or two, however, you'll have a good idea of which plants definitely need help holding themselves up — and

then you'll have no good reason for not taking action ahead of time! Whether you take the direct route of providing some kind of support system or you use a combination of pruning techniques to help the plants support themselves, you'll eventually be rewarded with a fantastic-looking fall garden.

🍂 *What's at stake?* The two secrets to successful staking are matching the support to the plant and getting it in place early. For tall perennials, choose single stakes or insert three or four stakes around the clump and connect them with twine or yarn. Lower, bushy perennials are ideal candidates for hoop stakes (circular grids of wire supported by wire legs) or "pea staking" (twiggy brush inserted around a clump, so the stems can grow up through the twigs). When you get these supports in place just as the plants emerge in spring, the plants grow up through and cover their supports in just a few weeks. To make the supports even less visible, paint them black before you put them in place.

🍂 *Try dividing or thinning.* Sometimes just a little assistance from you can help your plants support themselves. If the clumps have been in place for a few years, dividing them

Thin in spring for sturdier fall stems.

in spring may help relieve crowding and allow the stems to grow straight and strong. Or leave the clumps in place, but cut or pinch out some of the stems right at soil level. Leave 2 to 4 inches between the stems; that way, they won't have to compete so hard for space and light, and they'll stay sturdy and upright.

🍂 *A pinch in time.* For some perennials, you can find compact cultivars, which naturally produce shorter stems that don't need staking. You can help your existing plants produce the same effect by removing their shoot tips, which encourages them to produce bushy side growth rather than tall, lanky stems. Start in late spring or early summer, when plants are about a foot tall, snipping or pinching off the stem tips or simply shearing back the whole plant to about half its height. If desired, you can pinch or shear lightly again in midsummer. Different plants react differently to this technique, so it's worth experimenting to see what works best in your particular situation.

## Cut back long-bloomers

### LATE SUMMER

Flower-filled perennials are always a delight for gardeners, but sometimes these generous plants can be victims of their own beauty. In other words, they produce so many flowers that they actually bloom themselves to death! It can be hard to cut back plants in full bloom, but it gives them a chance to produce leafy new growth and store some energy before winter comes, instead of expending all their energy making more flowers and seeds. Good candidates for a moderate trim (by about half) in late summer or early fall are red valerian (*Centranthus ruber*), blanket flowers (*Gaillardia*), zebra hollyhock (*Malva zebrina*), and coreopsis. Sure, you'll lose some flowers, but you'll soon have fresh new foliage to enjoy.

# • SHEAR GENIUS •

Pruning techniques can do more than keep your perennials looking their best; they can also expand your options for fall flowers. Once you learn the basics of what, when, and where to cut, you'll be amazed at how easy it is to delay or extend the bloom season of many common perennials well into autumn.

First, there are the perennials that put on a fabulous show of flowers in late spring to midsummer, then repeat the performance in fall if you cut them back when the first batch of blooms begins to fade. A hard cut is generally in order if you want the plants to really look good in autumn, with fresh foliage and abundant blooms, too. (A light shearing usually delays blooming for only a few weeks, so the plants may be out of flower again by fall.) Here's a list of perennials to try cutting back by half to two thirds in mid-June to mid-July. If you think of it, also

Cutting back a sprawling veronica.

## Prop up sprawling stems

### LATE SUMMER TO MID-FALL

If you didn't take steps earlier in the growing season to support your plants, or if wild summer weather has blown over stems that would normally stay upright, don't despair; it's still possible to get your plants standing up for the fall season. Now don't be afraid of

letting your plants lean on each other a little, because mingled foliage and flowers gives your borders a lush, full look, and some absolutely delightful, albeit unplanned, combinations can occur. But if delicate companions are being completely shaded or crushed by bigger companions, then it's definitely time to take action. In recent

give them a thorough watering and add a shovelful or two of compost around each one to encourage vigorous regrowth:

*Anthemis* (marguerites)

*Calamintha* (calamints)

*Centranthus* (red valerians)

*Coreopsis* (coreopsis)

Dianthus (pinks)

*Gaillardia* (blanket flowers)

*Gaura* (gauras)

*Lavandula* (lavenders)

*Nepeta* (catmints)

*Origanum* (oreganos)

*Salvia* (salvias, sages)

*Tradescantia* (spiderworts)

*Veronica* (veronicas)

A number of later-blooming perennials benefit from some attention *before* they flower to improve their looks in autumn. Here's a list of plants you could cut back by about half in early summer to help reduce their ultimate height and minimize their need for staking. Or, cut them back by about a third in midsummer to delay their flowering season a bit:

*Boltonia* (boltonias)

*Chelone* (turtleheads)

*Chrysanthemum* (mums)

*Echinacea* (purple coneflowers)

*Eupatorium* (Joe-Pye weeds)

*Helenium* (sneezeweeds)

*Helianthus* (perennial sunflowers)

*Leucanthemella* (leucanthemella)

*Phlox* (border phlox)

*Physostegia* (obedient plants)

*Platycodon* (balloon flowers)

*Sedum* (sedums)

*Vernonia* (ironweeds)

*Veronicastrum* (Culver's roots)

Some leaners look great left alone.

years, garden-supply catalogs have started selling linking metal stakes in a variety of sizes and shapes perfectly suited for supporting starting-to-sprawl stems in late summer and fall. You can find other ideas for propping up your perennials in Providing Temporary Support on page 163.

## Remove faded flowers

### LATE SUMMER TO MID-FALL

From a maintenance standpoint, fall deadheading is a valuable tool for keeping some plants from getting out of hand. Specifically, it's useful for annuals, perennials, and shrubs that produce large quantities of seeds, which can sprout into masses of unwanted seedlings in your garden or even in local natural areas, where they may crowd out the existing native vegetation. By stopping these seedlings before they start, you're eliminating a lot of weeding work for yourself, and in some cases protecting the environment outside your garden, too. Some of the most notorious self-sowers to watch out for are border phlox (*Phlox paniculata*), butterfly bush (*Buddleia davidii*), fennel (*Foeniculum vulgare*), Japanese silver grass (*Miscanthus sinensis*), and some cultivars of fountain grass (*Pennisetum alopecuroides*).

Of course, sometimes you'll deadhead simply to make your plants look better (as for dahlias). And you don't necessarily want to remove *all* seed heads from your garden, because some of them are quite decorative. For more information on deadheading decision making, check out Deadheading: When, Where, and

Remove faded flowers to encourage rebloom.

How, on page 13, and Off with Their Heads! on page 173.

## Think twice about pruning woody plants

LATE SUMMER TO LATE FALL

Although most perennials are fairly forgiving about experimental pruning, flowering shrubs typically don't take kindly to being pruned outside of their preferred season. If you have the urge to do some pruning but are confused about the right timing, keep in mind this general rule: Spring- and early-summer bloomers typically flower on shoots they grew last year, so the best time to prune them is within a few weeks after their blossoms fade. That way, they'll have all summer and fall to produce new shoots and flower buds for next year. Later-blooming shrubs tend to flower on shoots produced during the current year, so spring is the ideal pruning time for them. If you wait until summer, you run the risk of cutting off the developing blooms. That may delay the flower display for several weeks, or even eliminate it (if the new buds don't have time to develop into blooms before frost). Fall itself usually isn't a good time to do routine pruning on most shrubs because it encourages new growth at a time when the shrubs are trying to slow down in preparation for winter, but there are two situations where it's okay to snip.

♣ *Snipping suckers.* On woody plants that are grafted onto the roots of another plant, you'll sometimes notice suckers: shoots that arise below the graft union instead of from the desirable top growth. The suckers may be obviously different,

Prune suckers off woody plants.

with a leaf or stem shape or color that's not at all like that of the main plant. Or, they may look just like the main plant until flowering time, when they produce a different bloom form or color. The smaller the suckers are, the easier they are to remove effectively, so always remove them as soon as you notice them. Snip or snap them off as close as possible to where they emerge from the roots or the base of the stem; repeat if new growth appears from the same spot.

♣ *Seeing green.* It's not unusual to see solid-colored shoots appear on variegated perennials, shrubs, and trees. As with suckers, it's critical to remove these shoots as soon as you see them; otherwise, they detract from the variegated effect. Plus, they tend to be more vigorous than multicolored parts, so they may eventually crowd out the variegated shoots. If plain shoots arise from an otherwise variegated stem, simply cut off the plain parts at the main stem. When all-green shoots arise directly from the soil, you're probably better off digging up and removing the solid-green part.

# KEEPING PLANTS HEALTHY

Having a healthy, beautiful garden isn't just a matter of knowing what to spray and when. In fact, if you choose plants that are well suited to the growing conditions your yard has to offer, do a good job preparing the soil before planting, and use a few simple tricks to stop problems as soon as they appear, there's a good chance you'll never have to bother with spraying anything at all.

## *Watch out for late-season pest problems*

LATE SUMMER TO LATE FALL

By the time fall rolls around, most pests have come and gone, but some — especially aphids, slugs, and snails — can linger long into the autumn months. Keep a lookout for signs of these and other problems, such as chewed leaves, distorted shoots, and sticky or slimy patches on the foliage. The quickest and easiest way to eliminate pest problems is to directly remove the pests by picking them off the plants, trapping them, or pinching off shoots that the pests are clustered on. Don't just toss these into your compost pile; discard them in a sealed bag in with your trash.

## *Be on guard for fungal diseases*

LATE SUMMER TO LATE FALL

Several fungal diseases thrive in moist autumn weather. Some, such as powdery mildew, may start in summer and linger into fall; others, like rusts, are active primarily in cooler conditions. Common symptoms include discolored areas on leaf surfaces or undersides; fuzzy gray or orange patches on leaves, shoots, and buds; dropped leaves and buds; and browned, weakened, or wilted growth. If you see diseased growth, pinch or cut off the affected parts immediately and carefully clean up any already dropped leaves to try to stop the disease from spreading. Dispose of diseased growth with your household trash, not on your compost pile.

## *Early fall to early spring: Keep cool-season weeds under control*

Weeds aren't as much of an immediate threat to your plants as pests and diseases can be, but it's still important to take action as soon as you spot them. Annual weeds, in particular, can produce hundreds or thousands of seeds without being obvious about it, and the sooner you break the seeding-and-sprouting

Snip off aphid-infested shoots.

Watch out for fungal diseases.

Pull annual weeds before they set seed.

cycle, the fewer of them you'll have to deal with in the future. Luckily, annual weeds are fairly easy to remove: simply pull or hoe them out as soon as you spot them (avoid letting them go to seed). With perennial weeds, you'll usually want to get the roots too; if you pull off the tops only, they'll resprout from the roots. Young weeds can go in your compost pile; those that are already flowering and setting seed are better off in the trash. Annual weeds that thrive during the cooler weather of fall, winter, and early spring include chickweeds, henbit, and lamb's quarters; some common cool-season perennial weeds are clovers, curly dock, dandelion, ground ivy, and plantains.

## STOP DISEASES BEFORE THEY START

In a well-maintained garden, serious diseases usually aren't a common problem. But if you find that certain plants develop disease symptoms every year, or that all of the plants in one part of your yard always seem to suffer, it's wise to take precautions so the problem doesn't happen again. Here are some ideas:

♣ Diseases can spread quickly where stems are crowded, so divide or thin overgrown clumps in spring or fall.

♣ Soggy soil is an open invitation for root rots. One option is to choose plants that are naturally adapted to "wet feet"; another is to build raised beds, so the crowns and upper roots of your plants will be in well-aerated soil.

♣ If fungal diseases frequently attack the flowers and foliage of particular plants, seek out cultivars that are naturally resistant to those diseases. Border phlox (*Phlox paniculata*), for example, is often bothered by mildew, but resistant selections such as white 'David' and pink 'Shortwood' are far less likely to show symptoms.

# PREPARING YOUR PLANTS FOR WINTER

As your fantastic fall flower display starts to wind down, it's time to start thinking about getting your garden ready for the return of cold weather. From bringing tender plants indoors to bedding down outdoor plants for their long winter's nap, the last few weekends of fall are the right time to shut things down for this season and make sure all is in good shape for when spring returns.

## *Consider bringing cold-tender plants inside*

EARLY TO MID-FALL

If you enjoy growing cannas, dahlias, or any of the other wonderful tender perennials that add so much beauty to fall borders and containers, you'll probably want to bring at least some of your favorites indoors for the winter as soon as frosty weather returns, if not before. (By the way, weather forecasts can be helpful in predicting possible frost events, but they don't tell the whole story; a good deal depends on your local conditions and on your particular site. Some surefire late-afternoon signs that frost might occur that night are clear skies, still air, low humidity, a dew point at or below 32°F, and, of course, dropping temperatures.) To learn more about the various overwintering options you have, check out Handling Cold-Tender Plants on page 102, Preparing Tender Plants for Winter on page 169, and Handling Tender Plants Indoors on page 188.

Keep in mind that sometimes the best way to overwinter marginally hardy plants (those that usually need some protection to survive the winter outdoors in your zone) is to *not* pamper them with warmth. Many perennials need a period of cold temperatures to produce vigorous new growth in spring; otherwise, they'll eventually get so weak that they die out. If a plant totally dies back to the ground, your best bet is probably to leave it in the garden and cover it with a 6- to 10-inch-deep layer of mulch in late fall. If the plant is growing in a pot, or if it has evergreen foliage, bring it indoors but keep it in a bright, cold spot (about 35° to 40°F) until spring.

Dig and label dahlias for indoor storage.

## Fill in holes in beds and borders

MID- TO LATE FALL

If you've dug tender plants out of your garden for winter storage indoors, you'll notice that your beds and borders are left with a number of ugly craters. Take a few minutes now to fill in those holes with some compost, or a mix of compost and topsoil, then rake the areas as best you can to level them. Besides making your beds and borders look a whole lot better through the winter months, this is a great way to build up the fertility of your soil. Whatever you plant in those spots next year will really appreciate the boost.

## Consider garden cleanup

MID- TO LATE FALL

Some gardeners don't feel their borders are ready for winter until they're totally tidied up; others prefer to leave the dead leaves and stems standing until spring. Both approaches have merit. For more details on ways to approach the fall garden cleanup issue, turn to Tidying Beds and Borders on page 134 and Grooming Your Gardens for Winter on page 152. Preparing Pots for Winter on page 126 and Handling Container Plantings on page 143 present tips on dealing with autumn pots and planters. And Handling Garden Debris on page 155 offers ideas on what to do with all the cleanup materials you may end up with.

### Get ready for spring planting

MID- TO LATE FALL

Even though winter hasn't arrived yet, it's not too early to plan for spring planting. Think about where you might like to add cool-season annuals to your beds and borders next year, then get those sites ready for planting *now*. Spread about 2 inches of compost over the sites, dig or till them, and then level them with a rake. If you'll be setting out transplants, you could even cover the sites with a few inches of mulch; then, in

Smooth bare soil for spring sowing.

spring, simply pull back the mulch in each planting spot, set in the transplant, and pull the mulch back around it. If you'll be sowing seeds instead, leave the soil bare. When the time comes to sow in spring, simply rake again and you'll have a perfectly prepared seedbed all ready to go.

### Raise the stakes

MID-FALL TO EARLY WINTER

This is a good time to remove all of the stakes you put out in spring, so you don't have to look at them all winter. Plus, they're likely to last longer with proper care. Rinse off any soil that's clinging to the stakes themselves, then let them dry and store them in a shed or garage. If you used biodegradable twine, it can go right in the compost pile; otherwise, you'll need to wind up any string or else toss it in the trash. If you use metal stakes or supports, it's smart to remove them *before* you do any cutting-back in fall. Accidentally hitting a metal stake with pruners or a string trimmer can cause serious damage to your tools — and maybe to you.

### Protect plants from cold and wind

MID-FALL TO EARLY WINTER

Providing temporary covers for short-term frost shielding is one thing (it's covered in detail in Extending the Season on page 178, by the way); preparing plants to weather the worst of winter's cold and wind is another. Winter protection takes a fair bit of time, and it usually doesn't add much to the

## WINTER WONDERS

Here's a short list of some perennials you may choose to leave standing in your garden for their winter interest:

*Agastache* (agastaches)

*Aster* (asters)

*Astilbe* (astilbes)

*Calamagrostis* (feather reed grasses)

*Chelone* (turtleheads)

*Echinacea* (purple coneflowers)

*Echinops* (globe thistles)

*Eryngium* (sea hollies)

*Eupatorium* (Joe-Pye weeds)

*Liatris spicata* (spike gayfeather)

*Miscanthus* (miscanthus)

*Panicum* (switchgrasses)

*Rudbeckia* (orange coneflowers)

*Sedum spectabile* (showy sedum)

*Vernonia* (ironweeds)

*Veronica spicata* (spike speedwell)

*Veronicastrum* (Culver's roots)

beauty of the garden; in fact, a yard filled with burlap-wrapped shrubs and mulch-smothered beds can be downright depressing to look at all during the winter months. That's why many gardeners skip this step altogether, trusting the plants to take care of themselves and replacing those that aren't tough enough to reappear in spring. Even if you don't normally protect established plants, though, it's smart to provide a little TLC for those you've set out this year (especially in autumn).

♣ *Mulch management.* Mulching is the most common — and probably the most hotly debated — type of winter protection for beds and borders. The traditional advice is to wait until the top few inches of soil are frozen; this can discourage critters like mice and voles from snuggling into the soil under the mulch and feeding on the roots of your plants all winter. Unfortunately, by the time the soil is frozen, your mulch or compost pile is probably frozen too. As a compromise, try waiting until there have been a few freezing nights; by then, the critters have (we hope) found other winter homes but your mulch should still be usable. A few inches of shredded bark, chopped leaves, or chunky

compost will usually serve the purpose; covering this with evergreen boughs provides extra protection and keeps lightweight mulches from blowing away.

♣ *Screens for evergreens.* Deciduous shrubs and trees typically don't need special winter protection, but evergreens are a different story, especially if they're growing in windswept sites or are newly planted. Use stakes and burlap or sections of bamboo fencing to shelter at least the west and north sides. White plastic is a less attractive but still functional option; avoid clear or black plastic, though, because these materials can heat up in the sun and damage your plants. Some gardeners build lumber frames topped with laths or plywood to protect evergreen foundation shrubs from snow sliding off their house roof. Out in the yard, winding some twine or rope around upright evergreens helps prevent them from splitting due to the weight of snow and ice.

♣ *Protect plantings from salt.* If you live where winter snow is common, it's smart to think now about how you will protect your plantings from deicing salt if they're anywhere near a road, sidewalk, driveway, or walkway. Traditional rock salt (sodium chloride) can seriously harm perennials, ground

Shield evergreens from drying winds.

covers, evergreens, shrubs, and hedges when it dissolves and washes into the soil next to the pavement, causing browning of the leaf tips or even killing the planting outright. If you must use it, apply it sparingly; for improved traction, try combining a small amount of it with sawdust, sand, or cat litter. Applying gypsum in fall (about 50 pounds per 1,000 square feet) to plantings adjacent to paved areas may help counteract any salt that does make it into your beds and borders.

## Keep critters at bay

MID-FALL TO EARLY WINTER

Protecting your plantings from animal pests is often a year-round job, but it's especially important in autumn. Even if they don't normally bother your plants during the growing season, hungry critters won't hesitate to treat your yard as their own all-you-can-eat buffet during the winter months. Sometimes their damage is immediately obvious; in other cases, you may not notice any problem until your perennials and bulbs fail to appear in spring. Worst of all, these marauders can strike without warning: One day your plants are fine; the next they are severely damaged or have disappeared completely. If you know animal pests are common in your neighborhood, taking precautions against them is a must.

Elsewhere, you might take the chance that they won't strike — but is that a gamble you're prepared to lose?

♣ *Oh, deer!* These four-leggers are a breathtaking sight in the wild, but the devastation they can cause in a home landscape provokes a much different reaction from gardeners. If deer are only an occasional threat in your area, you might choose to experiment with the wide range of repellent sprays on the market, or try home remedies such as hang-

ing bars of deodorant soap on your trees and shrubs to discourage browsing. You'll often see lists of "deerproof" plants, but remember: If they are hungry enough, deer will feed on or rub against just about anything they can reach, list or no list. Individual wire cages are a possibility for protecting small shrubs and trees but aren't especially attractive; often, the most practical (albeit expensive) option is enclosing all or part of your property with an 8-foot deer fence.

♣ *Those rascally rabbits* nibble on buds and shoots near the ground and particularly enjoy feeding on tender bark. If they gnaw off the bark all the way around the trunk, the plant is likely to die. As with deer, you can try repellents, but individual plant "collars" are a more dependable deterrent. Simply create a cylinder of small-mesh wire (often called hardware cloth) a few inches wider than the diameter of the trunk and fasten the free ends with wire ties. Make the collar at least 2 feet taller than your usual deep-snow level, with a few extra inches so you can sink it into the ground a bit to prevent bunnies from tunneling underneath. Secure it in place with two or three short stakes.

## ● ROSES IN THE SNOW ●

Of all the plants in the garden, hybrid roses are probably the most notorious for needing winter protection, and there's a whole range of specialized techniques and products related specifically to these floral prima donnas. Gardeners devoted to growing questionably hardy cultivars don't mind the time and energy it takes to mound soil or mulch over the crowns, cover the canes with insulated cones, or even bury the plants altogether. For most of us, though, sticking with roses that are naturally well adapted to our winters is a far more practical solution. For extra insurance, choose

Rosa 'Blushing Knock Out'

"own root" roses; that way, if excessive cold kills the canes, new growth can sprout up from the roots. (If the tops of grafted plants die, the new sprouts will be from the rose used for the rootstock, not the rose you wanted when you bought the plant.)

Protect tender bark with a wire-mesh collar.

♣ *Avoiding rodent woes.* Field mice and voles attack both above- and belowground. Like rabbits, they can gnaw off enough bark to weaken or even kill trees and shrubs. Below the soil or mulch, they tunnel around and feed on plant roots and bulbs as they go. You may not even notice they have been here until you see the rootless crowns of your perennials sitting on top of the soil in spring, or find that the plants are missing altogether. The wire collars you use to protect woody plants from rabbits can deter these critters too; just make sure the holes are no larger than a ¼ inch. To protect very special perennials and bulbs, line their planting holes with the same type of wire mesh. Also, try cleaning up your gardens thoroughly in mid- to late fall, then wait until the ground is frozen before you mulch.

# CARING FOR LAWN AREAS

Nothing sets off colorful flower gardens better than a backdrop of rich green grass. Take the opportunity to give your lawn some TLC this fall, and you'll enjoy fantastic-looking turf next year.

## Test your soil

### LATE SUMMER

Before you know how to proceed with fall lawn care, you need to know where you are soil-wise, so start with a soil test. At least check the pH, and ideally do a complete test for pH *and* nutrient levels. A complete laboratory test (available through your local Cooperative Extension office) is a little more expensive than a home-test kit, but the results will include specific recommendations for the kinds and amounts of materials you need to apply to fix any soil imbalances and encourage vigorous growth.

## Aerate lawn areas

### EARLY FALL

Aerating your lawn — essentially, poking holes into the soil so water and air can easily reach the roots — works wonders in perking up tired, trodden-down turf. Besides directly improving the conditions for root growth, aerating relieves soil compaction, and it also helps break down thatch (the buildup of undecomposed grass clippings and stems). A step-on core aerator can do the job on a small lawn; for larger areas, it's worth renting a power aerator. Make sure the tool you use pulls out small plugs of soil and grass; a solid-tined tool can actually make compaction worse. You don't have to aerate every year; every other year will keep your lawn in top form.

## Repair bare spots

### EARLY FALL

Does your lawn look good overall but have a few bare spots that need help? Fall is an ideal time to fix them. Remember: If you don't fill those areas with grass quickly, then Mother Nature will fill them with weeds instead. To ensure that your repairs work, and that they *stay* fixed, first figure out what caused the bare spots — tire damage, poor drainage, and repeated heavy foot traffic are a few common causes — then take steps to make sure that doesn't happen again. (If foot traffic is wearing a trail through your lawn, for instance, it's probably easier to install a proper path than to redirect the people and pets who want to walk there.)

♠ *Repairing by reseeding.* To fix a damaged spot with seed, use a hand fork or spading fork to loosen up the soil. Scatter a handful or two of sifted compost or organic lawn fertilizer over the area and fork it into the top few inches of earth. Next, make sure the soil level in the bare spot is even with the surrounding ground. Once it is, firm it with your foot, scatter some grass seed over the soil, and lightly rake it in. (Match the seeds or seed mix that you're using for repairs as closely as you can to the existing lawn, so the repaired site blends into the surrounding grass.) Firm the area with

Reseed bare spots in your lawn.

your foot, then water well and keep the soil there moist until your new grass starts to grow.

♠ *Patching gaps with sod.* For an "instant" fix, buy a piece of sod at your local garden center — try to match the grass that you already have — or use a piece from a less visible part of your yard. Cut a square or rectangle around the damaged spot with a spade or lawn-edging tool, then remove any remaining grass within the area. Loosen the soil and prepare it for replanting as you would for seeding (see above). Cut a piece of sod to fit the exact shape of the cut-out area, then lay it on the soil, making sure it sits at the same level as the surrounding lawn. Firm the piece of sod in place by tamping it with your foot or the back of a metal rake, then water thoroughly.

♠ *Fixing the highs and lows.* Uneven areas of a lawn are susceptible to damage (bumps often get "scalped" by the mower blade, and low spots tend to stay wet), and they can make walking or playing hazardous as well. To fix either condition, cut an "×" across the area with a spade or lawn-edging tool, then carefully fold back the flaps of turf. Remove excess soil to lower a bump; add topsoil to

raise a low spot. Once the area is level with the surrounding soil, firm it with your foot. Put the turf back in place, trimming away any excess, then water thoroughly.

## Fertilize wisely

### EARLY FALL (AND SPRING)

The best time to fertilize a lawn is when the grasses are getting ready for a burst of growth. And for the cool-season grasses — such as fescues, bluegrasses, and ryegrasses — that means in spring and early fall. (Hold off until spring for warm-season grasses, such as bermuda grass, buffalo grass, and zoysia.) If you let the clippings fall back onto the lawn when you mow, they'll do a good job returning many of the needed nutrients to the soil; in this case, a light topdressing of finely sifted compost or dehydrated manure may be all you need to add. If you prefer to remove the clippings, or if there is some nutrient imbalance, you'll probably need a commercial fertilizer; follow the recommendations on your soil test results.

# GIVING NEW LIFE TO TIRED TURF

If your lawn is looking a little sparse this year, fall is the ideal time to do something about it. But before you can decide *what* to do, you need to figure out *why* there's a problem in the first place. Otherwise, you could end up doing a whole lot of work and still have an ugly lawn after it all. Here's a rundown of some common causes for lawn problems, and what to do about them.

**Too much shade.** If you have any trees in or around your yard, you'll eventually have more and more shade, and that increasing shade will weaken a lawn based on sun-loving grasses, such as Kentucky bluegrass. Some people choose to prune their trees to let in more light, but that's only a temporary fix. Instead, consider overseeding with a more shade-tolerant grass, such as creeping fescue, to fill in as the other grasses die out.

**Compacted soil.** Heavy foot traffic, as well as repeated mowing with a riding mower, gradually packs down the top few inches of soil, making it difficult for water and air to get down to the grass roots. For a quick test, try to push the blade of a screwdriver about 6 inches into the soil. The harder you have to push, the more likely it is that compaction is a problem. To fix it, use a core aerator to loosen things up. (For more information, see Aerate Lawn Areas on page 221.)

**Soil pH or nutrient imbalance.** If your soil is too acidic or too alkaline (6.5 to 7.2 is about right for most grasses), or if the grass plants don't get the nutrients they need, their growth will be less vigorous and the look of your lawn will suffer. Take a soil test to see if anything is out of balance, and if there is, follow the testing lab's recommendations for getting your soil in good shape to support a healthy lawn.

**Poor lawn management.** Lawns can take an amazing amount of abuse, but eventually, even the best-looking lawn will turn weak and patchy if you don't take care of it properly. Some common care mistakes are overwatering, overfertilizing, and mowing too closely, all of which stress the turf and make it prone to other problems. Read up on lawn care this winter, and make an effort to treat your turf better next year.

**Pest, disease, or weed woes.** A healthy, vigorous lawn is seldom bothered by serious pests, diseases, or weeds, so if you see one of these problems, simply applying a pesticide, fungicide, or herbicide won't automatically improve your lawn's appearance. Consider one or more of the above causes, and take steps—such as aerating, liming, and fertilizing—to improve the overall growing conditions for the grass. Overseeding with grass varieties that are resistant to common pests and diseases in your area is good insurance against future damage.

Think your lawn looks too bad to salvage? If more than half of it is weeds, you're probably better off removing everything and starting over with seed or sod. In most cases, though, you can get great results by sowing seed right into your existing lawn (rent a tool called a slit seeder to get the seed directly into the soil) or on top of the turf (aerate first, spread the seeds with a drop seeder, rake them into the soil, and keep the area moist until the seeds sprout).

Improve turf with a scattering of fine compost.

## Adjust pH, if necessary

EARLY TO LATE FALL

Liming lawn areas in fall is ideal, because it takes awhile for ground limestone to do its job. Some folks make a habit out of liming their lawn every year without fail—but you shouldn't be one of them! At best, routinely applying lime without taking a soil test first is a waste of your time and money; at worst, it can drastically raise the pH of your soil and make it tough for any grass to thrive there. If a test does indicate you need to lime your lawn, it should also tell you what kind and how much to use. As a general rule, if you need to add more than 50 pounds of lime per 1,000 square feet of lawn, apply half of it at one time, then spread the rest in spring.

# CARING FOR TOOLS

We all know we should take care of our garden tools before we put them away for the winter — but how many of us actually do it? Well, let this be a challenge to you: Try it this fall, then see if you aren't delighted with the results when spring rolls around. Until you've experienced the treat of having sharp, clean tools right at hand and power tools that start up the first time you need them, you don't know what you're missing.

## Clean and store hand tools

MID-FALL TO EARLY WINTER

If you prefer to buy inexpensive hand tools and simply discard them when they break or rust, then you don't need to think about careful cleaning or storage. But once you have had the pleasure of working with a high-quality tool, you'll know that good garden tools are worth every penny you pay for them and every minute you put into their upkeep. A key part of proper maintenance is putting away your tools between uses. If your usual storage area is too far from your garden for convenience, fall is a good time to add a shed for easier storage of long-handled tools. An old mailbox mounted near or even right in the garden makes a perfect storage spot for small hand tools.

♠ **Protecting metal parts.** With any tools, the first step is getting rid of any clinging soil and debris by washing them with soap and water. (Use paint thinner or nail polish remover to clean sap off of the blades of pruning tools.) If large patches of rust are present, use a wire brush or even liquid rust remover; get rid of small rust spots by rubbing with sandpaper, steel wool, or wadded-up aluminum foil. Once all the metals parts are clean and dry, sharpen any cutting edges that are dull, or take the tools to a professional for sharpening. (For pointers on doing the sharpening yourself, turn to Winterizing Garden Accessories on page 140. Then wipe or spray the metal parts thoroughly with penetrating oil to protect them from rust during winter storage. Don't have proper tool oil handy? Cooking oil spray will serve the purpose.

♠ **Handling wooden handles.** Inspect all parts of each tool thoroughly, paying special attention to any wooden handle. Don't be tempted to fix cracks by wrapping a handle with electrician's tape; at best, that's a temporary fix. During the stress of digging or cultivating, a tiny crack can lead to a snapped-off handle — and possibly some serious damage to you! Fall is the perfect time to replace any handles that are showing signs of cracking. Small nicks and rough spots are common types of damage, and they are easy to fix: Sand them smooth with sandpaper or emery cloth, wipe off the sawdust with a damp cloth, and let them dry. Before storage, wipe or brush wooden handles with raw or polymerized linseed oil or tung oil. (Avoid *boiled* linseed oil; it contains toxic solvents and drying agents that can be absorbed by your skin.)

Treat wooden handles with oil.

**♠ *Storing your tools.*** Finally, tighten any loose nuts or screws, and treat all pivot points and springs with a bit of lubricating oil. Replace or repair any broken, damaged, or missing parts, so the tools will be in perfect working condition when you're ready to use them in spring. If possible, hang them up so they are not resting on the floor; besides being out of the way, they'll be less likely to pick up dirt and moisture from the floor. If that's not an option, try wrapping your hand tools in newspaper to keep them clean and dry. Store brooms and rakes with their handles pointing down, so the weight of the tools doesn't push the bristles and tines out of shape. Digging tools can be stored blade-down; to protect the sharpened edge, cut an old piece of garden hose the length of the blade, slit it along one side, and slip it onto the blade.

## Prepare power equipment for storage

MID-FALL TO EARLY WINTER

Treating hand tools as disposable items is one thing; neglecting your lawn mower, tiller, and other power tools is quite another. These items aren't cheap, so you'll want to give them the best care possible;

otherwise, they have a habit of failing you just when you need them the most. Well-maintained equipment will start without a struggle, run more cleanly, and make your whole gardening experience go much more smoothly. Here's a brief overview of basic fall care, but for best results, follow the manufacturer's directions that came with your equipment. Or take your power tools to a service shop for a complete going-over by a professional. As with hand tools, fall or winter is the ideal time to do this, so you'll get them back in plenty of time for the first spring mowing or tilling.

**♠ *Fuel and oil issues.*** For most power tools, the standard advice is to run the engine until all of the fuel is used up before you store it. This can allow moisture to collect in the engine and fuel line, however, so some experts prefer to fill the tank with gas that's been treated with a fuel stabilizer. If you choose this option, run the engine for a few minutes to evenly distribute the treated fuel through the engine. After turning off the power but while the engine is still warm, drain the old oil out of the crankcase and replace it with new oil. Then remove the spark plug, add several drops of engine oil to the cylinder to help prevent corrosion, and replace it with a new plug. Start the engine again to distribute the oil, then shut off the power.

♣ *Do a careful cleanup.* Before continuing with the service, disconnect the spark-plug wire and make sure it can't flip back and touch the plug. Begin the cleanup process with a good scrubbing with soap and water; use a wire brush, if needed, to remove any stubbornly clinging dirt and debris. Remove the blade from your lawn mower and the blades from your tiller and sharpen them, or take them to a sharpening shop. Cover all bare metal parts with penetrating oil to prevent rust, and lubricate any moving parts. Check all nuts, bolts, and screws, and tighten any that are loose. Don't forget to look carefully at the belts and cables, and replace or fix any that show cracks or other signs of heavy wear.

♣ *Finishing touches.* Clean any debris out of the air intake area and also clean or replace the air filter. Finish up with a thorough inspection of your equipment's handles, wheels, and other accessories. If you have a bagging mower, make sure you clean out the bag to get out any lingering clippings. Remove the battery from equipment that has a battery-powered electric starter and store it in a frost-free place for the winter. Wipe down the handles with soap and water, and dry them with a cloth; replace any grips that are cracked or worn. Replace any loose or wobbly wheels, too. When the service is complete, store your equipment in a clean, dry, well-ventilated area.

Secure the spark-plug cord before servicing.

# USDA HARDINESS ZONE MAP

The United States Department of Agriculture (USDA) created this map to give gardeners a helpful tool for selecting and cultivating plants. The map divides North America into 11 zones based on each area's average minimum winter temperature. Zone 1 is the coldest and Zone 11 the warmest. Recently, the zones were further divided into "a" and "b", with "a" being the colder portion. To locate your zone, refer to the map here, or for the most up-to-date information, visit the National Arbor Day Foundation's Web site: *www.arborday.org/media/zones.cfm*.

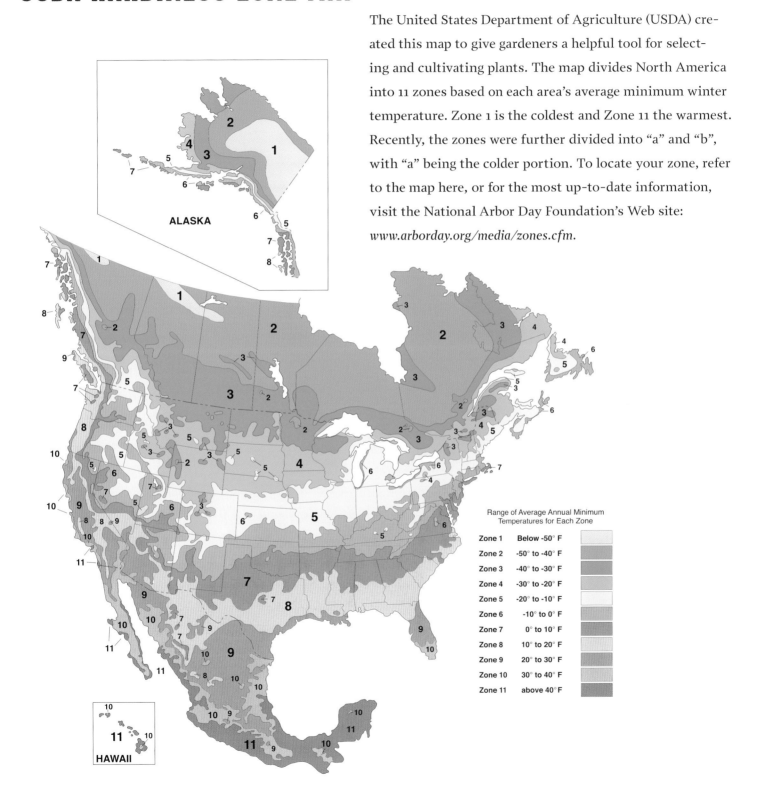

ALASKA

HAWAII

**Range of Average Annual Minimum
Temperatures for Each Zone**

| Zone 1 | Below -50° F |
| Zone 2 | -50° to -40° F |
| Zone 3 | -40° to -30° F |
| Zone 4 | -30° to -20° F |
| Zone 5 | -20° to -10° F |
| Zone 6 | -10° to 0° F |
| Zone 7 | 0° to 10° F |
| Zone 8 | 10° to 20° F |
| Zone 9 | 20° to 30° F |
| Zone 10 | 30° to 40° F |
| Zone 11 | above 40° F |

# INDEX

*Page numbers in italics indicate photographs.*

## Photographer's Acknowledgments

**With much gratitude to these talented designers, gardeners, and institutions, whose designs are featured throughout this book:**

Andalusia, PA, p. 61
Beaubaire-Cohen Garden, PA, p. 141
Beds and Borders, NY, p. 10
Bellevue Botanical Garden, WA, pp. 137, 183
Botanischer Garten, Germany, p. 81
Bryn Athyn Cathedral, PA, p. 143
Bunting Garden, PA, p. 101
Chanticleer, PA, p. 178
Stephanie Cohen Garden, PA, p. 118
Farmingdale State University, NY, p. 98
Fordhook Farm, PA, pp. 75, 95

Haverford College, PA, p. 37
Heronswood Nursery, WA, pp. 146, 196
Longwood Gardens, PA, pp. 34, 48, 117, 132
Meadowbrook Farms, PA, p. 104
Morris Arboretum, PA, pp. 97, 109, 112, 129
Mt.Cuba Center, DE, p. 5
Nancy Ondra Garden, PA, cover, pp. 2, 6, 8, 11 (bottom right), 25, 41, 92, 111, 115, 121, 123, 125, 139, 188, 189
Scott Arboretum, PA, pp. 107, 145, 194

**Thanks also to these gardens for allowing me access to their inspired fall displays:**

Ballymore Gardens, PA
Bedminster Organics, PA
Chicago Botanic Garden, IL
Dans la Foret, PA
Deep Cut Gardens, NJ
Delaware Center for Horticulture, DE
Frelinghuysen Arboretum, NJ
The Gardens at Ball, IL
Green Springs Gardens, VA
Henry Botanic Garden, PA
Hershey Park, PA
Hortulus Farm Gardens, PA
Huntington Botanical Gardens, CA
Landcraft Environments, NY
Landscape Arboretum of Temple University Ambler, PA
Linden Hill Gardens, PA
Marano Gardens, PA
Merryspring, ME
Minnesota Landscape Arboretum, MN
Minter Gardens, BC, Canada
Muir Garden, PA
New York Botanical Garden, NY
Nordic Nursery, BC, Canada
Ogden Garden, PA
Penn State Horticulture Trial Gardens, PA
Ravenna Gardens, WA
Regan Garden, PA
Royal Botanical Gardens, ON
Rutgers Gardens, NJ
Schmeider Arboretum, PA
Southlands Nursery, BC
Tyler Arboretum, PA
Weaver Gardens, PA
Welkenweir, PA
Winterthur, DE

**Many thanks also to** Gardener's Supply Company (www.gardeners.com) and Netherlands Flower Bulb Information Center (www.bulb.com) for providing tools and plant materials.